The

PRACTICAL
DREAMER'S
HANDBOOK

Other Books by Paul & Sarah Edwards

Best Home Businesses for the 21st Century

Cool Careers for Dummies (with Marty Nemko)

Home-Based Businesses for Dummies (with Peter Economy)

Home Businesses You Can Buy (with Walter Zooi)

Finding Your Perfect Work

Getting Business to Come to You (with Laura Clampitt Douglas)

Making Money in Cyberspace (with Linda Rohrbough)

Making Money with Your Computer at Home

Secrets of Self-Employment

Teaming Up (with Rick Benzel)

Working from Home

The PRACTICAL DREAMER'S HANDBOOK

Finding the Time, Money, and Energy to Live the Life You Want to Live

Paul and Sarah Edwards

JEREMY P. TARCHER / *Putnam*
a member of Penguin Putnam Inc.
New York

Most Tarcher/Putnam books are available at special quantity discounts
for bulk purchases for sales promotions, premiums, fund-raising,
and educational needs. Special books or book excerpts also can be
created to fit specific needs. For details, write Putnam Special Markets,
375 Hudson Street, New York, NY 10014.

Jeremy P. Tarcher/Putnam
a member of
Penguin Putnam Inc.
375 Hudson Street
New York, NY 10014
www.penguinputnam.com

Library of Congress Cataloging-in-Publication Data

Edwards, Paul, date.
    The practical dreamer's handbook: finding the time,
    money, and energy to live the life you want to live/by Paul
    and Sarah Edwards.
       p. cm.
    Includes index.
    ISBN 1-58542-055-7
      1. Self-realization. 2. Conduct of life. I. Edwards,
Sarah (Sarah A.) II. Title.
    BJ1470 .E39   2000   00-039254
    158.1—dc21

Printed in the United States of America

10 9 8 7 6 5 4 3 2 1

This book is printed on acid-free paper. ∞

Book design by Deborah Kerner

ACKNOWLEDGMENTS

We want to thank our friends and neighbors in Pine Mountain Club who have welcomed us into their community and are so generously helping us learn how to live in harmony with the National Forest, which is our home. We also want to thank the many practical dreamers who have shared their stories and personal journeys with us as we all strive to find balance and peace in these times of burgeoning complexity and change. Thanks, too, to Justen McCormack for her day-to-day assistance in getting this book ready for publication and to Roland Reuter for his editorial assistance. And, of course, many thanks to our editor, Mitch Horowitz, and publisher, Joel Fotinos, and the staff of Tarcher/Putnam, with whom we have worked for so many years.

We also express our deep appreciation to Lynn Andrews, author of *Medicine Woman* and *Love and Power*. Through Sarah's participation in the Lynn Andrews Center for Sacred Arts and Healing, Lynn has inspired us to tap into new depths of who we are and the message we want to bring to the world. Special thanks also to Kirsten Hermann, Sarah's mentor in the school, who was the first to encourage us to write more from the magic of our hearts, and to Charel Morris, who opened the door to our relationship with Lynn and her program, for their support each step of the way over the past four years along our journey as Practical Dreamers.

To the Spirit of Pine Mountain

CONTENTS

The

PRACTICAL
DREAMER'S
HANDBOOK

INTRODUCTION:
WALKING BETWEEN TWO
WORLDS—
THE PATH OF THE PRACTICAL
DREAMER

Aim for the ideal; understand the real.

JEAN JAURES

It's so easy. We have a desire. We do something to fulfill it. And once we do, we feel satisfied . . . until we have another desire. Then the cycle begins again, and again and again. Desire, action, satisfaction. We go through this cycle every time we take a breath. We do it every time we get hungry, or thirsty, or want to get up from a chair, or need to go to the store, or decide to look out the window. It's such a natural cycle, so much a part of who we are, that we don't even think about it. We've been doing it since the moment we were born.

But when we have to dream up some way to fulfill a desire, it's not so easy. The process is the same: We have a desire, we imagine how we might fulfill it, we take whatever action is needed, and once the desire is met we feel satisfied. But when it comes to fulfilling a dream, there's usually nothing automatic about it, because dreams are from another world. They come from our imagination. Taking a breath or getting a drink of water, walking over to the door or opening the blinds to let in some light are part of the world that already exists. No one questions whether it's practical to get a drink of water or whether we should get thirsty in the first place. But dreaming up something that doesn't exist anywhere except in our own minds is quite another matter.

Dreams are, by nature, not practical. Practical has to do with what is; dreams have to do with what could be but isn't yet. So we do question them, we question ourselves and so does the world. Should we have such a desire? Why aren't we satisfied with what we have? Is it appropriate? Is it possible? Realistic? Dreaming about a return to simpler times, for example, may be understandable when three out of four people report feeling stressed out, but do we dare think we could actually live a simpler life with time for family, personal fulfillment, nature, and meaningful work? To many that seems impractical, unrealistic, and even impossible.

Yet bridging these two worlds, the actual and the desirable, is the practical dreamer's challenge. The practical dreamer is both the architect and the builder, creating what could be from the reality of what is. So the practical dreamer must walk with one foot in the world of imagination, hopes, wishes, dreams, and possibilities, and the other firmly planted in the world of physical reality with all its limitations; like time, money, space, form, material, and the needs of other people. While our imagination is limitless, reality is not.

Many people choose not to walk the path of the practical dreamer, disliking the inconvenience and discomfort of having to straddle two very different, seemingly incompatible worlds. Some people prefer to live in the comfortable, imaginary world of their dreams, always talking and thinking, wondering and planning about what they will do, could do, or should do . . . someday . . . but never actually acting on their ideas. Without using some type of mind-altering substance, however, those who only dream are never truly satisfied with this choice. "Reality" has a perverse way of intruding into our awareness whether we want it to or not, reminding us again and again, often at the most unexpected moments, in the most unexpected ways, that our lives don't match our fantasies. So, as the Everly brothers' song bemoaned in the

50's, inevitably we realize, "Only trouble is, ghee wiz, I'm dreamin' my life away."

Others prefer to live strictly in the world of practical reality; they choose not to wander into the "unrealistic" and impractical realm of dreams. "It's never been done before," they say; or "That's not the way we do things here." But those who never dream rarely feel truly satisfied with life either. They become enslaved to what is, and sooner or later sense that there could be more, especially when someone else attains what they would have enjoyed but never dreamt possible. It's a tedious, gray, and gloomy world that's never lit by glimpses of a treasured dream.

How about you? Are you comfortable in both worlds? Can you dream? Do you dream? Can you accept and use reality as it is or would you prefer to ignore or fight it? Can you bring your dreams into reality and reality to your dreams?

Trying to walk between these two worlds can also put us at war with ourselves. The dreamer in us may thwart our efforts to be practical, realistic, and disciplined. The practical side of ourselves may squelch our dreams, declaring them impossible before we even have a chance to explore their potential. Thus it's easy to get stuck at some point in the cycle that turns desire into action and action into satisfaction. We can become disillusioned, stop dreaming, and bury our desires. We can fail to act or become consumed with action and lose our dreams in the busyness of always having to be doing something. We can dream or work our lives away without stopping to savor or feel the satisfaction we crave. Who hasn't done some or all of these at some point in their lives? But we may tend to get stuck more often at one place in the cycle than another. I know for me it's in doing. I can literally "do myself in."

Where do you get stuck? Can you hold on to your dreams through thick and thin? Do you get down to work on them or let them sit on the back burners of your mind? Can you stick to business and persevere? Do you allow yourself to savor the satisfaction of what you accomplish, each step along the way?

Practical dreamers embrace both the dreamer and the practical taskmaster within themselves, welcoming and encouraging their imagination while honoring their ability to face and live within the practicalities of reality. Their inner dreamer and their inner taskmaster become allies, working as a team toward a shared vision, drawing equally upon the unique perspectives and tools of their two worlds.

BRIDGING BETWEEN WHAT HAS BEEN, WHAT IS, AND WHAT COULD BE

If you want to get ahead in this world," my boss and would-be mentor advised me,* "figure out which way the wind is blowing and go stand in it." I was baffled by this advice since the prevailing winds I saw weren't blowing in any direction I wanted to go.

The prevailing winds said, "Get a good job, come in early, work late, invest wisely, and thirty years later you can retire and do whatever you want." Of course, by then our son would have grown up and we would have missed his childhood. We would have had so little time to spend together as a couple that we would probably have grown apart and could possibly have divorced. At least, we would have found ourselves married to someone we hardly knew and might not have wanted to know. Our bodies would most likely have become so run down and worn out that much of whatever money we'd acquired would have had to go for medical expenses.

But in past times that's what most people did. So few options

---

Throughout the book, unless otherwise specified, "I" and "me" refer to Sarah, and unless it's used in reference to all of us in general, "we" refers to the experiences of both Paul and Sarah.

seemed possible at the time that most people weren't motivated to take the world by its horns and turn their dreams into realities. You went along to get along, made do, and put up with. Only a minority of people were willing to wrestle the world into compliance with their dreams. Clearly this mentor was not one of them, but I soon met someone who was.

He was from the "new school" of success that can be summarized briefly as decide what you want, visualize it in clear detail, set specific, measurable goals for accomplishing it, write down those goals, make a plan for carrying them out, commit to persistently implementing your plan, do this relentlessly, and maintain an unshakably positive attitude in the process.

That sounded much better to me than standing in the prevailing wind, especially since it came with a guarantee. If you took this mentor's course, followed that methodology, and didn't achieve your goals—whatever they might be—during the program, you could continue taking his course until you did. Having left my job to start a home-based private psychotherapy practice, I was hosting a weekly radio show called *Here's to Your Success!* To stay on the air I had to sell advertising, but not being a salesperson by nature, I needed to triple my income to keep the venture viable. So I enrolled.

This program delivered on its promise. I did triple my income, in six weeks! Others accomplished equally astounding feats. But I was miserable, and as far as I can tell, so were they. Achieving my goal required me to get right back on the treadmill of working morning-noon-and-night. The only difference was that this time I was doing it for myself instead of for an employer. There was no time for family, no time for fun, no time to relax, no time for anything other than meeting our weekly goals, with which we had all inevitably become obsessed. In the end, we were triumphant but exhausted, or worse. My partner throughout the course, after meeting her goals, became critically ill and perilously close to death.

It was a huge lesson. The mind-over-matter, conquer-the-world, winner-take-all approach that has provided us with the benefits of so many marvelous modern conveniences and such unprecedented material wealth can never provide us with the kind of life so many of us are dreaming of today. It's modeled on the behavior of yesterday's winners, who got us to where we are now. Many people are still trying to use this approach to bring a sense of balance and control back into their lives, but it's a method at odds with the goals. We can't hammer reality into the shape of our dreams. We can't force ourselves to relax or drive ourselves relentlessly to greater happiness.

Forcefulness, drive, and dominance are the tools that have built the jam-packed, high-pressure world of today. They can't bring us the peace of mind of simpler comforts any more than always standing in the prevailing wind can ever take us to the destinations of our own choosing. But today we don't have to choose between the security of a good life with material comforts and the luxury of a sane and meaningful life with simple comforts. We can be the artists of our dreams without having to give up the best of all that we've gained in recent times. But to do so we need to honor the truth of both the world of our dreams and the world as it is.

To balance the needs of the body, the mind, and the soul, the practical dreamer must be equally at home with yesterday's ruthlessly practical tools that built the wonders of today as with a wealth of new tools that will lay the foundation for the wonders of tomorrow. Whereas in the past we looked outward to find what we desired, now we must look inward to find ways to bring what we imagine and aspire to into the physical world. Whereas the past demanded that we use logic, set goals, plan, and follow through on our plans step-by-step, today we must also learn how to let our dreams unfold organically within the context of fast-changing complexities over which we have little control. So, the new tools we must master include listening to our desires, using our intuition, following our beliefs, reacting spontaneously, and seizing on fortuitous serendipity.

ABOUT THIS HANDBOOK

This is a handbook about mastering the tools of the practical dreamer and learning to walk comfortably between the world we want and the world we have. It's a compilation of what we've learned about what could be called the "craft of life." Because finding the balance we've lost without losing all we've gained cannot be a simple, logical, step-by-step process, neither is the book. Instead, it unfolds as a series of queries, insights, discoveries, and reflections, along with specific steps to take; more like the process of practical dreaming itself. The threads of memories, our own experiences and those of others, research findings, facts, and fantasies are all woven into an exploration of the creative cycle that is so intrinsic to our nature as artisans of our own life—the cycle that takes us from desire to action and from action to satisfaction.

Part One, Desire, is about awakening our new dreams of a world that encompasses the best of both the past and the present. It's about listening to what we're yearning for, imagining it as possible, believing in our ability to create it, and committing to doing what we are intuitively guided to do.

Part Two, Action, is about finding and following the thread of truth that will take us from what is to what could be. It's about embracing the realities of space, money, time, and energy and using them in the service of our new dreams. It's about living spontaneously in the here and now as if it were the future we want and having the patience to allow the new realities we desire to unfold serendipitously.

Part Three, Satisfaction, is about finding pleasure in the creative process of crafting our lives. It's about appreciating this process and savoring our experiences moment by moment. It's about allowing ourselves to be fulfilled and renewed so we can go on to dream and create new dreams again and again.

Throughout the book you'll be presented with many of the questions each of us must answer in our own way if we are to reclaim the best of the past times while retaining the best of all that modern life can offer. In each chapter, you'll read about our own experiences in the creative dreaming process, as well as those of our neighbors in the village where we live and friends, fans, and colleagues from coast to coast, from all of whom we've learned so much. You'll also find sections called "TRY THIS" that suggest ways to start using the tools of practical dreaming in your own journey as you go through the book.

At the conclusion of each of the three parts of the book, you'll find a section called "REMEMBER THIS." It's filled with ideas and reminders we've collected and used over the past twenty years. You can turn to them, as we have, whenever you get stuck in your efforts to bridge the worlds of yesterday, today, and tomorrow. Or you may want to select one each morning or evening. Many such reminders also appear on our Web site <www.simplegoodlife.com> so you can also pick up one there anytime during the day.

It's an exciting time to be a practical dreamer because, you'll discover, as we have at the close of this book, you'll rarely need to dream alone. The ranks of practical dreamers are growing and the rewards of our journeys are great. In bringing the best of the past into the best of today, we can create the future we long for, one that's filled with the peace, happiness, and joy of serving others.

Part One

DESIRE—
AWAKENING
THE DREAM

*Dreams are the seedlings
of realities.*
James Allen

Dreams are born from the seeds of our deepest desires. In my heart there's the seed of a dream that's yearning to be born this very minute. It's been there a long time, perhaps all my life, but often we never get to know our dreams because we don't dare allow ourselves to feel their yearnings. We're afraid to know where our desires might take us, afraid they won't lead us toward what's realistic, practical, expected, and acceptable.

Is this why I haven't honored this yearning before now? I ask. It's true I've hijacked it for as long as I can remember, saying, "Oh, let's do this or let's do that instead. It's more realistic right now and it will be just fine. You'll see. It will be enough. Just wait and see." Yet such diversions rarely satisfy our true yearnings, and so we wonder why our accomplishments bring so little fulfillment. If we are to reclaim what we've lost and replace what's missing from our lives, we must dare to want what we want.

What are you yearning for? Do you know? Do you have a dream that's waiting to be born?

I read about a man who had created a lucrative business of fifteen years doing something he'd enjoyed since childhood—making dulcimers and teaching others to play them. "Wow!" I remember thinking. "Here's someone who is living his dream!" I eagerly called to set up an interview to learn about how he'd created such an ideal livelihood for himself. He laughed at my idea. "This isn't my dream!" he said with an edge of exasperation in his voice. "This is what I do for a living. This is how I support myself and my family. My dream is to produce my own music. Hopefully someday I'll do that."

Is this what's to become of my unborn dream? Will it be relegated to "someday"? At least he knows what his dream is, but he's already judged it as impractical. How odd. Creating a good livelihood making dulcimers would sound highly impractical to many people, yet he's done it so effectively, attending to all the practical details, finding the materials, crafting the instruments, marketing them at art shows across the country, recruiting private clients, scheduling sessions, and on and on. How and when did he conclude his real dream was impractical? Was it? Would he have to wait until he retired to discover where his dreams might lead?

That's what my father did. For most of his life, my father spent every day of the week except Sunday (and even some Sundays) doing work he disliked. What were his dreams as a young man, I often wonder, as he headed off to college shortly before his father died of a massive heart attack? Did that trauma and the responsibilities that ensued extinguish those dreams? Or was it World War II and his decision to join the FBI and take his new wife and baby girl from city to city, year after year, even long after VJ-Day?

I'll never know. What I do know is that when my father retired he became a magician. The frustrated, irritable, soft-spoken, ex-FBI agent and businessman he'd been evaporated and the gregarious, hilarious, cunning, fun-loving, and stunning Graybeard the Sage was born. No one would have ever guessed he harbored such a bizarre dream. Nor perhaps did he, until his brief someday arrived. Within only a few years my father died of cancer. But over the last six months of his life, while he lay wasting away in the hospital bed, he had only one wish. Tears would well up in his eyes as he'd tell us longingly, "If only I could do one more magic trick."

What happened to your parents' dreams? Do you know? How has their experience affected your willingness and ability to feel and follow your desires?

As I sit here filled with a yearning for who-knows-what, I can't help but wonder what my father would be saying to me now. What would he say about the fact that within the last year, my husband and I left behind life as we've known it with no clear plan for what we'll be doing, except to follow a yearning that seems destined to become a bigger dream? Would he roll his eyes and shake his head in dismay as he often did so long ago at my hare-brained, adolescent schemes? I think not. I remember on his deathbed the still-hungry-for-life look in his eyes so misty, gray, and glossy with morphine; and I know what he would say. Perhaps it's what he was trying to say near the end when all that remained was a glance and a touch:

"Don't do what I did, Sarah. Listen to the wild beatings of your heart and dance to them . . . before it's too late." I always wanted to hear them. I always wanted to dance to them. Sometimes I did. But like him, often I didn't.

Can you hear the beat? What's the pulsating desire that would move you to tears and to action?

The next four chapters are a journey into learning to listen to the heartbeat of our desires, for they are the well from which our dreams will spring. They are about learning to honor and welcome dissatisfaction as the door to a new and better future, about allowing ourselves to want and to yearn with abandon so we can imagine and see possibilities. They're about feeling the magic, believing we deserve it, and committing to follow wherever it takes us. That is the path of the dreamer. It's a journey from satisfaction to dissatisfaction and back again and again. It's about doing one more magic trick!

1

YEARNING FOR YESTERDAY
. . . OR SOMEDAY

. . . Suddenly, again, a feeling, known on more than one occasion as a child, an unbearable intensification of all senses, a magical and demanding impulse, the presence of something for which it was alone worth living.

VLADIMIR NABOKOV, *Glory*

Everyone has dreams, both day and night. Mostly, they're just that—dreams—entertaining, amusing, interesting, or distracting fantasies. We daydream about what we'd do if we won the lottery. We imagine what it might be like to live in Hawaii instead of just taking a vacation there. We wonder what would have happened if we'd married our high school sweetheart. We extrapolate about the kind of movie we'd make if we were a director or screenwriter. We fantasize about how great the hottest pop singer would be in bed.

But without the yearning of desire, a dream is only a diversion. Yearning brings dreams to life, wakes them up and plants their seeds in our hearts. It was yearning I saw burning in my father's eyes even as he lay dying. He wanted to perform. He ached for it. It was a burning desire, a hunger. When I saw it then in my father's eyes, I recognized it had been some time since I'd felt that kind of desire. At the time, I felt mostly tired, overcommitted, obligated, and pressured. When and how had I lost the beat of my heart's desire? How could I get it back?

LISTENING FOR RECURRING THEMES

Some of us are lucky. We seem to have been born knowing what we ache for like the professional singer who told us, "I don't remember a time I didn't want to sing." Or like hair colorist Diane Carolaw, who remembers, "From the time I was a little girl I always loved playing with colors." Mixing colors seems to be in her blood.

Others of us knew our deepest desires once upon a time but we've forgotten them. Jonathon Storm forgot his for a while, but only briefly. As a child and a young man, he spent many hours in nature. It was his passion. But like so many of us, when he entered college, he set out on a more "practical" course. He decided to become an architect. However, a three-month summer vacation traveling throughout Europe and in the wilds of Alaska changed the course of his life. While sitting on a glacier, taking in the sounds and sights of nature around him, he realized what he wanted and needed to do—to be in nature, listen to its sounds, and record and capture its music to share with others. And that's what he's done. He became a nature-recording artist.

Storm and his wife, Laura, live simply in a meadow near Port Ludlum, Washington. His life is a mixture of sunny fields, dewy forests, windy seas, and many bright, cold days and long, dark nights. He spends at least two months a year outdoors recording, four months in his studio creating albums, and the rest of the time administering his recording business, Earthtunes. But it's the field time Storm lives for.

Perhaps we're all born with some core of desires that will bring us such contentment, but we just don't recognize them. I remember, for example, having a peculiar fascination with my first English textbook. I had no idea what "English" was. It was just a name on one of the books my mother brought home from the bookstore on a hot August afternoon so I could start the third grade. But I remember feeling excited when I touched its shiny orange cover. Its smooth stiff spine seemed to hold some magic attraction. After school started, as I sat conjugating verbs and diagramming sentences, I couldn't imagine what the fascination had been.

But I was always an avid reader, and as a teenager I remember buying one new spiral notebook after another with the intention of writing my own book. I rarely got past the first few pages though, for at that stage of my life I had no stories to tell. But when it came time to declare a major in college, I chose English. For the life of me I don't know why I decided I would be an English teacher, but after one semester of practicum I knew teaching English was NOT FOR ME. Much later in life, however, after I'd been a practicing psychotherapist for six years, based on a serendipitous recommendation of a friend, I attended a conference on the future. To my surprise, it would rekindle my long-forgotten love of language and the desire to write . . . and alter the course of my life.

As I listened to the speakers describe the changes we could expect over the coming years, I had a sudden, startling realization. I wanted to write a book with my husband about new ways to live and work. This desire was as clear as if I'd always known it. I was ablaze with energy and rushed home to tell Paul that I wanted us to write a book together. He was equally excited. In that moment, yearnings that had woven loosely through my life like a recurring theme emerged as a full-fledged dream that we've been living now for over twenty years.

What are the recurring themes in your life? What dream fragments are woven through your lifetime?

FEELING DISCONTENT, DISSATISFACTION, AND DIS-EASE

As always, the seeds of my sudden desire to write a book had begun with a feeling of discontent. A feeling that there was something missing, something more I wanted. Although I didn't recognize it at the time as something I'd wanted to do all my life, a growing undercurrent of discontent led me to attend a conference I wouldn't otherwise have been interested in and to do so with an open heart and mind, willing to entertain new possibilities.

Often we don't allow ourselves to feel our desire for more. We believe we should be satisfied with the life we have. We allow school, a job, or family responsibilities to determine the nature and structure of our life without our ever actually considering if it's what we want. We may simply be living our lives the way we saw our parents live theirs. Or we may think we're living our dream, only to discover that the dream has run its course or turned out to be only part of the picture or even someone else's dream. For many years, for example, following my dream to become a writer was exhilarating and thrilling, everything a dream should be. We wrote ten books, all were still in print with over a million copies sold. We had other books in the making. What more could anyone want?

"You've had enough." "You can't ask for more." "What more can you expect?" "You can't have everything you want." "Aren't you ever satisfied?" How often do we hear such messages while growing up? How often do we say them to ourselves even now?

Each day I was feeling a little more tired at the end of the day, a little less eager to leap out of bed in the morning, a little less enthusiastic about doing more and more of what I'd once enjoyed so thoroughly. Then, three years ago, I got ill.

Often discontent, dissatisfaction, and dis-ease are natural precursors to some emerging desire. They're signals that we're hungry; alerting us that we're starving for something more. Think about it. When you start to get hungry, you feel a little uncomfortable and then you recognize that you want something to eat. The longer you go without eating, the worse you feel until you start to get irritable, maybe feel a little sick in your stomach, and before long you're ravenous. Of course, if you don't eat, eventually you get ill. That's how desire works.

Is it OK for you to want more?

If I'd been listening to the signals of discontent I might not have gotten ill. But sometimes we get so busy we don't notice that we're getting hungry until we feel really awful. That's what I had done. I was so busy doing what I thought I wanted to be doing, or felt I had to do, that I wasn't hearing the messages of discomfort and discontent that would have alerted me to the new desires I needed to pursue. The signals were buried under the details of my daily routine . . . until I got sick. Then I could no longer ignore the message that something was missing from my life. It seems there was another theme running through my life, one I'd long forgotten and hadn't listened to in years. Something alive and beating in my heart.

⟹ **Try This** ✩✩✩

Sit down now and complete these two sentences "All I want is . . ." and "If only I could just . . ."

In the classic musical *My Fair Lady* Eliza Doolittle tells us exactly what she wants—a room somewhere, far away from the cold night air. In fact, as the song goes, that's all she wants. What about you? Finding what you're yearning for often begins by paying attention to what you're muttering under your breath. When you hear yourself saying, "All I want is . . ." or, "If only I could just . . ." it's a sign that you're feeling frustrated, even desperate. The "all I want's" and "if only I could's" are almost always less than what we really want, but they are a doorway to our real desires. Once we give ourselves even a small taste of "all I want is . . ." we can move on to the other desires that underlie new dreams forming in our heart.

So how would you answer the question, "All I want is . . . ?" Get it out in the open right away, because you probably won't be able to get on with what you really want until you start to feel the undercurrent of dissatisfaction and discontent, large or small, that's permeating your life.

All I wanted was to get away for a while, to go someplace with no phone calls, no deadlines, no e-mail, no traffic, no long lines. Just some peace and quiet. But, of course, such protestations usually arise from deeper, more fundamental desires. They're a doorway to a deeper restlessness, dissatisfaction, yearning, or hunger from which a totally new dream will arise.

No matter how many days I set aside to relax, for example, no matter how many days I asked my assistant to hold my calls, no matter how many extensions I got on particular deadlines, that uncomfortable, discontented feeling just wouldn't go away . . . until it finally led me to do something I never could find the time to do.

Although various friends had invited us to visit them in retreatlike settings before, we "could never get away." We couldn't fit a nonwork-related trip into our schedule. But when some friends we hadn't seen in years asked us to come visit them in their mountain cabin, to my surprise we said yes. Even as we drove the hour and forty minutes it took to get there, I was concerned about taking such a frivolous trip. Little did I know that one three-day, Fourth of July weekend would change the course of my life forever by taking me back in time to experience firsthand just how much I was missing. Once again serendipity had presented me with exactly what I needed. But if I hadn't been at my wits' end, I would most certainly have overlooked it.

In his book *Finding the Hat That Fits*, John Caple calls such discomfort *"divine discontent"* and he identifies several signals that let us know when it's time to start listening for what it's telling us. We've elaborated on his list below.

SIGNS OF DISCONTENT

Here are sixteen signs that there's something missing in life and a new desire is waiting to be born. Are any of them familiar?

___ Not wanting to get out of bed

___ Feeling mildly depressed for days on end

___ Difficulty motivating yourself to do routine tasks

___ Overeating, using alcohol, drugs, or TV to feel better or escape

___ Losing interest in things that once engaged you

___ Feeling chronically tired, de-energized, and listless

___ Nagging doubts about yourself and the course of your life

___ Losing a sense of enthusiam

___ Worrying about how you'll keep things together

___ Getting frequent headaches, stomach upset, and other aches and pains

___ Feeling bored and restless

___ Sleeping too much or too little

___ Wishing you were someone else

___ Nagging, complaining, and bitching

___ Having frequently bad dreams or nightmares

___ Feeling constantly overwhelmed and irritable

As you read this handbook, let your feelings of dissatisfaction and restlessness surface and heighten.

As long as we dwell in complacency, as long as we won't allow ourselves to feel discontent, as long as we deny that things are less than we desire, as long as we drown our dissatisfactions in diversions like drinking, doing drugs, watching endless hours of television, overeating, sleeping long hours, or whatever, we will never connect with the desires and yearnings that can point us in the direction of the changes we need to make.

Once we acknowledge our dissatisfaction, we open the door to once again feel the magic of being alive we've known in times past and long to feel again.

REMEMBERING THE MAGIC

Remember when you were a small child? Remember that magic feeling you used to have sometimes when you first woke up in the morning of a special day? Remember the feeling of everything being fresh and new and tingling with possibility? Remember that almost electric feeling that anything could happen?

Maybe it was the morning of the first day of school. Or maybe it was the beginning of summer vacation. Maybe it was the night before a big game, heading off to summer camp, or Christmas Eve. Later in life, maybe it was getting ready for your first date with a special someone who made your heart stop. Maybe it was your senior prom. A graduation ceremony. Your wedding day. The birth of your first child. Or a moment when you not only achieved a long-desired goal but also surprised yourself by surpassing even your greatest expectations of what you could do. Sometimes you can pinpoint no reason at all for the magic you feel, but you remember the moment all the same.

Well, we were about to have one of those magic moments as we approached our friend's cabin in Pine Mountain. The trip began quite conventionally. Packing, lugging things to the car, hitting the freeway traffic that makes you wonder if you should have stayed home, the blasé scenery you could see along any six-lane highway in the U.S.A. But well into our trip, as we turned off the interstate to head inland, we began noticing a dramatic change in the landscape. The desert was morphing into a forest. The temperature was dropping. We turned off the air-conditioning and rolled down the car windows to a welcomed breeze and the sweet smell of pine trees. But it wasn't until we turned off the highway into the Los Padres National Forest that we knew something extraordinary was about to happen. As we rounded the first bend into Pine Mountain, we had to catch our breath at the sight of the towering trees and S-curved vistas and knew we were having one of those experiences we'd never forget.

We call such times Magic Moments—those rare turning points in life when suddenly you feel totally alive and vibrant. When time seems to stand still and everything seems to flow effortlessly. Everyday cares fall away and you feel unaccustomedly at peace with yourself and in harmony with life around you. We'd had such moments before, but it had been quite some time. Chances are you've had such moments in your life, although you may not remember them. It's the magic of these moments that most of us want and need to recapture in our lives.

The memory of such moments, however buried as they may be, lie beneath whatever restlessness and discontent we're feeling, connecting us to the best of our past. Capturing and remembering these moments provides an undeniable sense of what we've lost and enables us to begin the journey that will bring it back into our lives.

Try This

Take a few minutes to recall the Magic Moments, large or small, in your own past. Sometimes, as you can see from some of the following examples others have shared with us in our workshops, the small moments can be as powerful as the large ones.

"Those were the days, all right," he recalled with the gleam in his eye that lit up his voice. "Snapping the ball around the infield. Stirring up the chatter in the outfield. Running after fly balls till my legs hurt. Playing heads-up ball. Looking alive. That's it. That's being alive!"

"My grandmother and I would sit on the big swing on the front porch, and she would tell me stories about the teddy bear who traveled to China in an underground elevator." Years melted from her face as she remembered. "The locusts would be singing and the crickets would be chirping and she would braid my hair. Summer afternoons on Grandma's porch. Time would stand still."

"When I was little, I used to dream of being a circus star. My dad would take me to the circus every year and we'd walk through the tents and I'd close my eyes and smell the hay and the canvas and the rope and the animals and I could see myself on the high wire. I still have all the old programs on the top shelf of my closet. I can show you," she offered, hoping we'd urge her to go get them down.

"She asked me what I'd want if I could have anything and I said I'd love to have the bathroom redone with a Jacuzzi and she said, 'That's it? That's what you want most?' And I started to cry as I thought about all the dreams I had lost." She looked as if she would cry again as she spoke.

Not everyone has positive memories at first when they try to recall the Magic Moments of the past. If you have trouble, start writing about whatever you're experiencing as you think about the past and work your way through to the magic like this example:

"I didn't want to try to remember magic times from my youth. All I could think of were the disappointments, all the things that didn't work out for me, the embarrassments. But then I started to remember the magic I used to feel exploring new routes to get to school. I found at least ten different ways to cover that ten blocks. I remember the alleys and roundabout shortcuts that made me late to school so many mornings. I remembered how excited I felt every year opening brand-new textbooks. They smelled so good and were filled with the promise of so many things I didn't know. I remembered how excited I was to wake up and see the first snow of the year. How we'd all head for Chelsea Park with our sleds and pile on and streak down the steepest hill, and almost slide right into the Jersey Creek. How the snow would cake on our mittens and we'd always have to taste it."

THE INNER COMPASS

This magic feeling has been called many different things. Some people refer to it as "optimal" or "peak" experience.

Behavioral researcher Mihaly Csikszentmihalyi calls it "flow," because that's the term people often use to describe how it feels: "It's like floating"; "I was carried by the flow." Whatever it's called, it's accompanied by amazing bursts of energy. It draws out the best of our abilities and strengths we didn't know we had. Dedication and determination kick in. It's almost addictive, in that we want to experience it again and again.

We refer to the unusual level of drive and determination these Magic Moments inspire in us as the "Rudy Factor," after Rudy Ruettiger. His legendary efforts to make the Notre Dame football team despite the seemingly impossible odds of his slight five-foot-six-inch frame and a mediocre high school academic history inspired the movie *Rudy*.

You may have seen the Rudy Factor operating in young children at play or when trying to master some activity like walking or riding a bike, jumping rope, skateboarding, or playing jacks. They do it over and over, falling and tipping over and tripping and floundering, again and again, but undaunted and oblivious to time or who's watching. This is precisely the kind of energy "that magic feeling" can release. It transforms us into someone who can do just about anything we set our mind to; and it's just what we need to reclaim what's missing in our lives.

The more an activity captures that magic feeling, the more likely the Rudy Factor will start working for you, and your chances of doing whatever you're intent upon doing go up dramatically. And vice versa. The less an activity feels like one of your Magic Moments, the better served you will be to head in another direction. So, consider this magic feeling to be like a barometer, or better yet, an inner compass.

Throughout life we have many opportunities to weigh how we feel about one direction over another, compare one option to another, or consider one path against another. In weighing our choices, we can return every time to this inner compass. We can use it as a reference point to compare all options we consider in charting our future.

➡ **Try This** ☆☆
               ☆

Give your choices the "Magic Test." Is there any magic in them? Can you feel it? Poet Rusty Berkus calls it her Goose Bump Test. "When I get goose bumps from an idea or possibility," she says, "I know I better proceed that way."

We got goose bumps often over that Fourth of July weekend in Pine Mountain. I could feel the magic in the air. We had begun to remember . . . because what we had lost was right there before our eyes.

LOOKING BACK TO LOOK AHEAD

We can't miss what we don't remember, but we feel instead a vague sense of loss or yearning that only remembering can heal, an undefined nostalgia often triggered unexpectedly by a strain of music, a scene in a movie, or suddenly coming upon the very thing you're missing.

For example, I had forgotten about "dark," that is when you can't see your hand in front of your face. Years of headlights, clock radios, high-intensity streetlights, crime-deterring garage lights that glare in your bedroom window—all this light had erased my memory of dark. But when confronted with darkness I remembered how, as little kids, my brother and I were afraid of the dark because it was *dark*. We would whisper stories to each other in the void of night until we fell asleep, reassured by the sound of each other's voices.

I had forgotten stars, as in that thick, sparkling blanket that fills the nighttime sky outside the city. "Stars!" I exclaimed with glee as if meeting a long-lost friend. And I suddenly remembered hours of stargazing, lying on my back on the picnic table in my parents' backyard, pondering the mysteries of life.

I had forgotten friendly, as in making eye contact with strangers, greeting each other with a smile, a hello, or a wave of the hand. Can I remember that? Certainly not for years past. Head down, walking straight ahead, minding your own business. It's not polite to stare. You won't see anyone you know anyway. That's what I knew. But once upon a time I must have known something different, because the first friendly "hello" triggered some long-ago programmed reaction. "Oh, yes," I thought. "Friendly, smile, wave, say hello."

I had forgotten that once upon a time you could talk to children without that look of horror crossing their face: STRANGER!! DANGER!! Children laughing, running up to show you their winnings from a booth at the fair. But I remembered as I saw it once again.

I had forgotten wind, the sound you hear when there are a lot of trees and no traffic. What was that sound I kept hearing? Is there a highway nearby? Could that be the wind blowing through the trees? No, it wouldn't be that loud. Oh, that's the "roar" of the wind! I remember having heard the wind described that way.

I had forgotten about not having to lock the car when you ran in the store and about leaving your house unlocked while you went uptown. But now I remembered coming home from school in the midafternoon. The door was never locked even if Mother wasn't home. I remembered going over to Daddy Jim and Aunt Pauline's house. They were our next-door neighbors. My brother and I were welcome to walk in anytime, whether they were home or not, because they were like family, and the door was never locked.

And speaking of neighbors. I had forgotten knowing your neighbors as more than a polite "Hello, how have you been?" I'd forgotten about sitting on the porch, dropping by to chat, and stopping on the street to pass on some news. Oh, and I'd forgotten all about going over to help make a cherry pie for the Fourth of July. Frankly I'd forgotten about seeing anyone I knew without making an appointment. I could walk through the crowded malls near where I'd been living for hours or days and never see a familiar face.

Yes, familiarity. That's something else I'd forgotten. Seeing the same faces at the post office every day. Faces of people who knew your name and you knew theirs. People who talk to you as people, not as clerks.

I'd forgotten about community fairs where everyone can participate without applying, auditioning, or knowing someone who knows someone. A community that wants you to participate instead of pay at the gate, because they need you.

"Yes, yes, yes," my heart said. "I remember. I remember and that's what I want! I want trees, and wind and stars, and the songs of birds, and friendly faces that know my name, all that and more. I want to write in a place like that." The memory of those spiral notebooks I kept buying as a teenager flashed through my mind. I was sitting, notebook on my lap, pencil in hand, out on the porch or under the weeping willow tree yearning to have stories to tell and there was wind and there were trees and there were the songs of birds . . .

I began to hear it, a faint wild beating of my heart, a pulsating desire that moved me to tears.

➡ **Try This**

What have you lost? Or never had, but wished you did? What are you yearning to have in your life now? . . . Someday? Remember. Put words to them. Write them down and don't forget.

2

IMAGINING IT NOW

*Imagination is a preview of life's
coming attractions.*

ALBERT EINSTEIN

"You have such a vivid imagination," my mother told me
again and again. It wasn't a compliment. She found my
imagination exasperating. But it's turned out to be a godsend because there's nothing much worse than living day after day with a
burning desire that has no place to go. Desire is a powerful creative force, loaded and ready to fire at its target, but what if there's
no target?

What if you yearn to leave your high-paying, high-stress job to
simplify your life but you have a serious preexisting health condition and fear you'll never get another health insurance policy?

What if you yearn to be home with your new baby but you
need the income from working outside the home?

What if you want to live closer to nature but you're trapped in
the big city because your high-rise condo won't sell?

What if you yearn to spend your days creating the art that lives
in your heart, but you can't see any way to pay the bills if you do?

What if you're heartsick about the slaughtering of horses and
yearn to do something about it but you don't have the time to volunteer or the money to contribute?

What if you want to travel the globe, but your job doesn't leave you any time to get away for more than a couple of days at a time?

What if you're a doctor pressured by managed care to pack more and more patients into each day and you don't want to practice medicine that way, but you have two kids to put through college?

The list of unfulfilled yearnings goes on and on these days. Paul and I receive thousands of e-mail messages and letters every year asking us about such dilemmas. They're usually written in desperation and end with a similar plea: "Do you have any ideas for what I can do?" The frustration jumps right off the page and through the computer screen. And it's no wonder because a burning desire with no place to go can eat your heart away, burn you out, and tear your insides up. But, in the long run that's good because one thing all practical dreamers share in common is a sense of urgency to make things happen, and a burning desire can most certainly provide you with a sense of urgency.

Wanting something real bad is like sitting down on a hot stove. It'll get you moving real fast, but, of course, you've got to have somewhere to go and that's why many of the people who contact us are feeling so desperate. They have the desire, but no idea or dream for how to fulfill it.

The solution to each of their dilemmas is the same: imagination! Imagination paints a target toward which we can aim our burning desires. It gives us somewhere to go. And it's something we can all do, if we allow ourselves to. All of the above dilemmas and many others have been resolved with a little imagination.

PICK UP YOUR FOOT

I want to start a home business," the woman began in earnest, "so I can be home with my kids. But *I don't have any idea* what I could do at home. What do you suggest?" We used to answer this all-too-familiar question by asking a series of questions in return like, What have you been doing? What interests you? What have you thought of? And so on. Unfortunately this response usually produced a recitation of previous work history, all the computer equipment and software the person owned, the various hot home businesses the person had heard about, etc., etc. In other words, a snapshot of all the confusion the person was experiencing.

We discovered the best way to answer this question quite by accident. One day I decided to prescribe for someone what I thought she could do based on the litany of assets she had described. "You know, I think information brokering would be excellent for you," I declared with a sense of relief at having come up with something so seemingly well-suited for her. "Oh," she replied quickly, dismissing my idea, "what I've always wanted to do is . . ." She went on to tell me in detail exactly what she really wanted to do and as she did, her voice became animated and her eyes lit up with excitement. "But," she concluded, puzzled again, "do you think that would be feasible?"

Wait! I thought. This is fabulous! *She did have an idea!* In fact, she had a dream, something she'd been wanting to do but hadn't entertained as possible until I proposed something entirely different. How many other people, I wondered, have an idea about what they want in their lives but just don't take it seriously enough to entertain it as a possibility? We began to check it out and without exception, everyone who approached us to say they didn't have any idea what they could do to change their lives suddenly had an idea once we ascribed some particular direction for them!

Clearly, to come up with a dream for how to create what you're yearning for, you've got to pick up your foot—the one that's stuck in the world of practical reality—long enough to at least entertain the possibility of whatever dreams pop into your imagination.

What if we could live in Pine Mountain? for example. Now there was a far-out idea! At first it was just a crazy thought—which I kept to myself, of course, not wanting to exasperate anyone. Then, probably because I have such a "vivid imagination," I began to imagine myself living there. We could recapture so

much of what we'd lost without even knowing it. We'd be surrounded by natural beauty, right in the center of a national forest
with a sense of inner and outer peacefulness. The pace of daily life
would make more sense, no rush, no crowds, no ATM's, no cell
phones, no traffic lights, but pretty much every other modern
convenience anyone could want including satellite, cable, an Internet ISP, a nail salon, and even t'ai chi classes. All within less
than two hours of the heart of Los Angeles!

I was just playing with the idea, of course. I made that clear to
the practical side of myself. It was only Saturday, after all, and I'd
been there only one day, so "Hey," I told myself, "this is just for
fun. It's only make-believe, so don't freak out! Just let me hop
around on one foot over here for a while in my fantasy. I'll come
back to reality soon enough. Anyway, it's a three-day weekend!
Give me a break!"

After all, the practical dreamer is *walking* with a foot in each
world, not *standing*. We get to spend some time strictly in our
fantasies and some time strictly in reality as we step back and
forth from one foot into one world and then into the other.

*What if you could do what you really want to do? Pick up your foot
and just imagine. Pretend anything is possible.*

ENTERTAIN THE POSSIBILITY

My mother and I had an ongoing argument when I was
younger. She regretted she hadn't had the choices I'd had
to go to college and have a career. In her opinion she wasn't able
to do these things until she was well past forty and had finished
raising her family. In my opinion she'd always had the choice to
go back to school, but had chosen instead to stay home and raise
a family.

We went around and around on this point and neither of us
would budge from her position. "You just don't understand," she
would tell me. "I did not have a choice." Only years later did I un-

derstand that actually we were both right. Theoretically, she had a choice, albeit an unconventional and socially unacceptable one at the time, but there have always been those few mavericks who defy convention—the Annie Oakleys, the George Washington Carvers and Amelia Earharts of their time. So she had a choice. But actually she didn't have a choice, because she didn't entertain the possibility of having one.

Once her family was raised, she did entertain that possibility. At that moment her desire became possible and she actually had a choice, which she took. She went back to school, completed her B.A., M.A., and Ph.D., and became a college history professor.

We can imagine anything, but that can never be enough to fulfill our desires. As long as we only dream, we have only dreams, but the moment we entertain the possibility that a dream could become a reality, we've created that possibility. We can't see possibilities until we consider the possibility of possibilities. But once we do, our imagination can become a bridge between desire and reality.

The social order of my mother's time had impressed upon her over a lifetime that women had to stay home to raise children. The social order of today has impressed upon us that we must live harried, stressful lives in crowded, polluted cities or suburbs. It's just the way things are. If it is to be different we must entertain the possibility that it could be.

Do you have a list of reasons things have to be the way they are in your life? What if there were some as yet undiscovered way around them all? What if you were to pretend it's possible to live the way you'd prefer to live? Can you entertain the possibility without yet knowing how it could happen?

He wanted to leave his job. But everyone was depending on him, his family, the company. The anguish showed in his eyes. He could feel the yearning for a simpler, slower life. A job more reflective of his personal and spiritual values. A job that left time to coach his son's soccer team, or at least attend the games. Some time perhaps to plant a garden. He'd loved to garden as a boy, but he couldn't remember the last time he'd had his hands in the soil. But what could he do? Nothing came to mind. Every option he thought of was worse or at least no better than his current position. Why couldn't he think of any other possibilities?

Each time he tried to imagine what he could do differently, he felt terrible. Angry. Sad. Frustrated. It was almost worse than just putting up with the current situation. "Just knuckle down and stick it out," he told himself. But the feelings of discontent and yearning wouldn't leave. He began keeping a journal. Asking himself over and over what did he really want? Gradually he realized that he felt too guilty to really entertain the possibility of changing his life. He had been raised in a family where the man's role was to put the welfare and desires of the family before his own. In fact, desire was considered self-indulgent, even sinful.

But his misery was affecting his household anyway. Always grumpy, he was snapping at his kids and his wife. They were spending even less time with him and why not? He didn't like being around himself, why should they? Ultimately, sacrifice is resented even by those who benefit from it.

Finally one night he sat down and talked to his family. He told them how much he wanted to leave his job and probably his line of work. Their response surprised him. Everyone thought he should find something new to do and wanted to help him come up with ideas. After a while they were all brainstorming possibilities. Why not start a lawn and garden service? Or set up an Internet business? Or ask his boss for a flextime arrangement? "You always told us we could do anything we set our minds to, Dad," his youngest son reminded him, "so there must be a way."

 **Try This**

Set aside a dreamtime for yourself, a quiet time when you can write, think, or meditate about what you're yearning for. Ask often, what is it

I really want? Create a dream journal to record your thoughts. Allow
time to understand what you're feeling and to let new possibilities arise.
You may be surprised with what you discover.

"The more I asked myself what I really wanted, the less familiar the answers were," the executive told us. "I thought I wanted
more money, more success, more opportunity to shine on my job
and get to the top. Everyone had said a woman couldn't make it
in this industry, and I had. But I thought I wanted more. Having
a television show of my own was being discussed. I was being considered to oversee a new media campaign."

When she first began setting aside dreamtime, these were the
kinds of dreams she focused on. The television show. Maybe
an Emmy nomination. Definitely a twenty-six-week contract.
"That's really what I thought I wanted. But before long the more
I focused on what I yearned for, something entirely different
emerged. I kept having fantasies like these:

"I'm sitting quietly reading by the fire, a mug of tea on the table
beside me. A Chopin concerto playing softly in the background.
My mind drifting with fascination into a world of new ideas and
new possibilities. There are no other demands to distract me. Lift-
ing my eyes from the page to savor a thought too large for reading on, I gaze out the window at the trees that shade my walkway.
And I can feel the days flowing leisurely by from day to day."

Soon instead of strategizing what she could do to get the chance
to take on more responsibility at work, she was imagining how she
could cut back her hours to a simple forty-hour week. Then she'd
actually have some time to just sit by the fire in the new house she'd
built with her success, the house she rarely saw in the daylight.

Freed to imagine how we could create what we're really yearning for, we can begin to entertain possibilities we would previously have overlooked or discounted. And of course, knowing
about the possibilities others have come up with can help to spur
our imagination, too.

Flextime was the answer for Neil Teplica. A travel aficionado, he wanted to explore remote locales around the world and start an off-beat travel-oriented Web site, but his job as a real estate consultant left him with little spare time. Negotiating flextime hours with his company provided him with the freedom to pursue these new desires.

Lawyer Demaris Brinton knew she needed to get away from the madding crowd and wanted off the treadmill. But that meant leaving her $100,000 salary, which would double when she made partner. She chose to walk away from that opportunity and took a full-time job in an exurb of about 14,000 people seventy miles north of San Francisco. There she works for the nonprofit agency where she'd been doing volunteer fund-raising to preserve the rain forest.

Thirteen years ago, Jim Haggerty was feeling burned out on his job as a mortgage broker when, standing at a newsstand, he saw a magazine about model trains. The magical feeling he'd had as a child playing with his own model trains swept over him and he started to imagine how he could bring that feeling back into his life. He soon left his paycheck behind to start his own business creating limited-edition railroad buildings for HO-scale model-train kits, which he sells to collectors and hobbyists.

Mother of four, Liz Danzinger wanted to spend more time with her kids without giving up the work she loved and the income it provided her family. She began thinking about how she could repackage the writing skills she used in her job in public relations into a home-based business. She now works at home twenty hours a week doing technical writing and earns more than she did in her job. This leaves ample time for her kids, especially since another innovative possibility she entertained was to hire help, not to sit with her kids, but to take care of the house so she could take care of the kids.

When George Hoeing graduated from the Chicago School of Fine Arts, he didn't like either of the customary options presented to him. He didn't want to take a job pumping out layouts and logo designs for ad agencies and other organizations like most of the other graduates would be doing. But he also didn't relish the idea of becoming a starving artist, living hand to mouth until he got a break in local galleries or art shows. He wanted to share his designs with the world and didn't want to wait to be discovered. His interest in bodybuilding became the innovative bridge to his future. He created a line of his own clothing for bodybuilders based on his original designs and sells them at premium prices through gyms across the country.

Linda Moss was horrified by the fate of the 10,000 horses that are exported for slaughter each year from California. Her solution was to create the Equus Sanctuary, a rescue center on a forty-acre ranch she arranged to acquire in Antelope Valley, California. There she provides homes for 300 old, disabled, or unwanted horses. The sanctuary, one of several in California, is supported entirely through private donations.

A group of northern California doctors in family practice decided to challenge the assumption that doctors can't have a family life. They saw their young children growing up before their eyes and knew that soon they would have missed the experience of parenthood. By redistributing their workload and sharing patient responsibilities, each doctor now works only part-time.

It's amazing what can happen when you entertain the possibility.

PICK A TARGET

That Saturday afternoon in Pine Mountain, I began imagining how we could spend more of our life up there. Maybe we could sell our home and live there full-time. Or we could continue living in the city and buy a little cabin where I could write for part of each month. We could move up there and get a little apartment in town for business meetings. Or we could just stay where we were and rent a cabin for lots of long weekends.

I was just imagining possibilities, of course, so I was still standing on just one foot. I had yet to consider if any of these ideas would actually be practical. I gave my imagination free reign and the next thing we knew, Paul and I were brainstorming ideas for doing seminars up there. Setting up a nature-based Web site. Walking for hours in the forest. Thinking about how much calmer we'd feel. How much more productive and healthier we'd be. Imagining ourselves making new friends and becoming active in the community. That part of the fantasy was particularly appealing to Paul, who had been very active in the community years before when we lived in Kansas City and had missed the opportunity for community involvement.

With each possibility we imagined, a new shared dream was taking shape and growing closer to becoming a reality. But we knew as soon as we left Pine Mountain, we'd be swept back into the hectic, whirlwind pace of our life. Within moments of our return, our newly recognized yearnings and all the exciting possibilities we'd been imagining could be swallowed up by life as usual. Hadn't it happened before? Energizing, neat, new ideas, lost to an over-pressured, overcrowded schedule. It happens all too easily.

So even though we didn't know yet if any of our ideas were realistic, we needed a target we could start moving toward, something we could focus on. Our friend Mary Ann posed the perfect solution. "Would you like to go looking at houses this afternoon before you leave?" she asked first thing on Sunday morning. We jumped at the chance. And so began our hunt for a house in Pine Mountain.

➡ Try This ✫✫

Pick a target dream that could fulfill what you're yearning for. You don't have to know if it will work, or even if it's what you will ultimately want to do. But having a target will give your burning desire, a direction to go in. It will begin a process of exploration and create the momentum for discovering the activities that will ultimately take you where you want to go. If you reach a dead end with one target, pick another one.

GO IN THE BACK DOOR

There's nothing like picking a target to make the other foot drop, the one that likes walking in the real world! At the very hint of actually doing something about an otherwise ideal fantasy, reality usually rears its head with the same old, familiar refrains: "You can't do that." "That's just not possible." "It's not a good time." "We can't afford it." Most dreams sound, look, and feel unrealistic, at least at first. From a practical point of view, it's never a good time and you rarely think you can afford it. So, you can't turn infant dreams over to the practical side of yourself to be number-crunched and analyzed until you can make a cogent case for them.

A number of years ago, for example, we certainly couldn't afford, nor was it the right time, to get a *third dog*. But I decided I *had to have* a female whippet. At the time I was running a mile every morning through the streets of Sierra Madre. On my run one morning I came upon two doe-like creatures that looked like nothing I'd ever seen before. They were standing side by side on the sidewalk seemingly lost, but looking like they stepped right out of an art nouveau etching. I was enchanted and once I saw that their owner was coming to retrieve them, I ran home as quickly as I could to look the breed up in the American Kennel Club manual.

From that moment on, I had to have a whippet. So, first came Wiley. He was a marvelous dog, but I wanted a matched set. Now that, even I had to agree, was really impractical, considering we already had a second dog, a Scottish terrier, and these were thoroughbreds, thereby expensive. But when it comes to wanting the impractical I never try going through the front door anymore to get it. It just stirs up too many inner battles I can never win and buries my desires in too many solid arguments I can't yet refute. So I set a target and go in the back door.

The inner dialogue goes something like this: "I want to get a female whippet—not now of course. Right now I'm just going to go looking at whippets. Then we'll see, you never know what might happen."

This approach always pacifies the practical side of me, which instead of stomping all over my ideas with why I can't do what I want, just lets me go off and play make-believe. So I spent several Sundays reading the want ads and going to look at whippets. Sure enough, they were too expensive. But then one Sunday, I spied an intriguing ad. It read: "Whippet pups. Free." What? Free whippet pups? How could that be? Of course I couldn't get there fast enough, but, alas, the "free" pups were as unappealingly gawky to me as they were to their owner.

But there was one absolutely stunning pup remaining in the pen. "That one," I blurted out. "How about that one?" "Oh," the woman replied, "that's Pleasure. I'm keeping her." Crestfallen, I continued looking at the gawky pups she'd brought out for me to consider. Meanwhile, I started to tell her about how I wanted a female companion for our wonderful male whippet, Wiley, and got out his picture to show her.

"Wiley!" she exclaimed. "You have Wiley!" It turns out she knew all about Wiley and just loved him. She talked animatedly with me about how he'd been destined to become a grand champion when, at six months, he drew one of his testicles up out of the scrotum during a cross-country flight in jet cargo bay. There it remained, undescended, thus ending his much-anticipated show career. She ooh'ed and aah'ed over his picture and promptly decided to bring Pleasure out of her pen, "just so I could take a closer look." And thus it was that shortly thereafter I left carrying Pleasure, my free female Whippet, to my car, having gladly agreed to co-own and show her.

It was in this spirit that we began looking at houses in Pine Mountain. "Let's just go and look. Then, we'll see. You never know what could happen."

Try it. It works even if it doesn't always work out as intended, because often when you see what happens, you know what you need to do next, and next, and next.

CREATE AN ANCHOR

That Sunday afternoon we saw that there were some homes in Pine Mountain that we could afford and one we absolutely loved overlooking a pond but that we couldn't afford. But all too soon we were heading back to Los Angeles, wanting to make sure we could keep the momentum flowing once we'd got back to the practical realities of our day-to-day life. So, we scheduled a series of return trips to continue our search—just to see what might happen.

Meanwhile, unbeknownst to us, we'd already created a powerful anchor that would enable us to keep our desire alive and blazing. Mary Ann had taken some pictures of us in our favorite Pine Mountain spots, including our dream house on the pond. We carried these pictures with us everywhere and pulled them out at every opportunity. We told the story of our magical weekend over and over to anyone who would listen. The pictures and the storytelling became our touchstones. With them on hand we couldn't forget what we'd discovered, nor could we stop yearning to have it become a regular part of our lives.

These anchors pulled us back into our dream again and again so we could continue walking with one foot in the world we hoped would be our future.

 **Try This**

Find an anchor for your dreams and keep it with you or nearby. It could be a photograph, a picture, a clipping, an object, or any symbol that represents the target you've chosen to bring what you've been yearning for into your life.

3

BELIEVING IT COULD BE

*By choosing to believe something, we breathe
life into it and give it authority.*

CAROLYN MYSS

"I can't do it," she said. "I'm not artistic." We had asked a group of workshop participants to create a name tag that reflected where they were in their lives from a tableful of crayons, colored markers, glitter, glue, ribbon, and other art supplies. Looking down as she spoke, she obviously felt badly about herself, aware of all those who were sporting unique and interestingly decorated name tags.

"I did it," her seatmate volunteered quickly, "but it didn't come out like I intended." We quickly assured them both that we weren't having a contest to find the most unusual or stunning name tag. The goal was for each person to explore how they responded to the challenge of tapping into their imagination and using their creativity to turn what they imagined into a physical object.

The woman smiled in recognition. "I didn't believe I could do it, so I didn't even try, did I? I've already gotten my money's worth from this workshop," she asserted. "Give me that box of crayons!"

Why is it some people are willing to try to create what they imagine, while others cannot bring themselves even to try? We can dream up and entertain possibilities endlessly, but until we start to believe in them, they're simply entertaining. It's not until we begin to believe in our dreams that they take on a life of their own. Belief forms the bridge between what is and what will be. It takes us from "What if?" to "Why not?"

But, what is it that causes us to believe, or not, in ourselves and the possibilities we yearn for? Paul and I have asked this question of thousands of people who have created their dreams, from Olympic gold medalists to multimillionaires, from people who are improving the world through philanthropic endeavors to those who are enjoying a simpler, more rewarding life. On the surface, it appears as if their answers are as unique as their dreams.

From the time she discovered her true calling, for example, massage therapist Linda Miller dreamed of opening a day spa. First she worked in a resort, later in a chiropractic office, but all the while she believed that someday she would open her own spa. When Linda moved to Pine Mountain to marry her husband Ed she knew the time had come. Her mountain day spa retreat would be a place where people could heal both body and soul. "But," we asked her, "why did you think you would be able to open a day spa in such a small, remote community?" "Actually," she told us, "everyone said it would never work, but I knew I could do it."

First, from her knowledge of the field she knew that body work was a major trend and was expected to grow in popularity for years to come. Also, she knew people in the nearby urban areas of Los Angeles and Bakersfield were stressed out and eager to get away to relax. "And," she said, "I knew I could do it. I had experience over many years. I knew how spas operated. I'd done marketing for the chiropractic clinic, so I knew how to get business. I knew what I needed to charge, how much people would pay, and how much it would cost to operate as a business."

Linda sold most of her expensive belongings, kept her full-time job at the clinic that was an hour's drive away, and worked weekends to build her spa. A year later, when the business had grown to a level she could count on, she quit her job. She now works four days a week in her spa and has had as many as eighteen people on a waiting list for a given day.

Years before, Linda's husband Ed had been living in Los Angeles, operating his own business as a construction contractor. His work involved going into large apartment buildings to do repairs for management companies and, "Sometimes," he recalls, "I had to carry a concealed weapon in my pocket to protect myself." One day he was confronted by a ten-year-old boy who tried to rob and kill him. "I decided right then and there that the confrontation with this little kid wasn't worth my lifestyle and I decided to give it all up and get out of the city." He quit a very lucrative business and moved to the mountains.

"The mountains always had a magic appeal to me," Ed told us. "So finally one day I said there's got to be a better way. I left with my truck, tools, and one month's rent." He had no plan but just started "beating the woods" as hard as he could for business to see if he could make a living. "At first I was just doing piddling jobs for grocery money," he admits, "but I figured I could starve a little to make it happen." Aiming to do the best quality work he could, three years later he has a backlog of work, and says, "I'm too busy now to even think about any more business."

Best of all, he says, "When I quit working at the end of the day I don't have to take it home in my head anymore. I can just go home and stand out on the deck and look at the beautiful trees and animals all around and I can breathe again."

Across the continent, twenty-six-year-old Mark Hankins had risen from a job in quality assurance at JCPenney to become one of the company's well-paid designers. By chance, while riding a train in upstate New York, Hankins was reading an article about how Connie Chung had turned her career around by deciding to take control and do her own thing. Hankins got off the train at the next stop to call JCPenney and quit his job. Two weeks later he'd started his own company selling his own clothing line and had signed a licensing agreement with JCPenney that brought a million dollars into his new venture in the first year. He soon had other projects under way, too, including a contract with Vogue Butterick patterns.

After interior designer J. T. Taylor suffered a physical ailment that left her confined to a wheelchair, she knew she wouldn't be able to continue in her career. For many days while recovering, she lay in bed wondering what she would do, how she could re-design her life. A longtime collector of rare artifacts, she was in-spired throughout this period by a golden giraffe she kept on display in her bedroom, and one day, as she looked at that giraffe, the idea for what she knew she was to do popped into her mind. She would sell items like those she collected to interior decora-tors. The golden giraffe became the symbol for her business, One of a Kind, located in Irvine, California. No longer in a wheel-chair, Taylor loves her new business and never doubted it would be the success it has become.

Margot Andrew had never met a child with HIV or AIDS when she had an epiphany while working out at a gym. A painter with a master's degree in art working for a music video company, Andrew was talking with an HIV-positive man about children with AIDS when she remembered her childhood experiences at camp. Every summer while she was growing up she went to Camp Tanamakoon in northern Ontario for a month. As she re-membered how it had taught her to believe in herself, to her amazement she heard herself saying that she wanted to create a camp for children with HIV. Within four months she had estab-lished a nonprofit foundation, written 500 letters to foundations seeking funding, and secured a $5,000 donation from Hasbro—enough for a down payment on a location for a camp. Two years later, thirteen very sick children got off the bus at Camp Laurel. It was the first time Andrew had actually met a child with HIV. Shortly thereafter she quit her job to run the camp full-time on an annual budget of $650,000, serving 800 children and their families. She's a firm believer that "When chance is talking, you have to listen."

Although each of these stories is unique, they all have at least one thing in common. Each of these people had convinced themselves they could do what they yearned to do. They did this in their own way, based on some combination of facts and figures, past experience, trend tracking, intuition, the inspiration of others, or just pure faith. Sometimes quickly, sometimes slowly, they came to a point where they were able to stand in their dream and look over into reality and see that what they wanted was possible.

What do you believe? Can you stand in your dream, look into reality, and see it there? What would convince you to believe it's possible?

LOOKING INTO REALITY AND SEEING THE DREAM

However they convinced themselves, all these people and the thousands of others we've talked with who have shaped their lives to match their dreams had four things we need to have going for us to believe in our dreams enough to make them come true.

1. We need to have and recognize a burning desire.
2. We need to believe that desire is important.
3. We need to believe it's possible to fill that desire and that what has been can be different from what will be.
4. We must believe that, one way or another, it's possible for us to do whatever needs to be done to create what we desire.

Over the course of creating the life we're seeking, these beliefs will most likely be tested again and again. The strength of our belief in these four things will affect how we respond to these challenges. If our desire isn't strong enough it won't get us through the challenges of practical reality. If we don't believe that what we yearn for is important enough relative to the other demands, values, and priorities in our lives, it will slip from our daily agendas. If we don't think what we yearn for is possible, we won't be able to see what we need to do to create it. And while we may recognize that others have what it takes to live their dreams, if we don't believe that *we* can do it, too, that we deserve it and are worthy of it, we will defeat our best efforts.

Many years ago, for example, Paul and I discovered the coast of Oregon while driving up the coastline from Los Angeles to Vancouver. We were enchanted. It's a place where our greatest loves, the mountains and the sea, meet. We stayed up late one night imagining what it would be like to live there. Looking back we realize that even then we had a yearning to live in a place of such beauty, peace, and harmony. But relative to other desires in our lives at that time, the desire to live there wasn't strong enough, nor did we think it was that important for us then. Although there were some people living there, it was very remote, hours from the nearest airport and metro area. We couldn't imagine how we'd earn a living doing anything we knew how or wanted to do. So, our fantasy of living on the Oregon coast soon faded into a pleasant memory.

In contrast, we had a burning desire to write our first book, *Working from Home*. We believed passionately that it was important for people to know they had new choices for how to live and work that would give them greater freedom and control over their lives. Of course, we knew writing a book was possible, albeit a challenge, and we were confident that working from home was destined to be a growing and popular trend. So, we believed a book on this subject would be popular, and given our backgrounds, we believed that we had what it took to write that book. Paul was a lawyer by background, had run a company, and was a good researcher. I was a licensed clinical social worker and an English major. I had written many materials for the government agency where I'd worked. People were constantly encouraging us to write the book. "You should do it," we kept hearing.

Our belief was solid on all four points and that was a good thing because the strength of all four would be tested repeatedly in the years to come.

 **Try This**

Rate the strength of your belief in what you're yearning for. On a 10-point scale, with 10 being very strongly and 0 being not at all, evaluate the following: How strong is your desire? How important is it for you to reclaim what's been lost from your life or to find what you've never had but always wanted? Do you believe what you're seeking is possible? Is it possible for you as well as for others? Most people need to rate each of these issues at least as strongly as a 7 to believe that what they're seeking is truly possible.

THE GREAT DEBATE

Often the practical dreamer's first test is with the demons of their own doubt. Usually it's right at the point when we actually start to believe we could have a life that will fulfill and nurture us that the doubts begin to surface. Although some of us "just know," most of us need to be convinced before we can truly believe. When we start to look at what would be required, what we would have to give up, the implications, the consequences, everything that would be involved to create a simpler or more meaningful life . . . we start to wonder.

Our desire to live in Pine Mountain, for example, was high. And we were convinced it was important to make a change. I'd faced a life-threatening illness for the second time in my life, so I knew I needed to listen to my body's desire for a less stressful, more balanced lifestyle. We could see it was possible to live there; eighteen hundred people were already living there at least part-time, and as writers we could live anywhere within driving distance of a major airport. But as to whether we could pull up stakes

and move to a remote area an hour and forty minutes from anywhere, well, we had to wonder . . . ?

Of course, having doubts isn't necessarily bad. Doubts can
protect us from making serious mistakes. But we can't just suc-
cumb to them; we have to stand up to them and determine what
value, if any, they have. Fortunately, the best practical dreamers
are usually good debaters, particularly with themselves. While
there's no empirical research to prove it, I would bet the best
practical dreamers spent so much time debating with their parents that they could actually win a point or two at times.

I know I spent many hours debating with my father on just
about everything, but when it came to debating with myself,
there was a time when I couldn't stand up to my own doubts. I
had to either just give up on my ideas or ignore my doubts and
charge ahead rebelliously without regard for the consequences.

I thought I was a good writer, for example. After all, I was an
English major. I'd gotten mostly A's on the papers I'd written in
class and I'd written well-accepted materials for the agency where
I'd worked. But our first editor for *Working from Home* concluded,
after a year of many drafts, that we couldn't write. Assuming she
knew more than I did about our abilities, we went along with her
judgment and she hired a ghostwriter with forty books to his
credit to work with us. Another year and many more drafts later,
she concluded he couldn't write either. He was so distraught over
the situation that he left the field and the editor began looking for
another ghostwriter.

Meanwhile, a prestigious magazine asked us to write an article
about working from home. Despite the fact that I now knew I
couldn't write, with great trepidation I decided to give it a try and
sent in an article, certain that they would either reject it or have
to do extensive editing. To our amazement, the magazine editor
loved the article! In fact, she complimented us on how she didn't
have to change a word and wished all her writers would make her
job so easy.

It was an important lesson in learning to stand up to yourself and for yourself. If someone can undermine your confidence in your dreams, you haven't fully resolved your own doubts. Lesson learned and armed with the successful article, we went to the publisher to ask for the rights to our book back. He heard our case, looked at the article, and asked us to give him twenty-four hours. We were assigned to another editor, and *Working from Home* was accepted for publication six months later. We'd written every word ourselves.

Clearly, the more effectively we can stand up to and take on our own doubts, the stronger our beliefs in our dreams will become. But, if we don't face down our own doubts, they will hound us mercilessly. They will always be there, even if we proceed toward our goals. They'll be nipping at our heels, undermining our confidence, and constantly distracting us with having to fight them off. So, better to take a stand and make the best possible case for our desires. If we can't convince ourselves, how will we ever convince anyone else?

Can you stand up to your doubts? How do you respond to your dreams? Do you welcome your ideas with an open mind? Or do you fight them? Put them down? Debate them? Or just allow yourself to do whatever you please without question? Can you take a stand with yourself? Can you make and prove your case to yourself and to the world?

BUILDING A CASE

Our great Pine Mountain debate began the day we had to decide whether to make an offer on our dream house by the pond. We'd delayed it for as long as we could, basking in the excitement of playing with possibilities, but at that point we had to come to terms with whether or not we really believed our new dream was possible. The demons of doubt began yelling in my ear.

Actually there was little in our experience to suggest we could or would want to do this. The one time we'd lived outside the heart of a city was an eleven-year stint in a small suburban town. We HATED IT. "It's forty-five minutes from everywhere," we'd jokingly say to express our dismay. As we pondered this move, my mother reminded me, "You didn't even like living in Sierra Madre, how could you even think of living way out there in the boonies?" So my doubts went on from there.

"What if we were that unhappy again? It took two years to sell that house! How could you do this to yourself? You finally have everything you could want at your fingertips. Your life is working. How could you take such a risk? What if you don't like it? You could be very sorry."

"What about your equity? Your assets? Your net worth? Property values are sky high in Santa Monica, and rising. You always dreamed of living in Santa Monica. How could you give up your dream? You live two blocks from the ocean, for heaven's sake!"

"Santa Monica is one of the most desirable places in the world. There are only several other places in the world with an almost perfect climate. You're living with the highest temperature lows and the lowest temperature highs in the country and you want to move back to a four-season climate, with snow and slippery, icy roads, and mountain lions and bears! You've told your mother a thousand times that you and Paul would never again live anyplace where it was cold."

"There are so many opportunities in L.A. What if you get a chance to do your own TV show again? Who will take you seriously living in the middle of nowhere? What if you get snowed in and can't get to your speeches or media tours? How will you support yourself then?"

OK, so that's what we were up against, a barrage of doubts eating away at the fabric of our dream. But they also piqued my curiosity. I wanted to take them on. I wanted to build my case and take a stand. I was ready for the great debate. I wanted to convince myself this was the thing to do.

I had many sources of evidence to call on in defense of my

dream. Like Linda Miller, I had statistics, facts, and figures on my side. "Population growth in America's small towns and rural areas has been widespread," says demographer Ken Johnson of Loyola University. "The boonies are booming," scream the newspaper headlines—credit technology!"

"Old and young adults in pursuit of work and play are creating boomtowns away from the madding crowd," says *American Demographics.*

"Whatever name is used—'rural renaissance,' 'rural rebound,' or 'booming boondocks'—the American outback . . . is growing twice as fast as the non-metro gains during the entire decade of the 1980's," reports the *Cleveland Plain Dealer.*

"Knowledge workers are headed for small-town and rural America," says *The San Diego Union-Tribune.*

"Fastest-growing places you've never heard of," reports *Business Week,* "include Columbia, Tennessee; Moncks Corner, South Carolina; Gonzales, Louisiana; and Castle Rock, Colorado." Places, they say, where "romance and solitude remain but are joined by technology and commerce that allow professionals and entrepreneurs of all stripes to ply their trades from the prairies, the mountains, and the forests."

Technology, these articles emphasize, is making it possible for us to live and work from virtually anywhere via modem, fax, e-mail, teleconferencing, online meeting, tele-learning, and e-commerce. Soon we'll be able to buy almost anything on the Internet without ever having to leave home. Meanwhile, medical, scientific, and sociological research is showing we're better off in smaller communities closer to nature. Proximity to nature, we're told, speeds healing and boosts both creativity and the immune system. Smaller communities offer more meaningful and deeper experiences.

Journalist Joel Garreau says that we're living increasingly in what he calls "edge cities"—new urban satellites that not long ago were villages and cornfields. Or we're moving to what Jack

Lessing calls "penturbia"—small cities and towns interspersed by farms, forests, lakes, and rivers beyond normal commuting range of central cities. There, he says, "The stresses of acquisitive consumerism can be laid aside for new priorities of family life, environment and concern for people." More and more of us, it seems, will be living "blue jean dreams," say Tom and Marilyn Ross, co-authors of *Country Bound.* * So why not me?

Like the clothing designer Mark Hankins, who got off the train to tell his boss good-bye and chart his own course, I also could draw on the experience and inspiration of all the people we've interviewed who made daring choices to do what they truly wanted to even if it didn't seem practical. People like Randy Merrell, for example. For five years Merrell was a globe-trotting president of his own company manufacturing lightweight hiking boots. Although the experience promised riches, it emptied his spirits. His boots were selling well, but not wearing well. In the throwaway marketplace, consumers wanted new colors and new styles every year. His life had become a whirlwind of deals, debts, and financing. But Merrell missed the life of the craftsman he'd considered himself to be when he first began making boots. To him the important things in life are family, faith, and comfortable feet. So he left his business and returned to the workbench to make custom-fitted cowboy boots in the town of Vernal, in a rock-cliff farming valley in eastern Utah, where he lives with his four sons and his wife, LuAnn.

Merrell believes where you live is as important as the work you do there. Vernal, he says, is a place where his sons can learn about the outdoors and where "everything a man produces must please him first." And Merrell is a hard man to please; his reputation for creating the highest-quality boots earns him $1,000-plus for a pair of boots, and he never gets to the end of his back orders. Each customer must travel to Vernal and spend three to four hours get-

---

*See References at the end of this chapter for books by the individuals mentioned in this paragraph.

ting fitted not only with measurements, but via a videotape and a rubber stamp of their footprints. Then they must wait a year for their boots to arrive!

Randy and LuAnn also operate the Merrell Institute of Boot-making in Vernal, where students from stockbrokers to ballet dancers, police officers to computer technicians and business executives come from across the country for two weeks to learn the craft of bootmaking. Why do they come? The most frequent responses to that question, LuAnn reports, are to make something of quality with their hands, to gain control of their lives, and to escape office politics.

Similar motivations fill Michael Dunbar's courses on how to make the classic Colonial Windsor chair. Every two weeks a group of seven would-be woodworkers come from around the country to Dunbar's workshop in the small seacoast town of Hampton, New Hampshire, to learn to work with the antique smooth-hewing tools of the rough-hewn past that are required to craft these curved-back chairs. Students include accountants, programmers, public relations specialists, and laid-off information workers. One was Mark Blanchette. At age thirty-nine, after completing four classes with Dunbar, Mark quit his $36,000 job as a photographer for the Bangor, Maine, *Daily News* to build Windsor chairs. He builds two $550 chairs a week.

Closer to home, Stephanie and Rob Ladd were doing what they loved, but they didn't love where they thought they had to live to do it. Stephanie was a psychotherapist in private practice in Southern California, but she had grown up in the Midwest. A child of the country, she'd spent her childhood walking through the trees and having free rein to roam the woods. She was eager to leave for the big city when she grew up, but after twenty-plus years living in Southern California's San Fernando Valley, the stress was starting to get to her. She began wishing for the kind of life she'd had as a child. She especially wanted to provide her three-year-old daughter, Chloe, a life like that. "My dream,"

Stephanie told us, "was to find a place where I could live in the woods."

But Rob was a musician, so the Ladds felt tethered to Los Angeles. Rob had been a freelance drummer for his entire adult life, but he didn't want to tour anymore. Touring was very hard on his daughter, and knowing what he'd learned about parenting and child development from Stephanie, who specializes in child and family counseling, he'd concluded, "It just doesn't make any sense for me to be out on the road all the time. I want to do more recording work in town. My friends say, 'Well, that's nice, but someone has to put food in your daughter's mouth.' That's true," Rob admits, "someone needs to be able to put food in her mouth, but someone also needs to be her dad and her mom."

Unfortunately, the high cost of living in the valley seemed to preclude Rob's cutting back on touring. Then, friends invited the Ladds to visit Pine Mountain. It was remote but only a little over an hour from the recording studios. "I didn't even know this place existed," says Stephanie, "but I'd been envisioning it for a long time." Rob wasn't so sure. "Right away Stephanie said, 'We're moving,'" he remembers. "But I wanted to consider all of the possibilities and be the devil's advocate but each alternative I considered failed miserably."

The more they thought about it, the more it seemed the move could reduce their living expenses so Stephanie could have her home in the forest and Rob could stop touring. "I'm a believer that if things are meant to happen they will happen," Stephanie points out. "So we pretty much just made the plunge. For me it was a matter of letting go and letting it happen and it all seemed to just fall into place." She moved her part-time practice to the northernmost valley suburb and arranged with the forensic psychologist with whom she'd also been working part-time to telecommute. Within weeks of living in Pine Mountain she began a new career, one she'd never dreamed of. She's writing children's books about growing up in nature.

It wasn't until after the move that Rob realized just how much he hadn't liked where he'd been living. "The heat you're constantly trying to escape, the parking place you're constantly trying to find, the way you have to figure out how to get somewhere before the traffic gets bad, all this takes up a lot of your life. Now I'm not just doing what I want to do with my career, I'm doing what I want to do with my life."

So, I asserted in making my case, if all these people (and tens of thousands more) can do what they're doing to recapture what they've lost without losing what they've gained, why can't I? To this argument I also added the power of my intuition. It just felt right, and as futurists and market researchers Jim Taylor and Watts Wacker point out in their book *The 500 Year Delta*,* in times of rapid change and complexity, we must learn to develop and rely more heavily on our intuition. We can't get stuck in out-dated logical arguments.

Like Laurel Andrews, who started the camp for children with HIV, and J. T. Taylor, who found a new career as an art collector, I had the magic of a little serendipity on my side, too. By coincidence, a month before my birthday, my friend Mary Ann Halpin sent us a news release about her new photography book. I hadn't seen Mary Ann in years and was delighted to hear from her. I called and invited her to my upcoming birthday bash. She and her husband, Joe Croyle, came to the party and hooked up there with our neighbors Stuart and Helen Garber, who later invited the four of us over for dinner. That night at dinner, Mary Ann and Joe invited us up to their mountain cabin for the fateful Fourth of July weekend that was to spawn our dream. We were under so many deadlines! Normally we wouldn't have felt we could afford to take the time off for a visit, but something had told us to say yes.

Coincidentally, the house next door to Mary Ann and Joe's was for sale. This house was one of very few in Pine Mountain that overlooks a pond, making it one of the only places there that

---

*See References at the end of this chapter for information on this book.

would fulfill both my love for the forests and mountains and Paul's desire to live near a body of water! It was love at first sight. But the asking price for this house on the pond was beyond our budget . . . until the listing ran out and the owner took it off the market and decided to sell it himself at a price we could afford! How could we ignore all this fortuitous coincidence?

On all counts, the evidence was convincing. The doubts were losing the great debate. My dream was winning my confidence.

 **Try This**

To strengthen your belief, use your doubts to spur your curiosity. Gather your strongest evidence and prepare your best case. Draw as much as you can from your experience, statistics, trends, the experiences of others, facts and figures, examples in magazines, newspaper, TV, books, the Web. Include any chance coincidences and serendipity that suggest what you're seeking is meant to be. Evidence in hand, take a stand. Make your case. Present it first and foremost to yourself. Debate your doubts! Are you convinced? What would it take to defeat your doubts and believe?

A NOVEL EXPERIENCE

Fortunately, the best way to overcome our doubts and believe we can live in a world like the one we dream of is more like reading a novel than like passing an oral exam or obtaining a court ruling. We don't have to make our case before an omnipotent Judge Doubt and have our ideas for how we could fulfill our desires stamped with a swift and final "YES" or "NO." We don't need to force a decision. We can prepare and present our best-case scenarios and then allow the possibilities to germinate, much like what we do when we pick up a novel and find our way into the story. In reading a novel, we ease ourselves out of ordinary reality into an imaginary world that temporarily becomes real to us, and we then find our way back again to our ordinary life. We step in and out of these two realities each time we pick up or lay down the book. And so it is with dreaming. We need to step into a dream before we can really see it and believe in it.

In his book *The Gutenberg Elegies*, Sven Birkerts explains the process by which readers become engaged in a novel. It's very much like the process we go through in deciding to believe in a dream. Birkerts begins by describing the struggle of making the transition from the ordinary world of not reading to the make-believe world of reading. "I can't flip a switch and be *there*," he points out. As with our dreams, "There remains the larger dilemma—whether or not to invest myself in the book. I read the first few pages, try to read them well, to give them every chance." If he decides to stay with the book, he pushes on, trying to extinguish his other awareness as much as possible, "to pull the author's world around me entirely. I make myself susceptible to [it]. I can measure the difficulty of this by noting the extent of my distractedness. Until I feel a tug," and he's engaged in the novel.

At this point, Birkerts explains, he has occupied the book and the book has occupied him. "Its atmospheres bleed obscurely into mine. Because I am immersed, I carry the [book] with me every-where, returning to the narrative every time there is an opening in the day. . . . I will shift between two centers of awareness, the one required by my more worldly functions, the other . . . of my subjective, inward self. . . . Attending to two very different kinds of reality, reconnoitering between inner and outer focus . . ."

And so it is with our dreams. The evidence we've gathered, if persuasive, causes us to open progressively to the possibilities we dream of, and in our minds, we find ourselves slipping in and out of the dream as if it were reality. The edges between our life as it is and our life as we wish it to be begin to blur and we come to be-lieve in what we could at first only imagine.

In my case, I found myself imagining what each day would be like if I were living in our dream house in Pine Mountain. Each morning I'd awake to a memory of the cry of the ducks and the view of the pond from what would be our bedroom window. In my mind, I'd watch the sun creep down the hillside and filter its warmth into the room through the branches of that aromatic ponderosa outside the window. I'd pad in my slippers through the darkened living room, past the black iron stove on the way to the kitchen for breakfast. I'd sit at our dining room table over my bowl of oatmeal, and I would no longer be in our Santa Monica condo. I'd be in our new dining room gazing through the sliding doors onto the lush meadow below.

Each day as I'd go out to get our mail, instead of feeling the ocean breeze, in my mind I'd be walking to the post office in Pine Mountain, where the mail isn't delivered to the door. On Friday mornings while lugging the trash out to the curb, I'd imagine instead driving past the equestrian center, along the manicured greens of the golf course to the recycling center in Pine Mountain where you take your own carefully sorted trash.

When I grew weary from a tiring day, I'd walk in my mind through the forests on late afternoons. I'd sit on the redwood bench on our front porch, soaking in the beauty of the pines, secretly hoping I might catch sight of a deer and her fawn wandering by.

At 11:00 each night when we'd take our dogs out under the starless L.A. sky, I'd close my eyes and remember the sparkling Milky Way blanket that would cover our mountain home in the night. Before closing my eyes to sleep, I'd imagine sitting around the warmth of the fireplace late at night sharing a hot drink with the new friends gathered there.

I grew quite comfortable in my imaginary world of what could be. I felt at home there. Home. That's a word Paul and I often hear when people talk about having found work they love and doing it in a place they love. "It feels like home." That's what Stephanie Ladd had said about her move to Pine Mountain and her decision while living there to write children's books. Is that what I was yearning for, I wondered, a place that feels like home, a place to belong?

. . . As the days passed, my Pine Mountain dream came to feel so real I could not help but believe it would come true.

➡ **Try This** ☆☆☆

Create your own novel experience. Give your dream every chance. Give yourself over to it and wrap yourself in it entirely. Carry it with you and inhabit it as you go about your daily tasks. Occupy it and let it occupy you. Feel it. Hear it. Smell it. Taste it. Touch it.

THE LEAP OF FAITH

W hen it comes to believing in how the future will unfold, we can never *know*, but we can *choose* to believe, for beliefs are always a choice. No matter how carefully we plan or how much evidence we collect, we can never be sure that what we imagine will come to be until it does. Ultimately, pursuing our desires comes down to taking a leap of faith—or not.

Usually, as with a novel, a particular dream will either grow on us or it won't. We take to it or we don't. Like the book left unread on the nightstand, many dreams get laid aside, often without our even consciously deciding to do so. But if we take up a dream, sooner or later, we must make a leap of faith. Without faith we cannot step across the chasm between what is and what could be. Yes, that requires taking some risk because, by definition, faith is a belief that's not based on proof.

Should we? Dare we? The intensity of standing on the edge of that chasm, looking into the void toward what we hope will be a new life is exhilarating . . . breathtaking . . . and unnerving.

Do you dare?

Making a leap of faith doesn't mean assuming all will be well simply by wishing it to be. That ignores our role in the process of creating our own futures. Nor does it mean assuming that we can create precisely what we want, when, and how we want it by sheer force of our will. That's the old approach of trying to stamp our desires upon the future at all costs, without regard for our quality of life or that of others. That ignores the role that forces beyond ourselves play in the creation of the future.

So what is it the practical dreamer has faith in? What is it we must believe in? It's more than thinking positively and hoping for the best. In fact, if all we can do is "hope for the best," our chances of success are probably not good. We need to believe in ourselves and our ability to do what we intend to do *within the constraints of our existing reality*. We must believe we can create what we're seeking by working with or overcoming whatever forces of reality are involved.

That means trusting that we can respond to whatever we discover as we start down the path to our dream in a way that will ultimately meet our needs. In other words, making a leap of faith requires self-esteem and faith that we can handle the new possibilities that emerge from our interaction with reality. Often they're different from what we imagine when we take the leap, but we must be willing to take them on nonetheless.

Of course, the degree of certainty one requires to make a leap of faith varies widely from person to person. Like Laurel Andrews, who dreamed of the camp for kids with AIDS, some of us believe passionately in our hearts with little or no evidence at all. In fact, many practical dreamers operate from what Warren Bennis, author of *Leaders*, calls "unwarranted optimism." Despite the weakest case, even when things don't look at all promising, they have a sixth sense, an intuition that what they envision is possible. Others, like Rob Ladd, will take the leap only after accumulating a considerable body of evidence.

Some leap with the confidence of absolute certainty, the kind that I heard in Linda Miller's voice when she said she always knew one day she would own a day spa. Others, like Ed Miller, who decided to leave Los Angeles with only his tools, his truck, and one month's rent, admit they don't know if they can do what they're wanting to do but are determined to give their best shot to find out what's possible.

How about you? How sure do you have to be to believe?

After many rounds of debate between myself and my doubts, after much discussion of pros and cons with Paul, and many hours enjoying my novel experience, we decided to believe what I'd known in my heart from the moment I arrived in Pine Mountain. We made an offer on the house by the pond.

4

COMMITTING
TO CREATING IT

Without surrender realization
is not possible.

Lynn Andrews

Nights, he was playing piano into the wee hours of the morning in smoky, stale, crowded bars. The audience generally talked through his sets or was too inebriated to notice. Days, he was working as a telemarketer, making call after call in a crowded, noisy, uncomfortable cubicle.

"Everyone kept advising me to play it safe. Have a real job to fall back on," he told us. "But all the musicians I'd ever known who had a fallback strategy ended up falling back on it. I didn't want a fallback strategy. I wanted to earn a living playing my music and I didn't want to end up with lung disease or cancer to do it."

After his uncle died of emphysema at fifty-two, the pianist decided, despite all the well-meaning advice from others, to quit his job. He resolved to play only for New-Age expos, health fairs, or family-oriented festivals. "Quitting my job and taking a stand for the kind of audiences I would play for forced me to start living my dream. I had to make it," he remembers. "Before I quit the job, I was hoping and wishing and trying, but when I committed 100 percent, that's when my career took off." He now travels to and from places like Santa Fe, New Mexico, Rhinebeck, New York,

Maui, Hawaii, and Boulder, Colorado, supporting himself as a full-time musician.

He had everything to lose and everything to gain. He was hungry, both physically and spiritually. So, he'd made the commitment to step into the chasm between life as he knew it and life as he wanted it. So did Mike and Justen McCormack, with one difference—they had nothing to lose and everything to gain.

During construction boom days in Southern California, Mike's career was flourishing and the couple lived in a beautiful and pricey seaside community. Then the recession struck. There was no work. "We decided we had to do whatever we could to make a dollar," Justen recalls, "so we moved to where the jobs were." Unfortunately, the area where they moved had been voted the worst city to live in in the United States, and Mike was building roof structures in 110-degree heat. Within nine months they knew they couldn't stay there any longer. "We had already surrendered to making changes just to live," Justen elaborated, "so we decided to look at all our options."

Justen grew up in Cambria, a beautiful pines-by-the-sea small artists' community on the Califonia coast. "I didn't have a television," she remembers. "I made blackberry jam from blackberries I'd picked. At eight years old I was walking through the forest whittling out little snakes. This was my entertainment." She wanted to raise a family in that kind of place. Also, she missed being near family, so they looked into moving to Pine Mountain where her parents were living.

"Pine Mountain got me in touch with my roots," she recalls. "I knew it was possible to live away from the concrete jungle of television and video games, and hanging out at the mall, because I'd grown up with it." For Mike, though, always a city boy and an avid golfer, living in a mountain community with a nine-hole APGA-approved golf course looked idyllic, but not very practical. Since they had nothing to lose though, they decided to rent the apartment above her parents' garage for a year to see if they'd like it. Mike found a job as an assembler an hour away. This gave them the roots they needed to know they could stay.

A year later, the McCormacks bought a house and started a family. Justen now home-schools their five-year-old daughter, McClain, and works part-time as our assistant. On some days, McClain comes to work with her mom and does her schoolwork in the guest room near her mother's office. "This is my room where I study," she says with pride when we show guests through the large second-floor room.

"A lot of our friends from the city wonder why we would want to live in a place where there's no night life," Justen points out. "But at this point in our lives we were ready to put all that behind us. While we don't have dance clubs, we have a close-knit circle of friends. Our social life is simplified, closer, more intimate and spontaneous. You can actually say to your neighbor, 'How about coming over for dinner Saturday,' and they have the time to say yes."

The McCormacks also like being involved in their community. "I'm just an average person who wants to get involved to create better things for my daughter." Justen adds, "You can fight for years to see a change in the big city but here everyone's talents are needed and wanted. You can see results from your efforts quickly." Of his commute, Mike says, "It's all worth it to know I get to come home to this, to look out my window and see the trees and hear the birds and go play a round of golf at 'my' golf course after work."

THE LEAP OF ACTION

We got the message. We'd heard it before. If you're hungry enough, you won't have a problem with commitment. When everything's on the line or there's nothing to lose, the desire for things to get better nudges or pushes us to step into the unknown. But too often, as uncomfortable as we may be with our hassled and harried lives, we're not uncomfortable enough to make a commitment to actually changing our circumstances. Instead, we put up and shut up or we complain and talk about what we'll do someday. Meanwhile, our fallback strategies become our way of life. Why is that?

It's said that the certainty of misery is preferable to the misery of uncertainty. Would you rather live with the certainty of your life as it is or endure the discomfort of uncertainty for the possibility of a better life?

Paul had been told from the time he was four years old that he would be a lawyer when he grew up. He followed his prescribed script, graduating from law school with honors, passing the bar with flying colors, and joining a successful law firm. But it didn't take long to realize he didn't like practicing law. The money was good. The career was prestigious. His family was proud of him. How could he complain? He wasn't enjoying his work, but maybe that's just the price you have to pay for success. Who said work should be fun?

Then one day he was having lunch with a wealthy, prominent lawyer in his late fifties. The lawyer asked Paul how he liked the practice of law. Evidently Paul was less than convincing in expressing his satisfaction, because the lawyer advised him in earnest, "If you don't like it, you should get out now while you still can. That's what I'd do if I had it to do over again. For me it's too late. I can't leave now." He was bound to his profession by the golden handcuffs of a superb income and all the accoutrements it was providing, like putting the kids through college, the big cars, the country clubs, the philanthropic causes, and so much more.

Haunted by this man's tale, Paul took his advice to heart and left the practice of law within two years. But what of this man? Of course, it wasn't really too late for him. He still had choices and probably had considered them, but he wasn't hungry enough. He was anything but hungry. He was too comfortable to take the leap of action that follows the leap of faith.

How hungry do you have to get before you get around to eating? Do you have to be starving? How thirsty do you have to be before you get a drink of water? Do you have to be parched?

If we want to change our lives, we have to be hungry enough to take that leap into the unknown. We have to step into the chasm between the worlds. From the certainty of our existing life, we can stand on the edge in our imagination and look over into the future indefinitely, fantasizing about how great it will be. But until we commit to taking that step over the edge into the free fall between the worlds, we'll never know what could have been.

Saying you're going to do it doesn't do it. Commitment means taking the step of no return. It's an emotional locking in, a joining of feeling and will that leads to a leap of action. It's tying the knot. Handing in the resignation. Signing on the dotted line. Making the offer. It's an act that binds us to our desired course, an act that means there's no going back.

FEAR OF FALLING

We lay wide-awake late into the night. The excitement was too intense to sleep. Our offer on the dream house by the pond had been accepted and we had put our house on the market. We were moving. "This place will sell in three weeks," the agent said of our condo. Three weeks. I was struck with a near-incapacitating fear. I'd felt this fear before. We always think we're past this gripping, stomach-wrenching feeling, but then there it is again.

It was the fear I'd felt when I quit my job with the government to open my private psychotherapy practice. The day I turned in my resignation I was confident, almost bold, as I declared what I was going to do. I'd read everything I could, talked to everyone I knew, taken several classes. I was sure of myself . . . until things didn't go according to plan, which was right away. I'd been told to develop a business plan, and I had. That plan was my security blanket. It showed me exactly how many clients I would need each week and exactly how much I needed to charge per hour. According to plan, I'd established my business name, obtained my business license, set up my business bank account, printed my cards and letterhead, and even prepared my first brochure. I had been told how to announce the opening of my practice and I followed to the letter the guidance I'd received.

Then I waited for the phone to ring. It didn't. The only business call I got those first two weeks was a wrong number. That was when I realized there was more to building a practice than anyone had mentioned. The next few years were not pleasant ones. The shift from having a position of influence where I wielded the power and authority of the federal government to being a sole practitioner on my own was a jolt. I went from feeling powerful to feeling powerless. The logical and dependable world I had known had given way. I was no longer being controlled, but I was not yet in control. I had taken the leap and was free-falling in the chasm between what had been and what I hoped could be.

This was also the same fear I felt when I started my radio show. To break into radio I'd purchased the time for my first show— thirteen weeks, one hour a week. I was excited and so confident. I'd already booked six weeks of great guests. I'd been a guest on hundreds of shows myself. I'd read everything there was to read. I'd talked to reams of people. I'd lined up a salesperson to sell commercial spots on the show to cover the cost of my time, which was substantial. Again, I had a plan, and I'd cleared my calendar of other work to have time to put my plan into action. I was ready . . . until the next day when the salesperson backed out to pursue other commitments! There I was free-falling again.

That was the feeling. It was the fear of falling. Falling hopelessly and helplessly into the unknown where anything is possible from the dreadful to the delightful. As I felt its immobilizing grip close over me once again I thought of one of my favorite quotes from explorer Douchan Gersi.

I learned to master the trembling of my limbs, to control my heartbeat and my breathing, to wipe away the sweat that burned my eyes . . . I was intoxicated by the satisfaction of having overcome my fear.

GETTING OUT OF THE HEADLIGHTS

My chest still in the grip of fear, I'm sure I must have looked just like a doe caught in the headlights of an oncoming car. But everyone we talk with who commits to making a dramatic change in their lives experiences some level of fear and anxiety as soon as they step out of their comfort zone into the unknown. This is especially true when the stakes are high, as they usually are when we're making a dramatic change in how we live and work.

So give yourself a break: don't panic or get down on yourself if you're feeling anxious or fearful about leaving behind the familiarity of the life you've been living. It's only natural.

Fear and anxiety are normal reactions to a totally unfamiliar future. They're signals that we perceive danger ahead. They're warning us that the future we imagine could hold some threat and urging us to be prepared for possibly negative consequences. So trying to ignore our fears is foolhardy. Usually, once we become aware of what we fear, we either recognize it as harmless, or we can use the information to protect ourselves from whatever potential harm there may be.

As is true of all emotions, both fear and anxiety have several characteristics that can help us use them effectively. Fear, for example, is an intense, active, fast-paced emotion. It provides us with an incredible amount of highly charged energy we can use to take action, but sometimes it's so intense we become immobilized by it instead. Then we need to get out of the headlights and calm our fears by shifting our focus away from the uncertainty of the future to the actual reality of the present.

OK, I told myself, the house hasn't sold yet. I'm still right here in Santa Monica where I've been for eleven years. Taking several deep, relaxing breaths while concentrating on the present moment can help, too. So that's what I did and as my panic subsided, I became curious about just what my sudden gripping fear was trying to tell me this time. Was it a warning of trouble ahead? Was I about to make a mistake? Or was I just needlessly scaring myself with some imaginary bogeyman?

 **Try This**

When you're caught in the headlights, immobilized by your fear of the unknown:

1. *Bring your attention into the present. Fear signals a possible future danger, so when you start to feel anxious, shift your attention immediately away from thinking about the future and focus on the present. Concentrate on the here and now. We need to be in the here and now to take action anyway, so it's the best place to be when you feel apprehensive about the future.*

2. *Notice that all is well for the moment. For example, if you're feeling anxious about quitting your job, stop thinking for the time being about life without a paycheck and recognize where you are right now. You still have your job and you're just fine. Or if you've already quit your job, even if you're not sure how you'll be earning your living later, notice that you're OK right now.*

3. *Focus on what you can do now to prepare or protect yourself from whatever negative possibilities are frightening you. Once you begin feeling safe in the moment, click on your curiosity and ask yourself what you can do to safeguard yourself from the catastrophic future*

you fear. What could you do to prepare for the imagined future situation? What are you afraid will happen? How could you prevent that? Become intrigued and fascinated with answering these questions. Begin breaking down what you can do into small, specific steps. For example, if you're going to be quitting your job, what can you do now to make sure you'll have some income when you quit?

4. Recall times in the past when you've taken the needed steps to meet a future challenge. Keep thinking about these times until you begin to feel capable. Other than for the purpose of identifying what you need to do to prepare now, avoid repeatedly recalling other times when you were not prepared.

5. Then imagine yourself preparing to meet this challenge or threat. Mentally rehearse the steps you will take until you feel confident in your ability to avoid what you fear and achieve the positive future you deserve.

6. Begin anticipating the experience of success you've been rehearsing. As you anticipate meeting the challenge, you may well begin to look forward to doing it.

FACING THE FEAR DEMONS

The moment we commit ourselves to creating something we really care about, the uncertainty and pressure of the task ahead can trigger all kinds of other fears, real and imagined, old and new. They rise up like demons in the night, testing once again our belief in ourselves and our dreams. For example, there were any number of possible fears that putting our house on the market could have awakened in me, like fear of failure, fear of disappointment, fear of rejection, or fear of success.

What about you? What do you fear?

Fear of Blowing It

Commitment forces us to face ourselves. Once we've committed, once we've declared that we're going for it, it's hard to hide from ourselves. We've put ourselves on the line. We've revealed our intention for the world and ourselves to see. Our weaknesses and inadequacies are exposed. As long as we don't care, as long as we don't commit to a dream, we can fantasize that we would have done it or could have done it if we'd tried. But once we commit, we find out one way or the other. We either create what we set out to do or we don't. We could fail. We could be disappointed in ourselves and with life.

When Lionel left his job in mortgage banking to do investment counseling, for example, he had a wife and two children to support. The children were still so young that neither he nor his wife wanted her to take a job. He wanted, and needed, his new business to succeed. Their future and his dreams were on the line.

The truth of the matter was Lionel had been asked to leave his job and he was fully aware that he had engineered his dismissal. He didn't feel he could continue working for someone else. He'd always dreamed of being his own boss. He yearned for the freedom, the chance to pursue his own ideas, and to make more money so that, instead of just getting by, his family could enjoy a better life. This was his big chance. But he was terrified of failing. He just didn't know it. He was so afraid to look at the possibility of failure that he almost defeated himself.

"I was so afraid of failing that I didn't want to see even the most obvious potential problems," he remembers. "I couldn't face them. I took any work that came along, even if I didn't like it and charged much less than I knew I was worth. I pretended everything was fine. But it wasn't. My wife saw problems coming, but when she pointed them out I thought she wasn't being supportive. I was angry and resentful, and most of all, I was envious of the people I knew who were doing better than me."

Fortunately, Lionel wanted to succeed so much that he was finally willing to admit his fear of failure. Admitting his fear was the turning point. Once he began to look at what he feared, he was able to take steps to make sure he could handle those situations effectively. He sought the advice of colleagues and attended several marketing seminars. In the process, he realized that he had to take a stand on the type of work he was willing to do and the fees he needed to charge. He also got a lot of encouragement. "If I had just paid attention to the way I was feeling in the beginning, it would have saved me and my family a lot of agony," Lionel admits. "But the important thing is that I did it. I've been my own boss now for five years!"

Russell Seeley served as CEO for a major corporation before leaving to form his own consulting firm, working with other manufacturing companies. Seeley attributes his success to the fact that he never ignores possible problems. "You've got to be willing to look the problems square in the face," he told us. As with Lionel, accepting our fear of failing can help us look at the problems that can prevent our success.

Oprah Winfrey claims she's never failed, but she says she's learned a lot of lessons. That's the best way to view failure. If you choose to view it this way, there is no such thing as failure, only lessons, false starts, dead ends, and wrong turns. So we can't let ourselves off the hook just because we fear failure. Negative results are irrelevant to the ultimate outcome. They aren't a sign of what's to come; they're a signpost pointing where we need to go next.

No one wants to fail. But it never need be an excuse not to proceed. No one succeeds without the risk of failure. Without failure we'd all be crawling on all fours instead of walking upright.

 **Try This**

The best antidote for the fear of failure is to watch a toddler learning to walk.

Fear of Boo Hoo

It has been said that the key to happiness is not caring. We don't agree, but even if it were true, not caring is certainly not the key to building a new life. If you don't care, you won't dare. To dare we must have that burning desire and fan the flames regularly to keep ourselves committed. But, of course, when we care we're vulnerable. We can be hurt. We can be disappointed. Creating a new life can be fraught with disappointment . . . as we were soon to learn, once again.

Two days after our real estate agent announced that our house would sell at or close to our asking price in three weeks tops, the stock market tumbled! The real estate market in Santa Monica came to a screeching halt. In the weeks that followed, while the stock market gradually recovered, buyers remained wary, especially since the stock crash was followed by five sensational murders in Santa Monica, one only blocks from our house. Since Santa Monica has always been a city with very little violent crime, these murders headlined every newspaper and newscast for weeks.

Our November 20 closing date came and went, along with our dream of Thanksgiving in Pine Mountain. Fortunately we had a six-month contingency on the purchase of our pond house, so, disappointed but not discouraged, we set a new goal to celebrate Christmas in Pine Mountain. Then Valentine's Day. Then the first day of spring—all of which came and went. With each holiday our disappointment grew.

But managing disappointment is a basic survival skill for practical dreamers. Each disappointment we encounter further tests the strength of our belief in ourselves and our dreams. Each disappointment challenges our commitment. If we continue on despite them all, our belief grows stronger. Through disappointment we discover whether we care enough to carry on toward what we're seeking or whether it's time to let go, redefine, or redirect.

While disappointment can be helpful in accepting something that's not to be, it's not productive when what we want is still possible. When there's still a chance for our dream, we need to turn disappointment into determination and perseverance. Or so I told myself. Our house would sell. I knew it would. Wouldn't it?

➡ **Try This** ☆☆☆

When you're disappointed:

1. *Ask yourself if having what you want is still possible through your efforts. Is there still something you can do? Can you think of others who have done what you're seeking to do? Can you imagine circumstances under which you could do it? Is it only a matter of time? Will waiting help?*

2. *If what you're wanting is no longer possible, it's time to let go of this line of pursuit. It's time to imagine another scenario that could fulfill your desires and move on.*

3. *If what you want is still possible, use your frustration and disappointment to strengthen your resolve. Focus on the fact that what you want is still possible. Recall times in the past when you've persevered and attained your goals. Resolve to be patient and renew your determination.*

4. *Spend time living in your novel experience to fuel your desire. Focus on what you can do and anticipate yourself enjoying the new life you're striving for.*

As weeks passed with no one even coming by to look at our house, the agents, once so thrilled with its perfection, became its harshest critics. But hope lived on through my novel experience. It carried me through the months that followed. Every morning I awoke to the memory of the call of the ducks, the smell of the pines, and the whisper of the wind through the poplar trees. I imagined padding in my slippers past the black iron stove that would one day be mine, fixing my breakfast in the wood-paneled kitchen and enjoying it on the deck above the pond . . . and I thought of the others I'd known who had persevered.

Over ten years ago, for example, Susan Van Lier moved from Seattle to Beverly Hills. She'd been a career airline stewardess with Northwest Airlines and was raising two daughters with her husband, Norman. The family had agreed that it was time for Susan to fulfill her lifelong dream to become an actress and producer of feature films. I met her in acting class shortly after she moved to Southern California and we immediately became friends.

But the road to Susan's dream was to be a long and arduous one. The savings she came with were too quickly gone and she had to take a job. In her heart, though, she never gave up her commitment to creating movies. Always walking forward, optioning scripts, raising capital, but making little headway, she endured a seemingly endless stream of disappointments.

To my delight, right at the lowest time in our efforts to sell our house, Susan called to wish me happy birthday and gave me the most delightful gift—news that she'd produced her first film! Earlier that year, her daughter Heidi, then grown-up and living in Chicago, had called to say, "Mom, I've written a screenplay and I want you to produce it." Susan read the script and was impressed. She decided to invest all the money she'd saved and with help from friends, the mother and daughter produced a low-budget independent film together in conjunction with Susan's business partner, Michael Blaha.

The result was *Chi Girl*, a clever story about a guy who stalks a girl on camera while she is stalking her ex-boyfriend. But that wasn't the only news Susan had for me that morning. They had submitted the film to Slamdance, a prestigious independent film festival spin-off from the Sundance film festival in Park City, Utah. The film was among fourteen selected for screening from over 1,000 submissions. And guess what? It won best feature film!

Doors, so tightly closed to Susan for so long, flew open.

Opportunities came flooding in. She had endured and is at last living her dream.

Cry, throw a fit if necessary, but as long as you still want it and it's still possible, keep your dream alive. You, too, can endure.

Fear of Never Getting to Dance

Pick me. Pick me. As people came through our house one by one, looking it over, liking this but not that, that but not this, I was reminded of when I was in junior high school. Every Friday night there would be a dance somewhere. We girls would spend hours primping to look our best. Every hair in place, lipstick on straight. Nothing showing that shouldn't show and everything showing that should. We'd gather around the sides of the room in little clusters of friends, waiting as each new song began for someone to ask us to dance.

Pick me. Pick me. You tried so hard to look cheerfully casual and calm, but were dying inside. Your heart stops. They're looking you over. They're coming your way. Pick me. Pick me. Pick me this time. Then, when they didn't, to show you didn't care, you'd smile brightly and flip your hair aside as if to say, "I'm having so much fun!" . . . If only you were.

That was me six months into trying to sell our house. I was back in junior high. Forty-five minutes of "dressing the house" before the realtor would bring someone by, attending to every detail. No dust. All trash cans empty. All personal items hidden from sight. Lights on. Mirrors sparking. Bread baking. Fires flickering on the hearths. Beautiful. So beautiful, I'd think as I stood back to survey our home before going out the door, much as my mother must have done as she said good-bye to me with such pride in her voice on those Friday nights so long ago.

Pick me. Pick me, I'd think as we were leaving the house, knowing people would soon be walking through, looking here and looking there. Opening closet doors, peering behind chairs. Of course, the things they didn't like were things we could do nothing about . . . a bedroom located here, the view they didn't like there. Much like teenage bodies that are too tall, too flat, too small, too fat. But worst of all, once our home had been sized up and rejected again and again, no matter how hard we tried, we could never feel quite the same pride in the place we'd called home for eleven years. Just like when our teenage bodies don't measure up after being checked out again and again by adolescent eyes, we can never again feel that unquestioned confidence inside our skin we once felt as a child.

Whether it's waiting for a chance to dance or for a new owner to buy your home so you can move on with your life, being rejected is hell. And yet we wallflowers never missed a Friday night dance, and so it was that when the agent called to say someone was coming at noon, I would stop whatever I was doing and head off to dress the house once again. It would sell if we kept trying, just like most of us eventually get a chance to dance if we keep believing we will.

 **Try This**

When rejection starts nipping at your heels, ask yourself:

1. *Do you still want what you're going for? When faced with repeated rejection, it's tempting to say, "Hey, I don't need this!" And of course it's absolutely true. You don't have to pursue this dream. You have choices. You're free to quit anytime. Is that what you want? Or do you want to proceed?*

2. *How much do you want this? OK, so you still want it, but how much? Do you want it enough to put up with whatever it takes for as long as it takes?*

3. *Are you taking this too personally? Like other artists, it's easy to overidentify with our dreams when we're crafting a new life. There's*

a tendency to think that the bank or the home buyer or the customer is rejecting us and judging us personally as inadequate. In actuality, most rejections have less to do with us than with the circumstances.

4. *Are you being realistic? Selling anything, whether it's yourself, your ideas, your products and services, or your house, is often a numbers game. What looks like rejection may simply be a matter of not finding the right person, the right bank, the right clients, or the right house at the right time.*

5. *Is that "no" really a "no"? Before letting the claws of rejection impale you, always consider that a "no" isn't necessarily a "no." While we were growing up, most of our parents told us, "When I say no I mean no. And I don't want to hear another word out of you." So most of us learned to take "no" seriously. But in the grown-up world some people routinely say no at first simply to determine if the person is serious enough to pursue the issue. It's amazing how many people change their mind after thinking or talking something over a second, third, or fourth time. Times change. Circumstances change. I've come to hear no as meaning "not now."*

6. *Who's the best judge? Who knows the true value and potential of your dream? To feel rejected is to let someone else answer that question. Welcome whatever feedback you get and make valid changes. Then go back to those who made the suggestions, thank them for their input, and show them how you've improved.*

7. *Who thinks you're great? One of the antidotes for rejection is a little support from your friends. When you're feeling your worst, ask yourself, "Who thinks I'm great? Who always believes in me?" Then get together with one of those folk at once.*

8. *Can you take matters into your own hands? Nothing can finish off a venture more effectively than having to wait endlessly for someone else's OK to get it under way. Entertainers and writers often face this*

type of chronic rejection. They can't get a part until they're in the union, and they can't get into the union until they get a part. But practical dreams don't wait for someone to discover them. They find some way to proceed. So if you're not getting the break you want, rather than feeling rejected, take charge. Don't let your success rest in someone else's hands. Don't wait for another "no." Make your own breaks.

That's what Amanda McBroom decided to do. She'd always loved performing songs she'd written for friends and they loved her songs. They'd shower her with praise and exhort her to find some way to share her music with the world. At first she didn't want to get involved in the music industry. All the hassle. All the distress of trying to get a record deal was so unappealing. For many years she resisted their pleas. Ultimately, she knew she had to honor her creations. She owed her talent and her songs the effort to make sure they were heard.

She began trying to find a record company that would put her songs on an album, but faced one rejection after another. By then, though, she was committed. There would be an album. She would find a way. She raised the money herself and produced the album *Amanda McBroom—Dreaming*. That was only the beginning. Her music has been heard on Steven Bochco's groundbreaking television series *Cop Rock*. Her one-woman show, *Heartbeats*, has played at the world-famous Pasadena Playhouse. And she performs regularly on Broadway.

Fear of Making It

When Meredith left her job and moved to Venezuela to publish a magazine about her passion, traveling in South America, everything went smoothly. At last she was doing what she'd always wanted to do, and best of all, she'd returned to the country and the extended family she'd loved so much as a child. But to her surprise, just as she settled in to enjoy her new life, she was gripped with fear. "Why?" she asked. "It feels like I'm sabotaging myself."

As she talked with me about these feelings, Meredith remembered that when she was growing up, her father had died of a sudden heart attack shortly after moving his family to America and setting up a successful one-person business. Unbeknownst to her, as a child she had linked his death to having successfully accomplished his dream to come to America and start his own business. She recalled an aunt shaking her head and saying, "He worked himself into the grave for his silly American dream!"

As Meredith remembered these events, the thought "I don't want to be successful like my father" ran through her head. Once she realized this, her fear subsided. She reassured herself that she did not need to re-create her father's fate. She had ample evidence of many successful people who were living long and happy lives. She resolved not to "work herself to death," but to continue building her new life at a reasonable and enjoyable pace.

Mike's situation was different. He was living in near poverty in a "tree house" he'd built on a small but lonely patch of land in the foothills outside a quaint little suburb. There he was, doing what he loved, restoring antique automobiles, but his work produced only the barest income. When he talked with me about his fear that he would have to abandon his dream, I offered several suggestions for how he could make the business more profitable. Immediately, Mike began shifting uncomfortably in his seat. He grew highly apprehensive as he searched for valid reasons why none of these ideas would work.

As we continued talking, he remembered that his father had failed at his one attempt to start a construction company. After that his father had never been quite the same. "The light had gone out in his eyes," Mike recalled, and suddenly he realized the real source of his fear. He was afraid that if he were to start making money in his own business, it would be a painful, ongoing reminder to his father of that past failure. "If I were successful," he explained, "it would be like opening an old wound, and just seeing me would be like rubbing salt in the wound."

Mike had cleverly set up his business so he could do it without really succeeding at it! By doing it that way, in Mike's mind, his father could feel sorry for him instead of being threatened by him. Of course, before Mike talked this out, he had no idea that his own fear was sabotaging his success. He decided to speak with his father and was pleased to discover that he wanted Mike to succeed; so much so, in fact, that he volunteered to help out in the shop.

Jeaneen was a stay-at-home mom with two kids under four. She had a great group of friends about her age who were stay-at-home moms. They swapped baby-sitting, shared advice, and went to Gymboree and Mommy and Me classes together. Jeaneen loved her life, except for one thing. She'd been a literature major in college and had always wanted to write a novel. Encouraged by her friends, she decided to enroll in a writing class and, to her amazement, the instructor was so impressed with her writing that he recommended her to an agent who was equally impressed.

The agent received positive responses from several publishers and called to suggest that they might get a bidding war going. This could result in a hefty advance for a first novel. Instead of leaping with joy at this news, Jeaneen grew short of breath, her palms began to sweat, and she suddenly felt light-headed. "No," her mind was screaming at her. "This isn't what you want!" Recognizing her reaction as an anxiety attack, she sat down to calm herself and asked the agent to call back later so she could consider how she wanted to respond.

This is what she'd always wanted. It was a dream come true. What was the matter with her? she asked herself. When she called, I asked her one question: "What do you think will happen if you get this advance and write this novel?" The answer came tumbling out. She foresaw a speedy end to her happy domestic life. She wouldn't have time for her husband or kids or her friends. She would suddenly have so much more money than her friends that they would resent her. She would have nothing in common with them anymore. She'd have to put her kids in day care to go on tour. This dismal scenario went on to leave her rich and famous but overworked, divorced, and lonely.

Jeaneen had to laugh as she heard her own fantasy unfold. Of course, none of this had to happen and none of it did. After securing a modest advance, she writes part of each day and hasn't missed a Gymboree class yet.

What do you fear might happen if your desires are fulfilled? If you follow your fears to their roots, you'll discover what's preventing you from committing to your dreams.

PULLING UP THE ROOTS OF FEAR

There's usually no rational reason to fear success or failure or rejection; but if we fear them, it means we think they present some danger to us. Usually when we follow our fears to their roots, we find some thought or belief that's linked to a past experience or decision that convinced us to fear pursuing what we most want. I could find no rational basis, for example, for the fear that gripped my chest the night after we put the house on the market. But I did think of Meredith and Mike and Jeaneen and how they'd found the roots of their fear.

As I reflected upon the fear I was feeling, I thought of my father dressed in his long purple robes, as Graybeard the Sage. I saw the twinkle in his eyes as he pulled a coin from the air with a majestic gesture. I heard the delight and pride in his voice as he rehearsed the patter that goes along with each magic trick. I watched the satisfaction that came across his face as he carefully arranged the items on his black velvet close-up pad. He was happy, really happy . . . at last. Not long after that he became ill and died.

Yes, there was my fear. If I were to wake up each morning to the call of the ducks and the smell of the pines and the sound of the wind in the poplars. If I were to live somewhere I treasured as much as he treasured that velvet pad. If I were to find a community where I was at home, where I belonged . . . I could see the twinkle in my eyes just at the thought and I knew I would be happy, really happy . . .

CLOSING THE DOOR

Not long after letting go of that fear I walked into the kitchen of our condo to get dinner as I had so many nights for over eleven years. I was overwhelmed suddenly with a wave of grief. "I will be leaving all this," I thought. My kitchen that we'd so carefully remodeled over so many years; sparkling and bright, just as I'd wanted it. Shiny cabinets, stove top, dishwasher, refrigerator, and microwave, all new, all gleaming white. Glistening wood floors, refinished to perfection. Our town house in Santa Monica, the home we'd dreamed of and worked for and worked on. Right here on the street we'd picked out and driven up and down hour after hour so long ago, looking for some home for sale.

I'm leaving a life and a time of my life behind forever, I realized. I will be saying good-bye to so many things that have been central to my life, so much I've been proud of and satisfied with. My home, my life, a reflection of the person I'd been and the person I'd become. When I left that home I would no longer be that person. I'd be someone else, living another life somewhere else.

I felt a great sadness. I was losing all these things I cherished. Soon they would be only memories. The door was closing behind me. I glanced around me as if looking back in time and then after a moment turned my attention forward once again to the future. I was committed. I was moving on.

Can you let go of what has been? Are there attachments holding you back? Can you say good-bye and let the door close behind you? Can you make a commitment to the future you've been dreaming of?

REFERENCES

Country Bound: Trade Your Business Suit Blues for Blue Jean Dreams. Tom and Marilyn Ross. Upstart Publishing Company. ISBN 1-57410-069-6.

Edge Cities, Life on the New Frontier. Joel Garreau. Doubleday. ISBN 0-385-26249-3.

The 500 Year Delta, What Happens after What Comes Next. Jim Taylor and Watts Wacker, with Howard Means. Harper-Collins. ISBN 0-694-51860-3.

Flow. The Psychology of Optimal Experience, Steps toward Enhancing the Quality of Life. Mihaly Csikszentmihalyi. New York: HarperCollins, 1991.

The Gutenberg Elegies, The Fate of Reading in an Electronic Age. Sven Birkerts. Fawcett Columbine. ISBN 0-449-91009-1.

On Becoming a Leader. Warren Bennis. Addison Wesley. ISBN: 0-201-08059-1.

The Complete Idiot's Guide to Making Money Through Intuition. Nancy Rosanoff. Alpha Books. ISBN 0-02-862740-7.

Penturbia: Where Real Estate Will Boom After the Crash of Suburbia. Jack Lessinger. Social Economic, Inc. ISBN 0-9625182-5-5.

The Power of Place, How Our Surroundings Shape Our Thoughts, Emotions, and Actions. Winifred Gallagher. HarperPerennial. ISBN 0-06-097602-0.

Practical Intuition for Success. Laura Day. HarperCollins. ISBN 0-06-017576-1.

There Are No Accidents, Synchronicity and the Stories of Our Lives.
Robert H. Hopcke. Riverhead Books. ISBN 1-57322-681-5.

➥ PART I: REMEMBER THIS ✩✩✩

Anytime you have difficulty tapping into your desires, imagining the possibilities for fulfilling them, believing you can do what it takes, and making the commitment to do it, turn here to this section and remember . . .

"Expectations create our future," said John O'Donahue. We've all heard about the self-fulfilling prophecy, but perhaps we do not realize that it applies to our own expectations. Research has clearly shown that we tend to live up to what is expected of us. A study in a Colorado school district illustrated this point dramatically. The researchers shuffled the records of two groups of students so that those with the lowest grades were placed in a class designated as gifted, while those students who had the best grades were placed in a class designated as average students. Can you guess what happened? The poor students in the "gifted" class dramatically outperformed the gifted students in the "average" class. If a classroom teacher's misunderstanding about students' past performance can produce such a dramatic result, just think what effect your own expectations have on your performance! So, check your expectations as you start each day; they may well shape tomorrow's reality.

Take the unaccustomed path. Often the road we want to take is closed to us, but if we are to follow our hearts we must not turn back. Instead we must do as John D. Rockefeller urged, "If you want to succeed, you should strike out on new paths rather than travel the worn paths of success." That is what Selma Schimmel has done. At the age of twenty-eight she was diagnosed with breast cancer. Her mother had just died of the disease. Schimmel survived and decided to dedicate her life to helping young people with cancer. She created a nonprofit organization called Vital Options to do that. Ten years later, charitable funding dried up in the recessionary early nineties. Rather than give up and get on with her life as friends suggested, Schimmel took the unaccustomed path. She arranged for commercial underwriting to launch the first nationwide radio talk show devoted to on-air cancer support. The show is called the Group Room and is heard on the Premier Radio Networks.

Desire

Clarify what you truly want in this day. The world, it seems to many, grows more complex. Often we despair of this complexity and yearn for the simplicity of yesterday. But what is complexity but an increase in options? The greater abundance of alternatives we have, the more complicated things seem. Yet this is only so if we fail to make choices. When we don't make decisions about what we truly want and need, life gets complex.

You can simplify your life by clarifying what you want in it. You can have what you yearn for if you hold on clearly to what's important and valuable to you and discard the rest for others to whom it appeals. As H. L. Hunt said long ago, "Decide what you want, decide what you are willing to exchange for it. Establish your priorities and get to work." If you do this each day, those things that don't matter will fall by the way and you'll have room for plenty of what you want.

Listen to your highest desires. It's been said that desire prevents us fom being happy; and that if we could somehow let go of all desire, then we would find peace. Yet desire is as natural as eating and breathing. We get hungry; we eat and feel satisfied. We breathe in, we breathe out; then the cycle begins again. So it is with desire. It inspires us to right action, and right action leads to satisfaction. Pain and misery come not from desire, but from failing to act on your highest desires, from resigning yourself to dissatisfaction, instead of learning how to fulfill what you yearn for. Fulfill and enjoy your highest desires and in time, new desires will emerge and through this cycle you will achieve your destiny.

Follow your private path. Each of us has a sense of where we're headed in life. Some of us feel this sense of direction quite keenly. Others know it only vaguely, as an inner hunger or need. But the closer you are to walking this path, the more confident, at peace, and in sync you feel with life. The further you veer from your personal path, the more anxious, agitated, irritated, and distraught you become. In fact, problems that would otherwise thwart you become invigorating challenges when traveling along your personal path. On this path, no one can stand in your shoes. You alone can carve it from the moments of time.

Many of our immigrant ancestors never got to live their dreams. The road to a better life was often harder than they'd bargained for. For most, there was, and there is, no land of milk and honey. They had to toil for years to buy the cows and build the hives, so to speak, before there would be any milk and honey. But, right now, many of us are living the dreams that brought our ancestors here. We're enjoying the milk and honey of their labors: freedom, a decent standard of living, and a future of our own making. So here we are, living their dreams while pursuing our own.

Follow the magic. Our lives are always a reflection of who we are, but do they reflect who we really are? You know the old saying "Follow the money." In this case, the easiest way to orient your life to reflect who you truly are is simply to follow what most energizes, inspires, and enlivens you. When you feel excitement coursing through your veins, when your heart is filled to bursting, when you feel a touch of magic—you're heading in the right direction.

We never need be envious of others, for there is a time and place for each of us. We each have a path, a role, to fill. Feelings of envy are actually a sign that somehow we're missing our own mark. If we are on target with our lives, walking our chosen path, fulfilling our inner callings, we hold no envy. We're satisfied, even if we have less fame or fortune than others. Only when we are somehow out of step on our own path do we look longingly at someone else's. But only you can find and cultivate your path. You must resolve to find your way by following the clues within your heart and amidst your life. Sharing your observations with others along that path, as they share theirs, is how you can best understand the world.

Dream big time. "Our deepest fear is not that we are inadequate. Our deepest fear is that we are powerful beyond measure," Nelson Mandela said in his inaugural speech as president of South Africa. "It is our light, not our darkness, that most frightens us. We ask ourselves, who am I to be brilliant, gorgeous, talented and fabulous? Actually, who are you not to be? Playing small doesn't serve the world. There's nothing enlightened about shrinking so that other people won't feel insecure around you. We're born to make manifest the glory . . . that is within us. It is not in just for some of us; it's in everyone. And as we let our own light shine, we unconsciously give people permission to do the same. As we are liberated from our own fear, our presence automatically liberates others."

Take care. It has been said that freedom is having not a care in the world. Sometimes we wish we could be free from the cares of the world, but if we had not a care, what meaning would life hold? As Los Angeles *Times* writer Frank Bruni wrote, "It is continued hoping and continued striving that propel a person through life."

Imagine
Leave the past behind. Ironically, the blocks most apt to stop us are often ones that were placed on our path when we were chil-

dren or adolescents. Those traumatic early experiences took place around the dinner table, on the playground, in the class-room, and so forth. One of the greatest gifts you can give yourself is to identify how ancient decisions you made as a young boy or girl about what you can and cannot do, or will and will not do, are keeping you from doing what you most want to do now. The next time you get that feeling "Oh, no, not this same old thing again!" think about how this all too familiar, unwanted development re-lates to some decision you made long, long ago, and then leave the past behind.

And the actress. She decided to round up several fellow actors and put on a Shakespearean play on the beach. The entire cast invited agents, re-viewers, and all their friends and family to opening night. Suddenly she was on the map. She was acting. She had a credit and the impetus she took got her more work. The lesson is, we can make our own breaks by walking our talk.

Welcome the challenge. Marc Allen, founder of New World Li-brary, points out, "Instead of challenging themselves and their world to fulfill their dreams, most people limit their dreams to their perceptions of the world's constraints." How easy it is to see the world as a small room with no doors or windows. How often we build elaborate dreams within the confines of those four walls thinking we have no other choice. If you are happy and fulfilled and satisfied within those walls, then there's no need to change. But if secretly in your heart lie bolder dreams and you find your-self longing to push against the walls that limit you, that is what you must do. Look for the windows to glimpse what could lie be-yond the world's constraints and welcome the challenge of find-ing doorways to the new worlds you can create.

Cultivate a sense of wonder. "When you see a window of oppor-tunity, leap through it," says Michael Sayer, computer entrepre-neur. Opportunities abound around us. We simply have to keep our antennae up to detect them. Instead of waiting to see where everyone else is going and joining the parade, survey the landscapes others overlook, watch and notice, question and imagine. As Albert Einstein asserted, your imagination can be a preview of coming attractions.

Just imagine. Albert Einstein thought imagination was more important than knowledge because while knowledge is limited, imagination is limitless, embracing the entire world, stimulating progress, and giving birth to the evolution of what is not yet but could be. So let imagination be your guide. Imagine how you want things to be in your life and use your imagination to come up with what you could do to begin creating those things right now.

Dreams seem so fragile; yet they're strong enough to be the foundation for tomorrow. So it is with our imagination, our will, our intent, our purpose. Each seems ephemeral until we see the power of what it brings forth. Once upon a time, mankind dreamed of going to the moon. That seemed impossible. But that dream became an intent that took on purpose and spread into the will of many who devoted hours and dollars and energy to fulfilling that dream. In 1969, man walked on the moon. A feat once unimaginable, yet only decades later, transformed from the extraordinary to the ordinary. We take it for granted; now it's history. So, dream grand dreams and let their power build for you still more extraordinary tomorrows.

Begin each day with the premise that anything's possible. The way you approach your day will affect how you experience everything from dawn to dusk. You always have a choice about your expectations. You can assume the worst, or the best. You can dread the unknown or anticipate its mystery. Why not greet each day as an adventure in which anything can happen and look for the meaning, the blessing, and the opportunity in whatever occurs? The happy person is one who sees all things as possibilities.

Cultivate an attitude of unwarranted optimism. Unwarranted optimism is a characteristic shared by all great leaders. It's the ability to believe in one's goals in the face of a reality that says they're not possible. Since our dreams exist only in our minds until we create them, we must trust they're possible and make a leap of faith. Every minute of every day, you have the choice to believe in your dreams or to doubt them. Choose to believe.

Create a touchstone. In the midst of the hassles, details, and responsibilities of daily life, it's easy to lose sight of the call that beckons you down a new path. It's easy to forget the inner vision that's motivating you to create a better way of living and working. But if you create a touchstone, a physical representation of what you're working toward, it can spark your imagination of what could be and serve as a constant reminder to stay focused on your desires.

Be extraordinary. Several years ago we were honored to have the late singer John Denver as a guest on our radio show. He told us and our listeners, "So many people feel powerless. They feel that they don't make a difference. But great things have been done by ordinary people who have a sense of purpose and a commitment to living out of that purpose. People can make an extraordinary difference from their knowledge and their own inclinations and interests. That is available to all of us. You, too, can make an extraordinary difference. You can live from the highest sense of purpose that you can imagine and have that show up in all aspects of your life, in your work, in your community, in your country, and in your world."

Believe

Banish fear and doubt. Have you ever noticed how fears and doubts become like quicksand, sucking you deeper and deeper into a quagmire of indecision? But fear and doubt are only messengers, sent to alert you to potential dangers and mishaps. They aren't meant to be your guides. Just thank them for their message and send them on their way. Let your goals and highest desires be your guides. Check out the validity of your concerns; track down potential dangers. Take steps to protect yourself on your journey. By pushing fear and doubt aside into their rightful role, you can take charge and clear a safe path to your goals.

"Choose belief over doubt every time," wrote screenwriter David Kelly in a *Nothing Sacred* episode. Our ability to believe in our goals, ourselves, and the forces that be is what enables us to turn our imagination, hopes, and dreams into reality, even in the face of seeming impossibilities and impracticalities. Without our ability to believe in the triumph of what could be over what is there would be no progress. So when push comes to shove, choose belief over doubt and let new options, solutions, and doors open to you.

Follow the dream in your heart. "I don't know how to wake up and not do this," the young woman said. She is following her dream. It's a big one. It's improbable . . . but only to others. To her, it's as real as anything else in life. She has only $20 in the bank after paying her rent. But she's determined. She is filled with aspiration, the kind miracles are made from. Any day could be the day she gets her big break. But if it isn't today there's always tomorrow and the day after that and the day after that, because she doesn't know how to wake up and not follow the dream in her heart.

"Be the best at what you do best," advised cleaning guru Don Aslett. When Aslett began his cleaning service over twenty years ago, he started from home and was plugging along earning a decent income. All around him he saw people jumping into the real estate field to make big bucks. Perhaps, he thought, he, too, should get a real estate license. Then he had second thoughts. His greatest chances for success, he believed, were not in chasing af-

ter what others were doing, but looking instead to what he did best—and that was cleaning. He decided to become the very best cleaning service in the country. It was a wise decision. He is now known as America's number-one cleaning expert. He's written twenty-seven books, has affiliates all over the country, and is sought out regularly to appear as an expert on radio and television across the nation.

Discover what you do best. Make that your thing. Become the best in the world at what you do best and you won't have to worry about why others are doing so well at their thing.

Life without anticipation is merely existence. Anticipation of a desired future is like adding spice to a recipe. It gives flavor to our lives. While the ingredients of life may be OK on their own, they can usually be enhanced with a sprinkling of anticipation. During those times when your life leaves something to be desired, adding a dash of anticipation for what could be can make life not only palatable, but enjoyable. Being fully alive in the moment is the main course of life. But spicing up the present with a little imagination about what could be can make the experience of life all the more delightful.

Discover what you are looking forward to. Then, instead of hoping and wishing for it, begin to anticipate actually experiencing it and see how it affects the quality of your life and your willingness to start adding more of those things that matter most to you.

Claim your strengths. It's so easy to focus on our weaknesses. While we may try to overlook or ignore them, our weaknesses are persistently pesky at getting our attention. We're forever tripping over them or running into them as they block our way. But our strengths are simply there for us in the background, quietly taking care of business. To draw them out and lead with them, we must consciously recognize and appreciate our strengths, just as a good coach, mentor, or supervisor would do. We need to cultivate our ability to marvel at what comes naturally to us, at what we've mastered, at the person we've become . . . at the very things that make us unique.

You will be tested. Accomplishing anything of importance will test your will. In the pursuit of a dream we each must move through a necessary period of darkness and pain in which we feel very alone. But this passage is necessary and the only way to emerge on the other side is through the effort of your own will. "From your extraordinary isolation of will, you feel the first taste of true achievement," says Shakkai in *Women of the Secret Garden.* "This achievement looks like . . . knowing the silence of the night, but the day of wisdom will come and the sun will rise and there will be meaning to all the pain and to all the joy."

Commit
What you resist, persists. Have you ever noticed that the harder you try to avoid a fear or concern, the larger it seems to loom or the more insidiously it keeps hanging around? While it is often said that we must maintain a positive attitude, paradoxically, if we ignore nagging fears and doubts, the harder and harder it becomes to remain positive. On the other hand, if we can bring our concerns out of the shadows of our mind and subject them to the light of day, often they simply fade away. Concerns and doubts are usually about what could happen, and in truth anything could happen. The more pertinent question for us as practical dreamers is: What do we want to create and how can we do it within the confines of existing realities?

Don't let your true dreams slip away. The basic difference between dreams that fade and those that become reality is commitment. If you're not committed to an idea, it dies. Of course, we can't follow through on all our ideas. We have to choose the ones we can and want to commit to. But often expediency dictates what we commit to instead of what would truly nurture and support us. To distinguish your true desires, put your "great" ideas on a sticky pad and post them on your computer. Or list them on your daily "to do" list. If you don't get around to doing anything about an idea on a given day, ask yourself each day whether you want to carry this idea forward and keep it alive or scratch it off and let it die. If you still care enough about an idea, you'll take some action on it the first chance you get. If not, obviously it's not something you're willing to commit to right now. The day you realize that, take it off your list. If you do this every day, you'll discover what's really important to you.

Believe in your willpower. The word "willpower" is often associated with keeping ourselves from doing things we think we shouldn't do. Actually willpower is what enables us to do what we want to do. Our willpower is working every day all day long. It directs our behavior. As Edgar Cayce said, "The human will is the paramount factor in one's life path." We can look at our lives and see the results of our willpower. We can see if it's working in our service or if we've turned it over to what someone else believes we should be doing. Tap into your willpower and you'll be amazed at what's possible.

Let your brilliance shine through. Often while we're growing up, we learn to tone ourselves down so we won't stand out from the crowd. We fear that if we excel, others will take potshots at us and try to bring us down. And, in fact, they may, but if we don't have the courage to stand tall and give our all, we contribute to a world of mediocrity. The more brilliantly we each shine, the brighter the world becomes for all of us. As I see you achieving success, it inspires me, if I let it, to reach further into my own potential. We each can take responsibility to create the highest value in our own lives. As Stanford University student Selena Señora Saunders said as a winner of the *Glamour* magazine Top Ten College Women,

"You don't have to blow out anybody else's candle to make yours shine brighter."

Declare your intention. There's something almost magical about making a declaration of what you intend to do in your life. Of course, there is a certain safety in keeping your intentions secret, while wishing and hoping for the best. Certainly that way you won't have anyone questioning your intentions or discouraging you from achieving them. And, indeed, sometimes there are those who will rain on just about any parade. But if no one knows what you intend to do, no one can help you. You won't hear any criticism, but you also won't hear any suggestions. You won't get any guidance for avoiding painful mistakes. And you'll miss those serendipitous occurrences that come from seemingly nowhere when you cast your intentions on the sea of life.

Don't keep yourself in the dark. While you don't need to share your intentions with everyone, the most important person with whom to declare your intentions is yourself. By making a declaration to yourself about what you intend to do, you test your will. When you put your willpower to work for your intentions, that's when you can truly mobilize your inner and outer resources and set a course for success. Your intention can carry you to wherever you're headed. As Benjamin Disraeli said, "Nothing can resist a human will that stakes its heart upon a purpose."

"Your heart is free; have the courage to follow it," William Wallace tells the Scottish people in the movie *Braveheart*. Well, that's the opportunity that's open to each of us if we claim it: a free heart. Yet to follow your heart takes courage, and we live in a country and a time when courage is a concept most often reserved for special heroes. Usually it's not something we think we possess until tragedy strikes to test our mettle. If fortune has shone upon you, you may not have been called upon to be courageous. Yet to

do those things you yearn for in life, to follow the dreams that dance in your heart, is itself an act of courage to which you can commit yourself. After all, courage is not the absence of fear; it's caring for something with a passion greater than your fear of pursuing it.

"Have I done enough for the happiness of mankind? Have I done enough to further the knowledge of future generations?" Writing in his journal, explorer Lewis Meriwether asked these two questions of himself on the eve of his thirty-first birthday. Earlier that day he became the first man to stand on the continental divide. Might we each ask ourselves these questions from time to time and think each day about what we might do to assure that the answer is yes?

"A person without a goal is like a computer without a program," Steve Danish of the Life Skills Center at Virginia Commonwealth University told the Los Angeles *Times.* "It's just an ugly piece of furniture." But when you have a program, a goal in mind, to which you are committed, your days come to life, you become animated with passion and drive. With commitment, you're not just responsive; you're creative.

Take a chance on your dreams. "The only time you run out of chances," said Dr. Alan Shutt on *Chicago Hope*, "is when you stop taking them." Taking a chance doesn't have to mean throwing caution to the wind. It means setting your course and sailing there with skill and care on the prevailing winds.

Overcome fear with your passion to explore life. Who has not been gripped by fear as we step into the void of an uncertain future? But if we are to succeed, our goals must call to us more loudly than our fear. We must listen to fear's warnings, take all possible precautions, and step forward even as it screams on in our ear. As explorer Douchan Gersi has said, we must learn to master the trembling of our limbs, slow the beating of our heart, wipe away the sweat that burns our eyes . . . and become intoxicated by the satisfaction of having overcome our fear of the unknown.

Find your antidote to fear. Who doesn't live with fear some time or another when following a dream into unfamiliar territory? There is so much that's unknown when creating a dream that's all your own; so much that is an experiment. So much about success that we do not have control over. But if your intent never wavers, there's no room for fear. Fear creeps in when we take our eye off where we're headed to focus on what could go wrong. Dealing effectively with whatever each day brings can keep fear in bounds.

Make your life a work of art. Regretfully art is generally not considered to be part of the regular work world. As a term it's usually used to refer to the fine arts, as in arts and entertainment. The "artist" is thought of as some unusually gifted person. Yet that has not always been so. Once, craftsmen of all kinds were referred to as artisans, people who considered their work to be an art. There's no reason we can't create a life that allows us to approach our work and our lives in this way, as artisans—people who, in the words of George Bellows, "make life more interesting or beautiful, more understandable or mysterious, or probably in the best sense, more wonderful."

By using this as the definition of an artist, Bellows has described something we can each provide. As we do the daily tasks of our life, we can ask ourselves, "How can I make life more interesting or beautiful, more understandable or mysterious, or in the best sense, more wonderful?"

Part Two

ACTION—
BUILDING A
NEW REALITY

*Every artist dips his brush in his own
soul, and paints his own
nature into his pictures.*
HENRY WARD BEECHER

Most of us have a myriad of excuses
for why we can't do what we need to
do to improve our lives, at least not
now. These excuses usually boil down
to something like this: "I wish I could
get away from all this hassle, but . . . I
don't have the money." "I don't have
the time." "I just don't have the energy." "I don't know how I'd do it."
Or simply, "I can't do *that*!"

But right from our first weekend
visit, we noticed that people in Pine
Mountain think about time and

money and energy quite differently from the rest of us. They approach these resources the way other practical dreamers do. They don't have any more time or money or energy than the rest of us, but regardless of their age, their income level or socioeconomic background, they make quite different choices, every day and every hour, about how they will use whatever time, money, and energy they have.

Like all practical dreamers, having committed to a dream, they jump into reality with both feet and put their time, energy, and money to work on living their dream. Not later, not someday, but right now. For the practical dreamer, commitment is a call for action. Like the artist who applies his tools to bring his or her vision to the easel, practical dreamers apply the hours of the day toward the life they're longing for. The artist makes choices about which color, shape, texture, line, and form to apply to the canvas; the practical dreamer makes choices about how to apply time, money, and energy to the canvas of daily life.

Look at where you're spending your time, money, and energy and you'll see a portrait of your life.

Rosie Reuter provides highly regarded cleaning services to Pine Mountain residents. When we asked if she would be able to clean our house once a week, she told us yes, she could. But when I asked her which day of the week she could come, a look of puzzled concern crossed her face. "Oh, I couldn't commit to a particular day," she said cheerfully. She has another commitment that places varying demands on her week—raising her two teenage daughters, Melissa and Marina, who are a refreshing contrast to the troubled adolescents we hear so much about in the news.

My first thought was "What! You just work on the days that fit into your schedule?" I'd never heard of such a thing. But before responding, I countered my own surprise with a rousing "Well, why not?" Why did I think she had to clean on the same day every week? The only reason I could think of was that's the way everyone else does it. Actually we have no need for her to come on any particular day. A flexible schedule works out just fine.

This sounds a lot like Liz Danzinger, the technical writer and mother of four, who operates her home business during weekday mornings only. When her clients want afternoon appointments, she tells them, "I'm sorry, I have another commitment that afternoon," and they arrange to meet on the first available morning. It works out just fine.

Scott Rosen runs the Frazier Mountain Internet Service. When we asked if he would also do some computer consulting to help us get our home office set up, the ex-bank manager told us, "I don't do computer consulting anymore. I used to but the time came when I realized that if I helped everyone who needed my help with a computer problem it would consume my entire life. I'd be wealthy, but I wouldn't have a life. A couple years ago I tried raising my rates for consulting but that only showed me my time is worth more to me than what I can charge. So instead of saying, 'I could do that,' I ask myself, 'Why would I do that? How can I do this in a way that will keep me happy?' Making more money isn't that important to me. Having time to relax, being with family, going horseback riding with my eight-year-old daughter, that's what makes me happy."

This sounds like Rich Pope of Dexter, Oregon, or Sidney Schwartz of Portland. Both Pope and Schwartz are stay-at-home dads. Schwartz is a full-time dad, and when he made the decision to leave his job, undoubtedly more than one person thought, "You can't do that!" But for him and his wife, Sherrill, a psychologist, it works out just fine.

Pope made a different choice. "Our kids were at the baby-sitter's from six-thirty in the morning until five-thirty at night," ex-high school science teacher Pope recalls. "We felt like we were losing them." Problems at school, grades slipping. His choice was to work from home as a freelance indexer of science books. "This has given me total flexibility to be with my kids whenever they need me, be it for a school picnic at noon, to coach soccer after school, or to attend a play at night."

Once he made the commitment, Pope was surprised the transition was so easy. He no longer has the benefits and retirement plan he had on the job, but his income has climbed back up to about two-thirds of what he was making on the job. He points out, though, that considering they no longer need to pay $600 for child care every month and his gasoline bills have dropped by $150 a month now that he's not driving to work, they're breaking even financially. And that's OK with Pope because the real payoff comes in ways money can't buy.

His wife, also a teacher, is more relaxed now because Pope explains, "I can take care of the laundry, pack lunches, and make dinner." His youngest son, who's six years old now, started reading two years earlier than his older sisters because of their daily reading ritual after lunch right before afternoon nap. His oldest daughter's grades have jumped from C's to A's. "We feel like a family now," he says.

What's your relationship with time, money, and energy? How do you feel about them as tools for building the life you'd really like to be living? Do you appreciate and value the resources you have or resent those you lack? Do you allow what you lack to prevent you from jumping with both feet into creating your dreams? Are you using whatever time, energy, and money you have to improve your life or cursing and struggling with their limitations? Have you resigned yourself to not having enough or are you busily building a future from what you have?

We think of artists as sitting at their easels, word processors, or drafting tables dreamily crafting inspired creations. But in reality, like Rosie and Liz, Scott, Sidney, and Rich, they're busy solving problems. Sometimes they're stymied, sometimes they struggle, often they tear up an unsatisfactory attempt and start over and over, experimenting, observing, adjusting, redoing, and polishing until they find a way to get what they're working on to resemble what they imagined. So it is with practical dreaming. Often we must experiment, play with, problem-solve, explore, and adjust our choices about how we spend our time, money, and energy before we can create what we're missing and find the balance we're seeking.

Dreams are born from inspiration, but they're raised with perspiration.

As the months flew by and our house in Santa Monica didn't sell, I was growing increasingly frustrated. I didn't want to spend any more time and energy trying to figure out how I could get to Pine Mountain. I didn't want to problem-solve or play with possibilities. Time was running out! The escrow for our pond house could expire. How I wished I had enough money to just buy our pond home whether we sold our house or not. I wanted everything to fall into place the way I had imagined it.

But whether it's finding the place where you long to live or crafting the type of work you're longing to do, it's what you do with what you have, not what you want to have that counts. Just as in art, life is about making choices and doing it over until you like what you've got. We may not feel like this is true, but we do have choices about how we use the time, money, and energy we have and it's through these choices that we discover how we can craft a more balanced life . . . or not.

Now, over a year later, after nearly getting and nearly losing our dream home over and over again, as I contemplate the new dreams taking shape in my heart, I feel quite differently about the prospect of exploring my options with time and money and energy. I'm excited, not frustrated, by the thought of experimenting with and exploring my choices for how I might turn these new ideas into reality.

Can you feel excited about exploring the limits and discovering the possibilities for how to use your time, money, and energy to manifest your dream?

The next four chapters are about knowing what choices to make. They're about new ways of thinking about time, money, and energy so we can make different choices in how we use them to more easily build our dreams. And they're about discovering whether our dreams can pass the tests of time, money, and energy, for that's what all dreams are born of.

5

FOLLOWING
THE THREAD

Have faith and
pursue the unknown end.

OLIVER WENDELL HOLMES

For husband and wife Jon Bard and Laura Backes, the third time was a charm. Their creative process unfolded like this. Jon, a public relations executive, and Laura, a literary agent, got fed up with the daily grind of rushing around in the shadows of Manhattan skyscrapers on dingy, crowded cement sidewalks. So they moved first to rural Monroe, New York, about an hour away from their jobs in the city. But commuting from afar was a grind of its own, and since Laura grew up in Colorado, they decided to move again to Laura's hometown of Evergreen. But they found it too suburban, so they moved again, this time to Fairhope, Colorado, located, as they say, "in the middle of nowhere," about eighty miles west-southwest of Denver. There they operate Two Mile High Press, an Internet newsletter and resource center.

Tom and Marilyn Ross experienced the reverse of this continuum. In 1980, Tom and Marilyn had a thriving consulting business in San Diego with an office overlooking the Pacific Ocean. But a vacation to a mountain cabin on Big Bear Lake changed all that. There, surrounded by the wonders of nature, the blessed silence, the friendly squirrels playing on the roof, and the deer grazing next door, they began thinking about an alternative to the life they'd known. They decided that with today's technology they could operate their business from anywhere and set out to answer a call to nature.

The Rosses moved to a remote 320-acre ranch nestled in the Rocky Mountains. But that choice proved too isolating, so they moved again, this time to Buena Vista, Colorado, a town of about 2,000 people nestled in a beautiful valley surrounded by 14,000-foot-high mountain peaks. "The move was a major culture shock, a real socioquake!" Marilyn remembers. "We had some frustrating, funny, and humbling experiences. Being a city girl, I've had to prove myself in ways I would never have dreamt of."

While it's been both an adventure and a major learning experience, their new life also provides the Rosses with the sense of community and connectedness they were looking for. "We've found the many special treasures we'd been missing from urban living—things," they say, "that were once taken for granted; like trust, honesty, safe streets, clean air, and friendly neighbors."

Like most practical dreams, these two couples had to follow the thread of their inner desires around the bend in the road before they found what they were seeking. Only then could they see what they needed to do. Yet the number-one reason so many of us don't do anything about our hassled and harried lives is because we think we should know what to do right from the start, but of course we don't.

Just as few artists create a masterpiece in one sitting, few of us are able to create a simpler, more balanced life at the snap of our fingers. It can take several months to several years and often it includes some false starts and some wandering around in the woods. People often tell us, for example, "I read your books *Working from Home* and *Best Home Businesses* several years ago and I want you to know that although it took me a while to figure out how I would do it, I've started a home business now and it's going well."

FIGURE IT OUT

On the other hand, I'm always pained by a question hundreds of people have asked Paul and me. "I want to be my own boss and your books are full of great ideas," they begin with a contagious eagerness in their voice, "but tell me, what should I do?" I'm pained with this question because those asking never seemed to realize the inherent contradiction within their request, and even more so because I know how unpleasant it is to know what you want to do but not know how to do it.

I've been in that place again and again in my life whenever I've wanted to step out of what's already been done and create something original, be it a work of art or a life that works for me. Recently, for example, I decided to create a line of greeting cards. Having done virtually no previous art projects since sixth grade when art disappeared from the public school curriculum, I thought my card creations would simply spring forth from my inspiration. I had great ideas, glorious ideas, for my cards. If only you could see them as they existed in my head! But I had no idea how little paper and scissors and glue know about what I have in mind. Or how stubborn and uncooperative they and all manner of matter can be.

When I sat down to execute my creative ideas, I was shocked at the quandaries I faced. To name just a few: Where do you find gold pinecones? How do you attach them to a card? Why does the glue stick everywhere except where you want it to? How do you keep it from showing through as streaks underneath the foil? Why does the glitter insist on falling off and why did I think that a pinecone of any size would fit inside an envelope? . . . and on and on and on. "Uh-oh! I didn't think of that!" became my mantra.

Creating anything from scratch is so puzzling because it's like a puzzle. I was trying to fit pieces of material together in a novel way as I imagined them in my mind, just as we're trying to fit pieces of our lives together in new ways. Just like the men and women who ask Paul and me how to be their own boss, I wanted to ask my friends who are also artists how to solve these problems. "Tell me what to do," I wanted to ask. I'm sure someone has some ideas for me.

There are always people who are eager to help guide our projects. Some will even step right in and do them for us! "Oh, here, I'll show you how to do it." And they do. They show us how they would do it. And if we choose, we can copy them. But if we do what they would do, we'll have their creation, or their life, not ours. And invariably we'll end up wondering why we're feeling so dissatisfied with what we've created. Creating a copy is never as satisfying as creating an original. And that's what we're seeking— an original life that works for us.

So just as no one could tell van Gogh how to put onto canvas the images he saw in his mind, no one could tell me, despite many helpful tips, how to create the cards I saw in my mind. Nor can anyone tell us how to create the life *we're* yearning for. *We have to figure it out!* And that can be a bitch. It can feel like several months or several years of labor, as in giving birth to a child!

 **Try This**

Create something you've never made before. If you've never baked a pie, invite several people over for dessert and take on the task of baking a pie for the event. If you've never planted a garden, get busy and plant one. If you've never hosted a dinner party, send out the invitations and start planning. If you've never made a work of art or tried a craft before, do so. Make a gift for a family member or friend. It might be a basket, a model airplane, a doll, a piece of jewelry, a toy soldier, a quilt, a wood carving, a frame for a photograph you take yourself, or a handmade greeting card. You name it.

Whatever you decide to create, watch how you react to your project and how you go about doing (or not doing) it. How do you proceed? Do you jump in with gusto only to get sidetracked halfway through? Do you bemoan the fact that you can't do something like that, but after complaining, moaning, and groaning, do a masterful job?

Most of us will get bogged down somewhere along the way. Some people will get stuck because they can't come up with an idea for what to do. Others will have lots of ideas but will get stuck in figuring out how to implement them. Others will make great plans and get everything ready but never get around to actually doing it. And some of us can create something just fine, but if we had to earn a living from making it instead of giving it away, we'd be in trouble.

Chances are whatever your reaction to this project, there will be many parallels between how you deal with it and how you would deal with creating your life. So notice where you get bogged down and what you do about that. Do you scrap the idea or do you plug on until you get it finished? Does the project get lost in your other responsibilities or do you eventually figure out a way to work it in? If, one way or another, you end up with a creation of your own, chances are you can do the same in creating the life you're yearning for. If not, this experience can be a useful way to identify where you're likely to get bogged down, why, and what you can do about it.

PUT ON YOUR HIKING BOOTS
AND GAS UP THE SUV

There are no paint-by-number kits for creating a balanced life that fulfills our particular personal desires and values. Nor is there a procedure manual or cookbook for how to create a life that makes room for what we're missing. We each have to cook up our future from scratch if we want something different from the standard fare. We may wish someone would just give us a recipe, but we don't really want a cookie-cutter plan because we don't want a cookie-cutter life. That's exactly what we're trying to escape, the limiting confines of stuffing more and more into the narrow perimeters of the way things have been.

We're needing a life with a lot more breathing room, a lot less pressure, and a lot more balance; but to find it, we have to go off road and get off the map. If we're going to walk between the worlds of the life we want and the life we have, we probably won't know exactly where we're headed or just what we need to do to get there until we get off the road and start hiking out a ways. Fortunately, not knowing what to do needn't be a problem.

Practical dreamers often don't know what to do, but we usually have a hunch. The threads of our desire, like an inner compass, provide us with an inkling of what we need to do inch by inch, step by step. As with Jon and Laura and Tom and Marilyn, what comes next often won't be clear until we get to the bend ahead, but if we wait to start walking until we know precisely where we're headed and how we're going to get there, we'll never find out.

We need to start thinking of ourselves as explorers, or detectives or private investigators, following our instincts instead of some map or manual in our back pocket. Maps and manuals are great for going places where lots of people have already gone, but they're not of much use when you're heading into the uncharted territory of a custom-made life. Out there, we have to *discover what to do.* We figure out what we need to do by working our way through it.

 **Try This**

When you don't know what you need to do, get curious. Begin by asking yourself the questions that come to your mind, questions like these:

1. *How did I create this life I'm living right now?*
2. *How do I want what I'm doing now to come out?*
3. *What's important to me about this?*
4. *How will I know I'm on track, or not?*
5. *When have I done something like this successfully in the past?*
6. *Has anyone else done anything like what I want to do? Who? What?*
7. *What's an example of one possible way I could proceed?*
8. *How could I do that?*
9. *How do I know that?*
10. *What stops me from . . . ?*
11. *What would happen if I did (or didn't) do that?*

FOLLOW THE THREAD TO FORGE A TRAIL

Discovering what we need to do to fulfill our desires is more like going on a treasure hunt than taking a motor trip. The several thousands of people Paul and I have interviewed who are successfully following their dreams have told us again and again about the similar conclusion they've each reached: "I've learned to trust my instincts," they say. But just how do we recognize our instincts, that inner sense of knowing, the ability to discern what is true and right and wrong for us? How do we know the difference between our instincts and what we simply wish were true or what we fear is true? How do we distinguish our instincts from what we've been conditioned to believe and the myriad of should's and shouldn't's we've been taught?

That is perhaps at the heart of wisdom: the ability to sort out the cacophony of voices in our heads so that we can listen to our inner truth. Some people do this by finding quiet times during each day to contemplate, play, or meditate. Others learn to distinguish their "gut" feelings for what is true from all the rest.

Finding our own inner sense of knowing is actually much like the process of learning to use a mouse to guide the cursor on a computer. At first, zeroing in on your inner truth is quite erratic. You can't quite get a bead on it, but eventually, as we keep striving to perfect our sense of it, suddenly, we "just know" how to do it. No one else can teach us; we learn by attending carefully to the subtleties of our reality. We learn by listening for our inner truth and letting our curiosity be our guide. Until suddenly things just "click."

As we start wondering what we need to do to get our life the way we want it to be, we'll encounter first one clue and then another. As we check out each clue some will be dead ends, but others will lead to new clues that will lead to other clues and so on. As we follow the threads of our highest desires, they can serve as the inner compass telling us which clues to pursue and which to discard. They let us know when the trail is cold and when it's hot, when we're on course and when we're off.

There's an integrity to following our inner desires that rings true, if we pay attention to it. If we veer off course, if we lose the thread, we begin to feel out of integrity with ourselves. To be true to ourselves, we must reconnect with the desires that will put us back on a course toward the kind of lives we yearn for.

How do you know when you're on track and when you're off? Can you sense your instincts at work? Listen to your body. Are you hurting, tired, and weary with life? Consult your soul. Are you pleased and at peace with your path? Are you willing to follow the thread?

PLAY YOUR PART

I was willing to follow the thread of my desire, and I felt a deep sense of integrity about moving to Pine Mountain. But why wasn't it happening? Why wasn't our house selling? I hadn't seen many clues as to what more I was supposed to do, I remember thinking as I made up the bed, just in case there might be a showing. Where is this desire taking me and why is it taking so long to do something as simple as selling a house? I wondered as I fluffed the pillows and piled them up like you see in the magazines. Was I off the track?

I was starting to feel like I no longer had a home. We were living in a showcase. No piles of files. No smudge marks on the switch plates. The Vita Mix put away out of sight. No morning papers on the coffee table. Who worked at my desk? It couldn't be me. There was no sign of my projects, all stuffed inconveniently away in some file drawers somewhere. The house was being painted to look the way our agent said prospective buyers wanted it to look. Our favorite artwork had been banished to the closets, replaced by decorator choices of items that made the rooms more spacious and bare so others could imagine their belongings there. The house looked great, but it didn't look like us, so with each passing day it was less and less mine.

As I pondered why I was putting myself through all this I thought of my friends Gene and Toni Bua. They'd had it all. They met as young actors on the cast of *Love of Life*, fell instantly in love, and basked together for ten years in the secure fame and fortune of a daytime soap opera family. But for Toni, something was missing. In addition to being actors, Gene was a composer and she, a lyricist. She wanted them to create something together with their music, something that would serve the world in a way that did more than entertain, in some way that mattered. And for some reason she didn't understand, she believed that meant moving to Los Angeles.

"I had to go there. I was possessed with the idea. It felt like my destiny," she recalls. But Gene loved New York and was very happy there. "I had to drag him to L.A.," Toni admits. Since she wanted to go so badly, he honored her desire. Within six months, they'd left everything behind without a clue as to why they'd come to somewhere that had never appealed to them before. Movies? A television series? They tried all that after they arrived and really hated it. It was a rat race. They were miserable.

Through all the lonely, hellish days of staring at the phone and waiting for their agent to call, Toni never doubted she'd made the right decision. But Gene soon began to feel resentful about being taken away from the life he'd loved. Sitting in his tiny apartment, he felt totally powerless, so much so that he had to start questioning himself and his life. He realized he was creating his life each day as he lived it and if he didn't like the way it was going, he'd better do something about it.

That was the turning point. He stopped waiting for his agent to call. "We started doing things we felt from here," Gene said, touching the palm of his hand to his chest. They started writing musicals and screenplays and then Gene invited five people to his living room to teach his first acting class. "It was a freebie. I told them if they liked it they could come back." They did. For the past twenty years Gene and Toni have operated the Gene Bua Acting for Life Organization and Theatre. They have 100 students filling four classes every week, and together they've written, directed, and produced nationally acclaimed musical productions like the award-winning *Pepper Street*.

But Acting for Life is more than an acting class and their musicals are more than an evening of entertainment. "Acting for Life is about releasing one's talents," Gene explains. The classes and the productions take those on the stage and those in the audience beyond the limitations of their belief systems. "The wouldn't's, shouldn't's, and couldn't's begin to disappear so you can experience what it's like to have no limitations," Toni adds. "And that opens the door to being all you can be."

I'd thought of Gene and Toni often while wrestling with my own obsession to move somewhere I'd never even heard of only a few months ago. So when Toni called right before yet another showing, I knew it was a clue. She had some great news. Their film *348*, which Toni wrote and Gene directed, had been one of only ten films accepted at the New York International Film Festival and THEY WON BIG TIME! Best film. Best actress (Caia Coley, a student from Acting for Life). Best rising star and new filmmaker (producer and Acting for Life student Nino Simon).

They played their parts in the dream in their hearts even when they didn't know how the play would end, and their inner compass took them beyond what they could have imagined.

I didn't know where my desire was taking me or why, but I did know I had to keep doing my part, which at that point was to just keep showing the house.

What is your inner compass guiding you to do right now? What one step is it suggesting you take at this time? Taking that one step is enough for now. That's your part.

THINK LIKE A HURDLER

OK, so I hadn't expected any problems. That was the problem. Walking between two worlds is like running the hurdles: there are going to be obstacles on the path. But hurdlers expect the track to be strewn with hurdles and they know that getting over them is the only way to get to the finish line. So we shouldn't be surprised by the barriers we encounter. They're par for the course, part of honing our skills and carving out the path to a future of our choice. They make us more accomplished practical dreamers. But there's a secret to running the hurdles. I first discovered it while riding a bicycle. It applies to almost anything we set out to do.

Every morning Paul and I used to ride our bikes down to the bike path in Santa Monica. To get onto the path we had to navigate our way through a barricade of closely placed metal poles that had been put there to keep cars from driving onto the path. Each day as I approached this barrier, I would try to get between the openings without having to stop, but every morning I'd come perilously close to the pole on one side or the other, so I'd have to brake and put my foot down to avoid a collision.

One day I tried a different approach. Instead of looking at the poles I was trying to avoid, I just concentrated on the opening between them. From that morning on I sailed right through those poles without even having to put on my brakes.

If I were ever going to get to Pine Mountain, that's what I needed to do. I had to stop looking at all the problems we were having with selling the house and keep moving in the direction I wanted to go. With that in mind, we started researching the kind of generator we would need. We got estimates from moving companies. We decided what kind of help we'd need on moving day. We talked to contractors about what we would need to do to add a garage to the pond house. We created a series of file folders and sorted the phone numbers, price estimates, catalog sheets, and other records we were collecting for when we'd be moving.

We stopped thinking of our plans as a road map, because clearly they weren't. We had to keep following the clues to find out how we would get where we wanted to go. But by putting the details of our dream onto paper and into files, we took it out of our imagination and put it into its first material form. Just as the printed page represents the line between the real world and the imaginary one that's unfolding when you read a novel, materializing elements of a dream serves as a gateway between the life we're living and the one we want to live. So, the best plans aren't about what will happen. When creating something new that can only unfold as it proceeds, the best plans are written representations of what we're doing to prepare for and assist in the unfolding of the new reality we're creating.

We did two other things that helped us to materialize our stalled dream. First we bought two futons and asked the retailer to hold them in the warehouse until we moved. What, we often wondered as the months passed, were we going to do with two queen-sized futons if our house didn't sell? "Well," we'd say, "we'll see."

Later, when it seemed like there was no hope left of keeping our pond house (the only place we'd found that met both of our needs), we bought ourselves black leather hats for cold, snowy Pine Mountain days. We had to laugh. We'd never have an occasion to wear these hats in Santa Monica.

Are you focusing on the hurdles instead of keeping your eyes on the track?

GET CREATIVE

Jan Trimmer was feeling especially stressed the day we met. She's a court reporter, which means spending long, intense hours precisely recording every word of complex court proceedings. Actually, she loves her work. You can see that in her eyes and hear it in her voice as she talks about the cases she's working on. But coming to Pine Mountain with her husband, Jim, a semiretired cabinetmaker, is a refreshing respite from all that. As we talked, she mentioned often how much she wished she could spend more time on the mountain. She even fantasized jokingly about taking a job as a stable hand at the equestrian center to escape the city more often. But owning a home both in L.A. and in the mountains was a stretch.

Short of a financial windfall that sets you up for life, just about the only way one gets to live in Pine Mountain is to get creative. So like all practical dreamers, the Trimmers found a novel but realistic solution that would enable her to be there as often as she chose. Instead of owning two traditional homes, they bought a trailer in L.A. and a cabin in the mountains. They spend long weekends in Pine Mountain and stay in L.A. for Jan's work on court cases.

 **Try This**

When you don't have any creative ideas for how to proceed, start generating as many possibilities as you can for getting where you want to go. Postpone evaluating your ideas at first. Just let your mind come up with as many options as you can. Sometimes the more bizarre an idea, the better. Try some of these wacky ways to generate workable possibilities. They're distilled from Whack on the Side of the Head, *by the creativity consultant Roger von Oech.*

1. *Pretend you know what to do. Maybe you do.*
2. *Think of impractical ideas. They may lead you to practical ones.*
3. *Come up with illogical ideas. They may lead you to logical ones.*
4. *Come up with wrong answers; they may lead you to the right ones. In fact, come up with stupid, foolish, and absurd answers. They may lead to smart, feasible ones.*
5. *Turn the situation into a metaphor: What if it were a contest? An elevator? A cowboy movie? A vacation?*
6. *Propose solutions that break the normal rules. As von Oech says, "You can't solve today's problems with yesterday's solutions."*

7. *Play what if. Pretend you're a wizard. What if things could be any way you can imagine? What would you do then?*
8. *When you find what seems to be the right answer, look for a second one. It may be better than the first.*
9. *Imagine doing what needs to be done backward. This perspective may give you insight into how to move forward.*
10. *Consider how someone in a totally different field or other circumstances would approach what you want to do. What would an architect do in this situation? An actress? A farmer?*
11. *Pose the questions you're asking differently. What if the problem isn't what you think it is? As Emerson said, "Every wall is a door."*
12. *How would your idols handle this situation?*
13. *Turn what you're doing into a game. Play with it. What if your life depended upon your winning?*

JUST DO SOMETHING

I really didn't want to paint the central hallway and staircase white. Our Santa Monica town house had a woodsy, rustic décor, as did our home in Sierra Madre. Redwood siding and lots of wood inside, soaring ceilings, and large windowpanes. (Could this have been a hint about the kind of place we'd been wanting to live in all along?) But the message was clear. Too much wood. One buyer, a doctor, loved the house, for example, but stopped short of making an offer because of all the money she'd have to spend to paint the natural woodwork.

This seemed ridiculous to me. There must be somebody out there who still preferred natural wood to wallpapered wallboard! But as a rule, when you're up against the wall, it's better to do something rather than nothing.

For seventeen years suburbanite engineers Susan Ray and Steve Middlebrook had been saving and investing to follow their dream to buy a farm. Seven years ago, they decided it was time to act. They bought an eighty-acre farm and moved with their two young children to the Ozark foothills of northeast Arkansas, about 200 miles from Little Rock. They thought they were going to grow organic vegetables, but it didn't take long to realize that plan wasn't going to work. They were too far from a major city to grow perishable goods. They had to do something.

Coincidentally, they had purchased two angora goats as pets for their kids. At the time there was a good commodity market for mohair, so they began raising angora goats and selling their hair. But since they were small producers and the bottom fell out of the commodity market, once again they had to do something.

This time they decided that they would add value to their goat hair by blending it with wool and crafting products made from luxury fibers. They currently have 130 angora goats and 30 sheep. They shear the mohair, blend it with wool, send it to a mill in Vermont, and then when it returns, they weave it into natural, black, and walnut sweaters, accessories, and throws, which they sell through craft fairs.

"It was pretty risky for us ignorant city dwellers to start out on a farm in the first place," Susan Ray admits. They knew nothing about farming, animal husbandry, weaving, or design when they left Springfield, Missouri. "A lot of people thought we were nuts. It has taken a lot of effort and trial and error, but it's worked out well."

Would they have ever imagined they'd go from being engineers to farmers to goat ranchers to artists in the course of seven years? It would never have crossed their minds. But they followed the thread of their desire and tried something different each time they didn't know what else to do. Susan Ray's conclusion, "Once you learn how to raise angora goats you can raise anything four-legged, even children!" Next, they plan to add their own mini-mill.

When you don't know what to do, but it's time to act, try something. Test whatever you do in as small a way as possible, and then assess your results. If it doesn't work, your results may suggest something to do next.

Once the central hall was painted white, we never heard anything but praise about the house. "Oh, it's so light." "It's so bright!" "It's so large." Nary another word about all the rest of the wood.

DON'T GET HOOKED

The layoff had been completely unexpected. She was a respected authority in her field with more seniority than anyone else in her department. Her performance evaluations had been outstanding. She'd recently had a paper published in a leading professional journal and she was invited regularly to speak at national conferences and symposia. But she was the only woman on staff and older than anyone else.

That was five years ago. She had sued immediately for age and sex discrimination, certain she would prevail. Two years later, she did, but it was appealed. She wasn't yet reinstated, nor had she received the compensation she'd been awarded. She lost the next round, but won the next, which also was appealed.

Meanwhile her career was on hold, her family finances were suffering, and she was becoming increasingly depressed. Friends and professionals urged her to continue her career as an independent consultant. She liked the idea and began to make plans for a new future she could pursue whether she won the lawsuit or not. But her plans remained on paper only. When she came to see us, she seemed excited about starting her consulting practice, but was frustrated with not being able to get it off the ground. After several consulting sessions, it became clear, this woman was hooked . . . hooked on the past.

The thread of her desires for the future was hopelessly tangled in the past. Until she was able to unhook her focus from the past and the ongoing lawsuit, she would not have a future.

It was a painful choice. She had been wronged. At least she deserved the satisfaction of having that wrong officially acknowledged. Also, she felt she should be compensated for the damage that had been done to her career. She could either hold out in hopes of vindication or move on. Only she could decide. When she chose to drop the lawsuit, within weeks her consulting business began to bloom. She was off the hook that had kept her in the past.

You can't manifest a new future if you're hooked on the past. Are there any attachments or unfinished business from the past that are keeping you from moving on?

For the past nine months, Paul had been under the most severe deadlines to finish the revisions of the twenty-first-century edition of our book *Best Home Businesses.* He was working morning, noon, and night and most weekends. I was devoting half time to this project, too. On February 23, we delivered the finished manuscript to the publisher. Not even a day passed after turning in this project before we got word of a pending offer on our home. Another developed within the week.

FINISH THE STORY

The optimism of late February faded as a continual stream of rumored offers either didn't materialize or were too low for us to consider. The clock was ticking. The contingency on the purchase of the pond house would expire April 5. As the day approached, we talked with our agent. We offered a bonus. He pulled out all the stops. Our town house appeared in Hot Properties in the *Los Angeles Times.* But nothing stopped the progression of days. April 5 arrived and the phone rang.

Our sale had fallen out of escrow, as they say. The seller was putting the house back on the market with a real estate agency at the original asking price and there was already an offer in hand. We'd lost our pond house. It seemed our Pine Mountain dream had died. I was griefstricken. I tried to imagine my life going on as it had before. After all, until the past July 4th, I'd been quite happy living in Santa Monica. So I tried putting down the novel I'd been writing for our future over the past nine months. I tried to stop imagining waking up to the call of the ducks by the pond and padding in my slippers past the black iron stove to fix my breakfast and sit on the deck. It was time, it seemed, to return to the reality of living in Santa Monica with a freshly painted white central hall. Or was it?

I felt lost in a story I thought I was writing. The plot had taken a twist from the one I'd had in mind and was unfolding on a course of its own. I stood on a desolate stretch of land with no exits and no U-turns. I could stop the journey by closing the book and leaving the novel unfinished alongside the road, but if I did that I'd never know where the story I'd begun might have taken me if I'd let it unfold on its own.

There comes a time in the birth of every dream when it takes on a life of its own. As long as your dream lives principally in your mind, you have 100 percent control of its nature, its content, and its unfolding. But as it becomes more and more of this world, it begins to slip away from you until suddenly you're no longer in charge anymore. You can influence it and play a major role in how and even if it continues to unfold, but a dream with a full head of steam is a force of its own.

You may still hold the power of life and death over your dream because if you walk away, most likely it will die without the continued investment of your energy and your time. But once your dream gets its legs, so to speak, you may even have trouble walking away. Forces of reality come into play and can sweep you up, even unwillingly. There may be others who are depending on you to proceed. You may have signed legal documents, made agreements, or committed funds you need to recoup.

It's at this turning point that we come to understand the meaning of the saying "Be careful what you wish for, because you may just get it." Think, for example, of Randy Merrell. He's the boot maker who built a company to manufacture lightweight hiking shoes. The company was his dream, his idea. But once he'd created it, once it was of this world, it took on a life of its own. He found himself swept up in his creation, jetting across the country, wheeling and dealing and manufacturing shoes that met market desires but not his own. He wasn't liking the way this dream had turned out, so like the artist who crumples up and tosses away an unsatisfactory draft, he decided to walk away and built a new dream more to his liking.

But we decided not to bail. Over the last ten days before the contract with our real estate agent ran out we decided we would continue to play out our part in the story we'd begun the past fall; no longer as the authors of the tale, but now as two characters whose fate life would author. That meant doing two things I didn't think I could do.

First we went up to the mountain to see if we could find another house. And to our surprise we did! Some days I could even imagine living there. It was beautiful—4,000 square feet, four-car garage, huge kitchen, massive stone fireplace two stories high in the living room, wood-burning stove in the master bedroom and dining room, large walk-in closets, luscious master bath with Jacuzzi ("We could have a party in here!" I joked to Paul as the agent walked us through.), a fenced backyard, large front veranda. And best of all, we could buy it FOR LESS MONEY than the pond house.

Paul promptly named the house Soaring Spirits. But there was no pond, no green belt of pines on all three sides, no dear friends next door, no ducks to wake us up in the morning, no brick fireplace with a black cast-iron stove. Our dream didn't need to die. We could move to Pine Mountain. But it wouldn't be the same.

The second thing I did right after we returned from the mountain was to write the owners of the pond house, Ben and Marie Jacquet. I gave myself over totally to that letter, pouring everything I had in my heart into words on its pages. I thanked them for their kindness, and their patience and understanding through the past six heartbreaking months. I explained how we could never have imagined having such difficulty selling our house. I let them know that, as disappointed as we were that our Pine Mountain dream on the pond was not to be, we understood their relief at having found another buyer, who we hoped would love and treasure their home as much as we would have.

Of course, I told them about how I'd imagined awakening to the call of the ducks and padding across the living room in my slippers, the whole novel experience I'd been living. I closed by saying that despite how difficult it can be to have the faith to keep a dream alive, it's far more difficult to have the faith to know that losing a dream is ultimately for the best. Finally I added that for their sake, "we hope the new buyers had already sold their house!"

Upon receiving the letter Ben called at once to say that he had turned down the other offer because it, too, was contingent upon the sale of the buyer's house. So his house was still on the market, and he would exclude us from his real estate agency agreement, so if our house were to sell before his did, he would sell it to us himself at our previously agreed upon price without forfeiting our deposit.

The story wasn't over. Our dream was alive again.

What is your role now in the dream you're writing? Are you willing to play out your part to the end?

➥ **Try This** ☆☆☆

Should you become lost between worlds, writing or talking out your situation can help. In talking with a caring individual, or expressing yourself in a private journal, the answers you're seeking may emerge almost magically. Articulating your situation for yourself or someone else to understand is like holding up a mirror to your thoughts and beliefs. It gives you a new perspective and allows you to see what you may have overlooked or couldn't see before.

On Monday, April 5, we relisted our town house. That Tuesday our agent held a caravan for other agents. Wednesday, one of those agents brought over a prospective buyer. His first comment upon arriving was, "I hope it's as rustic and woodsy on the inside as it is on the outside."

He made a cash offer on Thursday, we countered, and he accepted on Friday. The house, we were told, could have sold three times over that week.

We moved to Pine Mountain on May 19.

6

FINDING THE MONEY

Money, after all, is just a vehicle
to take you to your desires.
JERRY GILLIES, *MoneyLove*

Isn't it interesting that what's missing from so many of our lives doesn't cost a penny, but we nonetheless can't afford to make room for these simple things? The satisfaction of being with family, friends, and loved ones, for example. The sense of community that comes from sharing and giving and helping others. The gratification of a job well done. The joy of touching the heart of someone through the mastery of our work. The promise of a free afternoon to read a novel, go for a stroll, play with the dog, or hold hands under a tree after a picnic in the park. The solace of silence. The beauty of a star-studded midnight sky. The refreshing touch of a breeze through the forest or the song of a lark in the meadow.

Although such pleasures are free, for most of us money plays a role in whether we can make them a regular part of our lives or must instead squeeze them into crowded weekends, save them for the all-too-rare holiday vacation, or just forgo them altogether. We struggle with how we can support ourselves financially in a life that includes them.

"I'd like to start a home business so I could be home with my kids," the young woman explained, as she glanced at our book *Working from Home* on the table in front of her. She ran her fingers along its thick spine as if she wanted to pick it up. "What do you think, honey? It's eighteen dollars and ninety-five cents," she said, shifting her glance to her husband, who was standing beside her. She wanted his permission, but he said nothing. "Well," she concluded, looking back at the book and then turning to walk on, "we'll have to think about it. We have lots of expenses this month."

"I've won several awards," he pointed out as he showed us his artfully displayed portfolio of portraits. "But I'm still an amateur; someday though, I'd love to earn my living as a photographer. There's a great workshop coming up this summer outside of Paris that could help me a lot. I'd go if I had the two thousand dollars-plus airfare."

"I haven't had a day off in I don't know how long," the frazzled reporter told us as she shuffled through her papers to prepare to interview us. She stopped briefly and twisted her neck from side to side to relieve some of the tension that showed on her face. "I'm thinking of joining a simplicity circle so I can leave this job and do some freelance writing." Then, laughing, she added, "But, you know, somehow I just can't see myself clipping coupons and sewing my own clothes." Glancing at her beautifully manicured hands and expensive tailored suit, nor could we.

"I keep seeing myself living in New Mexico working outdoors in some way," the man commented during a break from the workshop we were teaching. He had a pained expression on his face. "I really don't like accounting, but the income is so good. I just can't imagine how I could afford to start over in some new place and learn a brand-new career."

"We've always wanted to operate a bed-and-breakfast inn away from the city somewhere," the woman told us, her voice animated with excitement. Then she rolled her eyes and shrugged, and added with a lopsided smile, "We found this place outside New Orleans. It's only two hundred thousand dollars. But even that's

not realistic for us. We couldn't afford the down payment." Imp-
ishly winking at her husband she added, "Unless we win the lottery!"

IF IT WEREN'T FOR MONEY

Each of these individuals is ready to follow the thread of a desire, but they've been waylaid by one of the earliest realities
we learn as children: money doesn't grow on trees, so you can't
have what you want, do what you want, or be what you want. Evidently this lesson is being ingrained in yet another generation
because, to my horror, I read recently that the number-one desire
children ages three to twelve have for their parents is for them to
earn more money! We've come to regard money not as a tool
with which to craft our dreams, but as the gatekeeper that allows
us to pursue them or not. If we have money, we can pass "Go"; if
not, there's nowhere to go.

Whether it's $20 for a paperback book, $2,000 for a workshop,
$200,000 for a mortgage on a house, the amount doesn't matter.
Many people believe if they DON'T HAVE THE MONEY,
they're out of luck. This belief is so firmly entrenched in our culture that when Paul and I first started teaching our courses on
how to change your life, we had to move the section on financing
your dream ahead of the section on discovering your dream. Like
the five people above, most of those in the courses simply
wouldn't explore pursuing a dream unless they not only had the
money in the bank to do it, but also saw how the dream would itself be a moneymaker.

Practical dreamers have a different attitude toward money. For
them pursuing a dream is not about money. It's about following
the thread. They don't wait to win the lottery, or to inherit a lot
of money, or to stumble into a stock windfall. Nor do they expect
the money to somehow be provided for them. If they have money,
great. They'll put it to work. But usually they don't already have
it, so instead of bemoaning the fact that they don't have the

money, they get busy figuring out how they can come up with it. To the practical dreamer, finding the money to create the dream is part of the job, another test of their belief and commitment to what they desire in life.

What would it cost to finance your dream? How could you come up with that much money? Does it seem impossible? Consider this.

IT'S NOT ABOUT MONEY

Who hasn't at least thought about shucking everything and hitting the road in a giant RV. It's a popular fantasy undoubtedly harking back to some magical sense of wanderlust we share from ancient ancestral ties to our collective nomadic roots. But with today's computer and telecommunications technology a vagabond life on the open road is no longer a pipe dream. How many of us wonder these days, could we do it? Should we do it? Husband and wife Megan Edwards and Mark Sedenquist undoubtedly asked these questions six year ago, before they hit the road in their custom, seven-ton, four-wheel-drive mobile home office. The nomadic life had always held an alluring pull for them, but the change they'd planned to make in their lives in 1993 didn't include life on the road.

Megan, a fledgling writer, and Mark, a real estate sales manager, had just opened a new home business selling retail merchandise when everything they owned went up in smoke in a California wildfire. As Megan stood beside the concrete slab that had been their home, her reaction was not what she might have expected. "We're cleaned out," she said. "We can do anything we want. Anything. Do you know what that means? We can go anywhere, Mark, do anything, start over again. Let's hit the road. We've got no stuff, no business, and no house to worry about. Let's just start driving and see what we find." Five months later that's what they did. They headed off on what was to be a six-month sabbatical. Now, 126,000 miles later, they refer to themselves as "dashboarders," living and working wireless, connected, and rolling. "Home is where the dog is," Megan says. "It's wherever we happen to be."

Of course, everyone assumes Mark and Megan are retired, independently wealthy, or cashed in on a giant insurance settlement. But none of the above is true of these virtual vagabonds. The insurance settlement paid off their business debt and a down payment on their 200-square-foot mobile home. Three banks rejected the idea of financing the balance before one finally agreed. Meanwhile, they've used up their savings, they've worked, and they've borrowed to cover the costs of the gas, living and business expenses, and the $15,000 worth of technology it takes to keep their rolling home office connected to the world.

Megan is a columnist and has written a book about their experiences on the road, called *Roads from the Ashes*. Mark runs their business, MTA Marketing, which designs and produces national public relations tours for corporate clients. Together they also publish an online magazine www.RoadTripAmerica.com. "Money isn't what enables you to do things," Megan points out. "It actually keeps you from doing things if you believe it has to come first. What really has to come first is resolve."

Over the years the couple reports having felt hopelessly short on cash at times and flush at other times. "We've been scared and we've been confident. We've come close to giving up and we've ridden high on abundance," Mark adds, not unlike most location-based lives.

Their nomadic lifestyle sounds intriguing, if not somewhat crowded and a bit challenging. There are no neckties or panty hose. Megan doesn't even own a purse. They might office one day in Flathead Lake, dine in the Blue Ridge Mountains, and fall asleep in the Acadian surf. Mark claims he meets ten new people a day, including many fascinating characters they include among the new friends they've made across the continent. But they also must contend with traffic tickets and tornadoes, floods, snowstorms, and insects. Without e-mail they couldn't last for long and there are still places where getting connected is a hassle or just not possible. "The worst part," says Mark, "is getting a good haircut. You never know what you're going to look like." Still, they have no plans as yet to settle down, but as Megan emphasizes, whether they will or not someday, "It's not about money."

Take the Job

"So don't tell me you don't have the money!" I admonish myself whenever a dream seems hopelessly impractical. Most people don't. We're each the parents of our dreams, and just as Mark and Megan have done, it's our job to figure out how to support them! There are plenty of ways short of winning the lottery or some other long-shot-in-the-dark to raise our dreams so they will eventually support us in the more balanced life we're seeking, but only if they . . .

Pass the Money Test

Where we spend whatever money we have is a snapshot of what's most important to us. For any dream to make it into reality it must first pass the money test—is what we desire important enough to invest whatever financial resources we have to make it come true? We can't expect it to be given to us. The Lord won't provide the Mercedes-Benz. If we don't have the money required to create the dream, we must ask if it's important enough to work for. If not, we should be honest with ourselves and put the dream aside, realizing that it's OUR CHOICE not to invest in or work toward this dream.

We faced that choice in deciding to move to Pine Mountain. We'd carefully planned out the financial aspects of moving. We'd calculated what it would cost to move, how much we would need to sell our house for, and how much we could afford to spend for a new house, including interest rates, closing costs, remodeling, etc. Early in the process, when the real estate market was strong, it looked like our Pine Mountain dream would pass the money test easily. All seemed well. But when the real estate market changed, the financial score of our Pine Mountain dream began to fall. We had to ask ourselves difficult questions about what we were willing to take on to have this dream. How much were we willing to pay?

How much are you willing to pay for your dream? How strong is your desire? How strong is your belief? Strong enough to pass the money test?

Cut Back, Reallocate, Save Up

Practical dreamers put their money where their dreams are. They know where their money is going and they make sure that where it's going is consistent with their dreams. Debbie, a stay-at-home mom, is a good example. Like the woman who couldn't bring herself to spend the $18.95 to learn how to work from home, Debbie wanted to start her own business. Ever since she was a child, she'd dreamed of being a chef, but marriage and family intervened and her life took a different path. When the last of her three children went off to grade school, however, her childhood dream started itching away at her peace of mind.

She didn't want to take a job working at night, nor did she want to work her way up the culinary ladder in a hot sweaty restaurant kitchen by day. But working as a home-based personal chef seemed like an ideal solution. She could cook on other people's premises in the mornings while her kids were in school. Just one problem. She "DIDN'T HAVE THE MONEY" to get the business under way.

At first, she was discouraged. "If I had a job," she thought, "I could set aside my salary until I had the money I need." But she didn't have a job, and didn't want one. Or did she? She did have a job—raising her family! What if the family paid her for doing her job? She proposed the idea to her husband. Together they reworked their budget and decided to cut back on expenses like the number of cable channels they subscribed to and how often they went out to movies. Every week she wrote a $30 check to herself and deposited it in her new interest-bearing account. Within three months she'd purchased a color printer and printed business cards and menus. A month later she was in business.

 **Try This**

Track your money each month with a software program like Quicken or Microsoft Money and print out a monthly report that shows all your expenditures. Take a close look at where your money is going. Is it consistent with living your dream? How could you reallocate your budget to invest in your dream?

Would you put your money on anyone who wouldn't bet on themselves?

Decide What's Most Important and Put Your Money There

When Elaine St. James and her husband took a look at their lives and where their money was going, they decided to prioritize what they were spending their money on so that they could get more enjoyment from life. They decided, for example, to:

- Make the things in their lives like their cars, home, diets, and finances small enough, few enough, and simple enough that they could easily take care of these things themselves instead of paying other people to do it for them.
- Buy in bulk.
- Resign from organizations that were unrewarding and unproductive.
- Drop magazine subscriptions they didn't actually read.
- Get rid of all but one credit card.
- Drop call waiting.

- Get a secondhand car.
- Buy clothes that don't need dry cleaning.
- Replace their Dayrunner with a simple one-page calendar.

Making these and other simple decisions so greatly improved the quality of their lives that St. James decided to write a book about their experience called *Simplify Your Life*. In this book, she shares *"100 Ways to Slow Down and Enjoy the Things that Really Matter."* Of course, the fact that these things simplified St. James's life doesn't mean they would simplify yours and mine. Many of the decisions the St. Jameses made would just complicate my life. For example,

- Using only one credit card would create unpleasant tax-time hassles for us when we need to sort and separate our business from personal expenses item by item. The small added cost of having two cards (actually we have three, another one for travel expenses) is well worth the investment when compared to how much it simplifies our record-keeping.
- We'd love to drop call waiting, but the resulting game of "telephone tag" would complicate our lives all the more and we might miss rewarding business opportunities.
- We prefer, if at all possible, to buy new cars. We don't enjoy inheriting other people's problems.
- Clothes that don't need dry cleaning need washing, drying, pressing, and folding, so for us giving up the dry cleaners gets a big "Ugh!"
- Using a simple calendar would be a double "Ugh" for us. We use a calendar and daily planning software program to keep our mind and our day focused on what's most important to us.

Simplicity is only simplicity if it simplifies your life. Clipping coupons and running from discount store to discount store can make life more harried and complex than working a few extra hours or raising your prices so you can shop leisurely nearby. Doing several extra loads of laundry to avoid the cost of dry cleaning so you can work less is only a good trade-off if you dislike your job and love doing laundry. Making your kids' clothes instead of working with an additional client each week will only simplify your life if you're exhausted by your clients and energized by sewing.

Clearly what may be important or simple in one person's life can be unimportant or complex to another. We must each decide what will make our lives most enjoyable and invest our money there.

What's most important to you? What makes life easier for you? Can you cut, save, or reallocate to have what you want most, or do you need to bring in more money?

Bring in More

Practical dreamers have an uncanny ability to generate income when they need it. They work a part-time job. They take a second job. They moonlight by providing some needed service like computer consulting, after-hours child care, programming, public relations, snow removal, or word processing. Sometimes they even find ways for their dream to pay for itself like taking preorders to launch a new business, or getting payments up-front or signing up contracts before leaving a job for an independent career. Or they may sell valuables they've owned that are no longer as important to them as having the things they're missing or needing in their lives. When we needed a computer to write our first book, Paul sold his Hasselblad camera to buy one. Later, we sold an exercise machine we rarely used to buy a color printer.

Sometimes, of course, working to bring in more money makes life temporarily more stressful. Some people aren't willing or simply can't add any further to their stress, so this is too high a price to pay. Then, of course, they need to find another way to finance their dreams, but often there is a creative way to generate the money we need to save a dream, even if it's having a yard sale, a bake sale, or a car wash. Here's an imaginative example.

It was a stretch for Bob Wallace and his wife, Ellen, even to think they could pursue their dream to create a line of skin care products called Arizona Sun. No one thought this home-based mom-and-pop team could compete in a field like skin care, where the major players are all big established companies with big bucks to develop, produce, and market their products. But Wallace had developed a unique moisturizer and sunscreen he believed would appeal to the sun-soaked, thirsty-skinned patrons who frequented nearby Arizona resorts. So Bob and Ellen launched their skin care company as a sideline business.

Even they were surprised when one of their first orders was for 500,000 bottles of their hand-labeled product! How could they possibly fill this order, particularly since the customer needed it delivered within just a few weeks? First, he "DIDN'T HAVE THE MONEY." Filling the order would cost $200,000 and, like the couple who wanted to buy the bed-and-breakfast, Wallace couldn't borrow $20,000, let alone $200,000. Second, even if he were able to arrange for the $200,000, he'd have to move at a near inhuman pace to hit the delivery deadline. If he missed the deadline, he'd have to repay the $200,000 he'd borrowed as well as pay for the $200,000 worth of ingredients, packaging, and other costs involved in filling the order. Third, he didn't know how he could get the labels on the bottles in such a short time frame because all 500,000 labels would have to be put on by hand. He didn't have and couldn't afford to buy the machine that would put them on for him.

Being a practical dreamer, however, he decided he would go for it. He began by convincing the manufacturer to have their trucks standing by and ready to ship. He convinced the label company to stop their presses and make up and ship him 500,000 of his labels. Next he convinced the bottle cap supplier to drop what they were doing and send him 500,000 caps ASAP. Despite having no credit history with these companies, he convinced them to do all this on credit!

Then, he came up with a novel idea for getting the labels on the bottles in only eight hours. There was a large church near his home that he figured had several youth groups, so he called the church and made them an offer. If they would have 200 teenagers in their social hall on Saturday, he would supply pizzas, a disk jockey, and a check at the end of the day for $1,000. The church thought this was a blessing! It would take them years' worth of car washes to bring in that much money. So it was a deal. The kids finished putting on the labels by 5:00 P.M. that Saturday. The truck drove the bottles to the manufacturer and the entire order was shipped within two weeks. Wallace got his $200,000 from the customer, paid everyone the money they were due, and his new skin care line was launched big time.

Does your dream require money you don't have? How could you bring in the money you need to proceed?

Ask for Help

Life hadn't been going well for Joe. He'd lost his job in a merger and over 100 résumés later he was still looking for a new one. To lift his spirits, a friend recommended that Joe attend a personal growth workshop. The workshop changed his life. He went from powerless to empowered in only four days and he wanted to share the experience he'd had in this workshop with the world! So he talked to the organization running the seminars about becoming a trainer for their company.

Like the photographer who needed $2,000-plus expenses to study in Paris, Joe learned he could enroll in a training program to learn how to teach the seminar by attending an initial $2,000 workshop in another part of the country. The next one was only weeks away, but there was one problem. He "DIDN"T HAVE

THE MONEY." From the moment Joe heard about this opportunity, though, he was on fire with determination. He would *find* the money. His plan was simple. He called everyone he knew and asked if they could each lend him $200 with the promise that he would pay them back within the next two months after he began conducting the training seminars.

"I only need ten people," he thought. His enthusiasm for the program, along with his past history as a reliable and trustworthy friend, did the trick. He was soon on his way to a new and far more rewarding career than the job he'd lost.

 **Try This**

When it isn't feasible to reallocate, save, or generate enough money to launch your dream, if you have a good plan for how you'll repay the money, you can ask for help. Make your case to yourself first, debate your doubts, go to battle with them, lay out the facts and figures. Demonstrate why you are a sure bet and once you've convinced your own doubts to get on board, make your case to people who know and care about you personally and who have the financial resources to help you out.

Trust Falling

There's a training exercise called Trust Fall that's used in many corporate team-building programs in which participants fall backward into the waiting arms of their colleagues. Some practical dreamers are quite accomplished at their own version of trust falling. They have a sixth sense or a spiritual connection to a force that's guiding them to make certain changes in their lives. This inner knowing operates much like what we've described as an inner compass and enables them to take a leap into their dream, trusting, without knowing, that it will work out financially.

In her book *The Anatomy of Spirit*, Carolyn Myss points out that this sense of faith or divine guidance allows some practical dreamers to take action that others would consider financially risky or even foolish. She describes, for example, a twenty-seven-year-old man who, like the man who kept seeing himself in New Mexico, had a recurring dream that he had moved to Montana with no job, no home, and no friends or contacts.

Since he'd never been to Montana and had no desire to go there, he ignored the dream at first. But as it continued to recur, he began to realize that he was only living where he was because of his job and he was only in his job because of its financial benefits. After six months of these dreams, he came to feel that staying in his job was compromising his integrity. One morning as he walked into the office, a powerful feeling came over him and he felt he had to act on it. He walked into his boss's office, quit his job, and announced to the world that he was moving to Montana "to follow a dream."

Within a month, he was in Montana. There he rented a room in the home of a couple who owned a ranch. They needed help with chores, so they hired him to become a ranch hand. That Christmas, the couple's daughter came to visit for the holidays and the next summer this young man and the daughter were married. He went on to learn to manage the ranch he and his wife would one day inherit.

There are times when we can't know where the money for our dream will come from before we act to pursue it. Such times require great faith and great courage.

Is your inner compass leading you to act without financial certainty?
Is your faith sufficient to take such a risk?

DON'T WAIT

Stuart Wilde was living and working in New York, but he had a mission. He wanted people to start taking better care of the environment. He was making headway, having catalyzed the first curbside recycling program, but he was getting tired of preaching to people about what they should do. He decided he could be of more use to the world by setting an example with his own life for how we can live in harmony with the environment.

His first plan was to continue working in New York until he saved enough money to buy some land in a remote area of the Pacific Northwest. But he concluded, "the more money you make, the more you spend. If I waited until I could save enough to buy the land I'd still be waiting." So instead, he sold his comic book collection for gas money, and this single dad headed for the northwest with only a few hundred dollars in his pocket.

Along the way his car broke down while he was passing through Taos, New Mexico. He liked it there—the beauty and the land and the environmental consciousness of the people he met. So he stayed, got a job, and rented a five-acre tract of land at the western base of the Sangre de Cristo Mountains along the southern end of the Rocky Mountains. While backpacking one day with his son, Zach, he found lugging the diapers and all the camping gear to be a lot of hard work. That's when he had the idea that was to fulfill his dream—Wild Earth Llama Adventures, a wilderness guide service and llama trekking company. Wilde takes tourists on wilderness treks using eight 80–120-pound llamas as pack animals so hikers are free to enjoy the pristine beauty of the wilderness and be inspired to protect and preserve it.

The ideal pack animals, these gentle, sure-footed creatures can carry 25 percent of their body weight, but they're quite expensive. So how, we wondered, did Wilde come up with the money to buy eight llamas? Again, he didn't wait to save up the money. To buy his first two llamas, he convinced the owner to sell them to him on a payment plan. He put $200 down and paid the rest off month by month. Since then, most of his other llamas have been given to him, because he's now known as a "llama whisperer" and desperate llama owners, eager to relieve themselves of the care of their unusual pets, call Wilde for help. He's traveled as far as 1,000 miles to rescue a llama.

"Our clients range from self-proclaimed couch potatoes and experienced mountaineers to groups of children and seniors," he explains. When we talked with him, he and his string of llamas were shepherding a group of professional photographers through the wilderness near Yosemite National Park. Eleven years after arriving in Taos, Wilde is now buying his own land, at last, twelve and a half acres for his llamas to roam when they're not off trekking.

What are you waiting for? How could you move on?

VOWS OF POVERTY NOT REQUIRED

When I decided to leave my government job, like the frazzled journalist who worried about having to clip coupons and make her own clothes, I thought my desire for a less hectic and more balanced life meant I'd have to tolerate living on a lot less money. I was prepared to sacrifice many of the comforts my government salary conferred. No more eating out. No more cross-country vacations. No more shopping sprees or cell phones. No more maid service to clean the house. Then, like so many people attracted to the simplicity movement, I unintentionally set out to make it so.

Fearful that I wouldn't have enough clients, I set my fees at near subsistence levels and I didn't think beyond seeing the number of clients I could comfortably work with privately each day. Before long I was working so hard that simplifying my life became as exhausting and complex as it had been before.

I noticed right away that not all psychotherapists in private practice were taking vows of poverty and that their lives were actually much simpler when they made more, not less. To supplement his income from private clients, one therapist had lined up a consulting contract with a forensic psychologist testifying in court cases. Another cut back the number of days he worked by seeing fewer private clients each week and doing weekend workshops where he could earn considerably more per hour. Both of these therapists were charging more than I was.

I raised my prices, started a group, and arranged to consult with a medical facility. Was I working harder? Was life more complex? It's all relative. For me, the answer was no. Having money to eat out periodically, use my cell phone instead of playing telephone tag, and having a cleaning service once a week made my life much more enjoyable than working fewer hours so I could play telephone tag and do all the cooking, the cleaning, and the wash myself.

IT'S NOT EITHER OR

It's not necessary to choose between money and simplicity. Often having money can enable us to simplify our lives. On the other hand, killing ourselves to make more and more money to have more and more "conveniences" can be a source of unnecessary complexity. It's up to us to find the balance. Actually balancing between the effort required to have costly conveniences and the effort they save us is a large part of how we make room in our life for what we're missing.

Janean had to make such a choice. She was a psychology professor at a small liberal arts college. Her salary was minimal. "Saturday shopping money," she used to say. She knew her salary wouldn't support her, let alone her four children, should anything happen to her husband's income. But that's exactly what she was faced with when he unexpectedly took ill and was unable to work for several years.

Janean sat down and looked at their expenses: $20,000 a month went to the mortgage on their large home, private school tuitions, a maid and garden service, expensive dental work for one of her children, weekly trips to their mountain cabin, nursing care for her husband's ailing mother, and much more. Under the circumstances, most people would "accept reality" and tighten the budget. Truthfully, she did consider that. Most families survive on far less than $20,000 a month, she reminded herself. So could hers.

But she and her husband were living the dream they'd spent

their lives creating. Both had come from families of limited means. She'd been the first person in her family to attend college. His mother, widowed during the Korean War, had worked two jobs to put him through school. They'd worked for twenty years to create the life they were enjoying. Janean didn't want to see all they'd worked for go down the drain.

They cut back temporarily on spending, but Janean resolved to find a way to generate the added $15,000 per month they'd need on top of her salary and his disability income. She knew that many other faculty members supplemented their income substantially by taking on corporate consulting jobs. But who, she wondered, would hire her to consult? Stress management was her specialty and she had written a number of articles on the effect of the man-made work environment on stress levels of workers. So she decided to put out some feelers about speaking to corporations on stress management.

As she knew nothing about corporate consulting, she started calling several companies each day just to gather information and explore possibilities. Within a few weeks, an amazing thing happened. One of the managers she spoke with mentioned that a public relations firm had been looking for an expert to talk with the media on behalf of one of its clients. They needed a spokesperson to explain the effects of natural versus synthetic fabrics on stress levels both at home and at work. She contacted the company and after reviewing her credentials, they hired her to work three days a week for a fee of, yes, $15,000 a month. Working on such an interesting and lucrative project was far less complex and stressful to Janean than cutting back on the hard-won pleasures of their family life.

Have you traded a complex grind for a simplified grind? What complicates your life? What would you be willing to work harder for in order to enjoy your life more? What could you gladly give up to work less? How could you enjoy both a financially rewarding, as well as a psychologically fulfilling and balanced life?

CHOOSE YOUR WEALTH

For Janean the wealth required to fulfill and live her dream involved substantial financial resources. But that's her dream, and her choice. Wealth need not involve substantial financial resources. We become wealthy when we fulfill the dreams that fulfill us. Our perception of wealth is independent of how much money we have, as Eileen Applegarth discovered in deciding to leave her job and live full-time in Pine Mountain.

As Applegarth's husband lay dying of a terminal illness he asked her to promise him that she would use the life insurance money to buy property in Pine Mountain. It had been a fondly remembered romantic retreat for the couple when they were dating and since property there was affordable, he wanted Eileen to have a place where she and their grown children and grandchildren could come together for family gatherings. So upon his death, as promised, she bought a weekend cabin.

But after her husband died, Applegarth felt as if her life had ended, too. Their friends ceased to call. Her best friend moved to Colorado. Her children were busy with their lives. Only forty-nine, she continued working at Disney studios as she had for twenty years but, she recalls, "There was no laughter, no happiness, no peace." At first she came to Pine Mountain about one weekend a month just to get away, then every other weekend, and finally every weekend.

"It got harder and harder to go home," she remembers. "I hated my life in the city. I hated getting up in the morning. There was a lot of depression. The doctor said my blood pressure was too high and that I had to find inner peace again." On weekends in Pine Mountain she felt at peace, so one day she called up her boss and said, "I quit." Within two months she was living in Pine Mountain full-time and she says, "I haven't looked back."

A neighbor introduced her to people in the community and "I haven't been lonely a day since then," she says. "I found peace. I sit and read a book, play with my puppies, and don't do anything unless I absolutely want to." She survives on a widow's pension. But, she says, "That's all I need. I don't need a lot in life. Money is not happiness to me. Happiness is how you feel inside. Here I can laugh. Here I have lots of people to talk to. I never thought I'd be so busy.

"I don't need Starbucks coffee," she admits. "I see the snow and smell the pines and look at the millions of stars in the sky at night and the Big Dipper." Like in the farm country of Tennessee where she grew up, she can appreciate Mother Earth and work the land in her own garden. "If I need extra money, I can clean carpets, clean houses, or I can sew," she points out. (She was working on a wedding dress at the time we talked.) "And," she adds, "I can barter. Everyone up here genuinely cares about one another and if you need help, everyone is there to help."

Her eyes filled with happiness as she spoke and I knew I was talking with a truly wealthy person.

How much money do you need to feel wealthy? Why? How do you feel about the money you have, or don't have? Are you comfortable with having as much as you want and need? Are you fulfilled with the money you have? Could you be? Or is money an unpleasant aspect of your life?

CHANGE YOUR MIND

"How are you?" I asked the woman I'd met briefly the day before in a workshop we were leading. "Well," she responded quickly, "tell me how the stock market is doing and I'll tell you how I am. If it's up, I'm up. If it's down, I'm down."

This woman has given money the power to determine her happiness and well-being. Unfortunately, she's not alone. The average American wastes twenty-four hours a month grappling with money woes, according to the National Institute of Personal Finance. More than half of us report worrying about debt and feeling dissatisfied with our financial condition. "Money," says Max H. Brazerman, author of *Smart Money Decisions—Why You Do What You Do with Your Money,* "is an emotional issue."

Do your happiness, well-being, and self-esteem rise and fall with your bank balance?

The way we feel and think about money plays an important role in how much we have, how difficult it will be to have more, and how we feel about whatever amount we have. Unfortunately, negative attitudes about money can actually prevent us from having as much of it as we might want, or from enjoying however much we have.

We have a very schizophrenic attitude toward money in this country. In the media and in our daily lives, we frequently hear disparaging comments about people with money, comments like, "I bet she's making a killing on that!" or "Well, he has all the money in the world! What do you expect?" In some circles, "money " is a dirty word and as a result many of us feel embarrassed to have or want money. But such negative beliefs and feelings can keep us from fulfilling our dreams and we've all been exposed to them.

What negative beliefs do you have about money? Where did you learn them? Do any of these sound familiar? Could they be preventing you from having the money to create your dreams?

Money is the root of all evil.

Money is hard to come by.

You make money by doing work you dislike.

You can't squeeze money out of a turnip.

Money is your master; you work for money.

How much money you make is out of your control.

Someone else, or luck, or fate, or the economy, determines how much money you make.

Money is a touchy subject. It's not nice to talk about money.

People who want money are greedy.

How can we expect to have the money we need to create and enjoy living our dreams, if this is the way we think and feel about money? How can we attract that which we resent others for having? How can we enjoy having what we're embarrassed to want having plenty of? How can we enjoy the fruits of our labor if we hate the labor or think the fruits will make us evil?

Practical dreamers don't work for money; they put money to work for them. They feel good about having and using and enjoying money as a way to fulfill their dreams. They don't mind thinking about money. They pay attention to how much money they have and where it's going. They're at ease talking openly with excitement, interest, and gratitude about this valuable resource.

 **Try This**

List your negative attitudes about money and replace them with new, positive ways of thinking about money like these:

You don't work for money; money works for you.

Money is a resource for creating what I want.

I can do great things with money.

The more time off I take the more money I make.

Money is a measure of results, a barometer that tells me how well I'm serving others.

I am a money generator.

The money I spend comes back to me multiplied.

Making money is like planting a garden; what you plant will grow in good time.

First, you support your dream; then it will support you.

I need to spend money to make money, but I choose to spend it on things that will fulfill my dreams.

People will gladly pay me for what I most enjoy contributing.

Throw your money in the direction you want to go and the rest will follow.

REFERENCES

The Anatomy of Spirit. Carolyn Myss. Three Rivers Press. ISBN 0-609-80014-0.

Moneylove, How to Get the Money You Deserve for Whatever You Want. Jerry Gillies. Warner Books. ISBN: 0-446-91009-0.

Money Troubles: Legal Strategies to Cope with Your Debts. Robin Leonard. Nolo Press. ISBN 0-87337-231-X.

Roads from the Ashes. Megan Edwards. Trilogy Books. ISBN 1-891290-01-0.

Smart Money Decisions. Max H. Bazerman. Wiley. ISBN 0-471-29611-2.

Simplify Your Life. Elaine St. James. ISBN 0-7868-8000-7.

7

MAKING THE TIME

*This day has been given to us fresh
and clear to either use or throw away.*

MARVA COLLINS, *Educator*

The woman was sitting on her front porch, reading. A breeze rustled through a nearby stand of Jeffrey pines. Periodically the cranky chatter of stellar blue jays would draw her attention from the page. She'd smile as she watched their antics, then lazily turn her gaze back to the book in her lap. Clearly, this was a person at peace with a plentitude of time. It was a pleasant but otherwise unremarkable scene, unless one knew what this person's life had been like only three years before.

In 1996, Mary Ann Halpin and her husband, Joe Croyle, were operating a 5,000-square-foot photography studio in downtown Los Angeles. Although they shared the studio with another photographer, the high overhead it represented had become a tough taskmaster, forcing them to work long, ten-hour days, six days a week. The pressure to be creative under such a grueling schedule was fatiguing and yet no matter how hard they worked, they were always a little behind.

"We were so stressed," Mary Ann remembers, "but we thought if we kept focused on our goals and worked harder things would eventually get better." But dedication wasn't enough. Their stress mounted when they learned that their partner hadn't paid his half of the rent for the past six months. They feared any morning they'd arrive to find the studio locked and their equipment impounded.

Then the forty-two-year-old husband of a close friend was diagnosed with terminal lung cancer and they dragged their exhausted bodies to and from the hospital and the studio to sit by his side into the wee hours of the night. "That was the turning point for us," Mary Ann recalls. "Our friend's graceful death taught us a lot about living. It gave us the courage to put happiness in life above all other goals."

Immediately after the memorial service, Mary Ann and Joe packed up the downtown studio and set up shop on a reduced scale in their home. Then they headed for a weekend retreat with friends who had a home in the mountains. "The mountain air cleared our minds and gave us a new perspective," Mary Ann told us. Although they had no money for a down payment, in June of that year they began looking for a weekend cabin of their own. By September they'd moved into their own log cabin. To their surprise, the lease-purchase offer they made on the cabin was accepted!

They now work four days a week in their L.A. home/office/studio and relax and enjoy life the other three days a week in Pine Mountain. "People are always saying to me, 'You're so lucky!'" Mary Ann points out, "But it has nothing to do with luck. It's figuring out what you value, what makes you happy, and what brings you peace, and then slowing down your life enough that you can find a creative way to make the changes you need to make. So many of my friends in the city tell me they don't have time to get away. But we all have time; we just have to decide how we want to use it."

HAVE THE TIME OF YOUR LIFE

Halpin is having the time of her life, not just on those rare occasions to which this phrase is most often applied, but every day. Isn't that what we all want . . . to feel like we own the time that constitutes our lives? That we can shape it, define it, and decide what goes into its moments, days, and years. Perhaps "free time" is the essence of freedom. To be free to do what we choose with the time that is our life. For in many ways, our time is our life. What we do with our time is what we do with our life. In this sense, becoming an architect of our own time is the greatest gift we can give ourselves. Time is both the fabric from which me must weave our dreams as well as the medium through which we will ultimately experience and enjoy their reality. If they are to be, they can only be in time.

Theoretically, in a free country, what we do with the minutes of our day is up to us. But it's the rare person today who doesn't feel as if they haven't mortgaged their time and thereby their life to a job or other obligations. It's the unusual person who doesn't feel that day after day, week after week, and year after year, large quantities of their time are imprisoned by activities they'd rather not do.

Sixty-three percent of American workers say they'd like to work fewer hours, reports the Family and Work Institute. Instead we're working 3.5 hours a week longer than we did just twenty years ago. Thirteen percent of us have more than one job. Seventy percent of working parents want to spend more time with their families. Instead, a study of 250 families by San Jose State University anthropologists found that families spend little time together. Each of our days, the study reports, is scheduled down to the minute with children hopping from day care and school to after-school activities while parents work ten- to twelve-hour days, often with hour-long commutes each way.

We're so starved for time, in fact, that many of us are going hungry—at least at lunch. Thirty-nine percent of workers surveyed by the National Restaurant Association report they don't have time to take a lunch break. Most others take only fifteen minutes to gulp down some lunch. And while for many of us vacation time is the only "free" time we have, more than sixty percent of full-time workers would consider dropping vacation plans if "something important came up." And should we manage to get away, over half of us will either check e-mail, voice or answering machines, take our pager, or use our cell phone to call work while on vacation.

Louis Harris Associates reports that leisure time in America shrank from 26.2 hours a week in 1973 to only 16.2 hours. Almost a third of people feel rushed on a daily basis while two-thirds feel rushed at times. Even weekends are no longer our own. An R. H. Bruskin survey of 1,008 people found that the typical adult spends fourteen weekend hours on chores. And, according to Bruskin, nine out of ten people feel no more energetic on Sunday evening than they did on Friday evening. One result of these time pressures is that increasing numbers of us are stressed out. *Prevention* magazine's "Prevention Index" claims that 63 percent of Americans suffer from frequent stress. That's up from 55 percent.

Husband and wife Evan Thornley and Tracey Ellery of California's Silicon Valley, who were interviewed about their lives by cell phone for *USA Today,* are prime examples of today's 24-7 time crunch. Evan and Tracey describe their lifestyle as being on the "bleeding edge." Cofounders of their own Web company, you would think this couple would have the freedom to structure their lives and that of their five-year-old twins any way they want. But they've found the pressures of starting a company to be enormous. Their workdays often stretch until midnight and their lives are for the most part "outsourced." While they work, a nanny raises their twins, a personal assistant runs the details of their life, a service cleans their home, another cares for their lawn and shops for their groceries; meals and laundry are ordered and delivered to their door.

John Faith of New Jersey now has what could become three full-time jobs. After his boss was laid off, Faith says, "It makes you stop and think." He made the cut, but he knows he could be fired tomorrow. So on the side, he's become a real estate agent and a financial services consultant. He considers this constellation of careers to be his economic safety net, but it leaves him little time for anything else.

In our society, these are people who would be considered financially secure and successful. They consider themselves to be in control of their lives. But at what cost? Being successful, secure, and in control are no guarantees of fulfillment if they come at the cost of the freedom to pursue those things we claim to want most. Fulfillment is all a matter of quality, according to the noted University of Chicago psychologist Mihaly Csikszentmihalyi. In his landmark studies on the quality of life, he found that the one most important factor in determining happiness is how good we feel about the quality of our lives, whether they're harmonious and satisfying to us. "Each of us has a picture, however vague, of what we would like to accomplish before we die," he writes. "How close we get to attaining this goal becomes the measure of the quality of our lives."

How do you feel about the quality of your life? Are you feeling pressed for time or enjoying the challenges and experiences it presents you? Are time pressures interfering with the harmonious, satisfying flow of your life?

WHERE DOES THE TIME GO?

How often we hear ourselves or others say, "I just don't have the time!" Usually it's said as a way to explain why we can't do those things that would make our lives more harmonious and satisfying. It's why we can't spend more time to be with loved ones. Why we can't create the masterpieces we intend to create someday. Why we can't get away to rest and relax and enjoy the beauty of nature. Why we can't pursue the dreams we have tucked away in our hearts. We believe that our work and other obligations must come first, but by monopolizing our time, they run our lives.

Driven by fear of what might happen if we did otherwise or by blinding ambition to succeed in accomplishing our goals at all costs, we become enslaved to the tyranny of the clock, working into the wee hours of the night and right on through the weekend. I know, because I had done that most of my adult life.

 **Try This**

Note the comments you make about time. How often do you hear yourself saying, "I don't have the time," or "There's just no time for that." Ask yourself what's preventing you from using your time in this way? Do you really want to, or is it an excuse? What would you rather be doing? What would bring you closer to your dream?

My fondest memories of childhood were the hours upon hours of time that seemed to hang suspended endlessly around me on warm summer afternoons while playing beneath the weeping willow trees or along sunny alleyways lined with hollyhocks. Tears sting my eyes as I recall the silent smell of heavy dew on the grass beneath my bare feet. The hum of locusts on a late afternoon. The serenade of crickets at twilight and as the daylight faded into night, the soft glow of the streetlight beneath the arching limbs of the Dutch elms along the sidewalks that lined our neighborhood.

In such moments there seems to be no time, only flow. No sense of self as separate from the world, only a feeling of union and harmony with the environment and all around us. Such moments are what Csikszentmihalyi describes as optimal experiences, when we're so involved in whatever we're doing that we're aware of little else. These experiences are so engaging and alive that we want to repeat them just for the sake of experiencing them again. At such times, we're in complete alignment with our desires.

Do you remember having the feeling of time without end? When? What were you doing?

Unfortunately, as I grew up such moments became fewer and fewer. Too soon my life was ruled instead by the clock. Getting to school on time. Getting home on time. Getting my homework in on time. Getting papers in on time and studying enough in time for final exams. Such school-day time tyrants were soon replaced by workday time tyrants. Getting to work on time. Getting back from lunch on time. Getting to the meeting on time. Getting the project done on time. Picking up my son from day care on time. Getting to the store in time to get dinner on time. And finally getting to bed on time so I could get up on time to do it all again.

When I decided to leave my job to go out on my own I thought I'd declared my independence from the tyranny of the clock. Everything about my decision to become my own boss was related to being able to set my own hours. It was about having time to be with Paul. Time to be with my son. Time to slow down and breathe. Time to go horseback riding or visit with friends. Time to do work I cared about and believed in. But once those pale green government payroll checks stopped coming, panic replaced my good intentions. I stepped right into the role of my parents, teachers, and employers. I became my own dictator, living once again by the clock.

Terrified that I wouldn't have enough business, I booked clients whenever they could come, morning, noon, or night. Like Mary Ann and Joe, I thought if I worked unceasingly I'd have to succeed. It was what I'd seen my father do. It was what the success gurus were espousing—you've got to give it 100 percent! But my friend and colleague Richard Nadeau found a different way.

When Richard went into private practice as a psychotherapist he also worked madly to ensure his success, cramming his days with clients, his nights with groups, and his weekends with workshops. But eventually he began talking about his growing unwillingness to work so much. He began setting limits on the number of hours and days he'd work. He told me he wasn't willing to give up his life for "success."

"When I first went out on my own," he recalls, "I had a feast-

or-famine attitude. I think sometimes we're like petrified children. We have this fear that if we say no we'll be out of business the next day. My great terror was that all my clients would conspire to cancel their appointments at one time. I feared that somehow these thirty unrelated individuals who didn't even know one another would all decide to cancel. It was ridiculous, of course. I had to take out my appointment calendar regularly just to assure myself that I had plenty of clients, and I wasn't going into Chapter Eleven."

I watched Richard summon the courage to cut back his hours and saw him become even more in demand. I watched him raise his fees so he could afford to see fewer clients. I watched him pass up lucrative opportunities to do out-of-town workshops so he could enjoy more free time. While he was working less, he was earning more. He'd developed a new outlook on time—the practical dreamer's view of time.

A NEW OUTLOOK ON TIME

Instead of thinking of time in terms of twenty-four-hour blocks into which we can never quite fit everything that needs to be done, the practical dreamer sees time as a plentiful resource from which we can create what we desire; an endless, flowing supply that never runs out. As long as we're still alive we have plenty of time. All we have is time, in fact, all the time in the world. It greets us anew with each new breath, to waste, to savor, to manage, or to invest.

Practical dreamers see time as the most democratic of all resources because we all get the same twenty-four hours every day no matter who we are, how rich or poor we are, who we know, or what other resources we may have. We get this fresh supply every day no matter how well or how poorly we've used yesterday's supply. To practical dreamers, time is like a brand-new shopping bag that's waiting beside the bed each morning to be filled with whatever we'd like as we shop through the day. We can take some of this and some of that, sampling whatever seems closest to our dreams and passing over that which we'd prefer not to have in our lives.

That's how I wanted to think of time, but often, even years later, that still wasn't the way *my* day went! More often than not I'd get up in the morning to find my day was already filled with deadlines and other leftovers from the day before. Sometimes I'd awake to find someone else had filled my bag with things *they* needed me to do. Often, too often, I had placed a standing order, so I'd awake to the anticipation of the same, less than desired routine as the day before.

Do you start each morning afresh, free to create a new day from your desires? How do you go about filling your day? Do you approach your day like a cafeteria line, taking some of everything that's presented to you until your life is chronically overstuffed? Do you pick and choose how you will use the hours of your day with your dreams in mind or are you taking potluck and just accepting whatever's dumped into your life? Would your life be fuller if you emptied it out? Or do you need to exchange its contents?

➡ Try This

Look at the contents of your day and try playing with them. Arrange them differently. Try taking out less appealing things and putting in more appealing ones. Whenever you say, "I can't do that," ask yourself, "Why not?" The answer will show you who or what is running your life. Would you like to take it back?

PINE MOUNTAIN TIME

Before we went to visit our friends in Pine Mountain, I'd never met adults who lived their lives in the kind of suspended flow of time I'd known as a child. I'd met plenty of people who "managed" their time quite well, parceling it out as if the minutes of their days were dollar bills or silver coins. They carry a time-management system like Filofax and DayRunners, or use calendar software as I do. They break their days into fifteen-minute scheduled increments and track seemingly endless "to do" lists to be reviewed and carried forward day to day. Often they also have large scheduling calendars along their office walls and sometimes posted on their refrigerators at home to chart their tightly packed agendas down to the minute.

I found that the more successful I became, the more challenging shepherding the varied aspects of my life through the day (and, unfortunately, often into the night) became. Despite all I'd learned about time management, my life was still ruled by the clock. I was just getting better at serving the ruler. In fact, the better I got at managing time the less I seemed to have of it. Because we can't be "in time" and be thinking "about time" at the same time, it was the rare activity I could give myself over to fully. I always had an eye on the clock.

By the time Paul and I visited Pine Mountain, we were starting to lose our battle with time. It was getting out of hand, slipping from our control. It was getting harder to beat the clock. We'd always been meticulously punctual but we were getting behind and missing deadlines, and the further behind we got, the more out of control our lives became. I edited manuscripts in the parking lot during one friend's wedding. I missed another friend's wedding altogether because of a last-minute deadline. Once having prided ourselves on taking regular vacations so we could be relaxed and energized, we hadn't had a vacation in years. One year we even worked on Christmas Day!

I began canceling meetings with friends, then business associates, then my annual Academy Awards party fell by the wayside, too, slain by still another deadline. Why we ever agreed to take off that Fourth of July weekend to visit our friends in Pine Mountain, I'll never know, because we really didn't have the time! I never wanted to be one of those people who say, "I really need to get away." Get away from what? I used to wonder. Your life! But truth be known, that's probably exactly what I was feeling when we agreed to take a four-day weekend.

Do you often feel like getting away? What are you wanting to escape? What's chasing you? What's holding you back? Could you send it away instead? How could you make your daily life into the life you're wanting to get away to? Would that be more like living your dream?

Within an hour and forty minutes, we'd left our superstressed, superfast L.A. time schedule for our first immersion in Pine Mountain time. It's somewhat of a joke up here, but Pine Mountain really does operate in a different time zone. My first experience with it was when Mary Ann and I went up to Diana's to make a pie for the Fourth of July party. The party was at Mary Ann's house at four o'clock that afternoon. I was somewhat apprehensive when we left for Diana's to make the pie at three o'clock. But what the heck, it wasn't my party. If it had been, I wouldn't have made a pie in the first place. I wouldn't have had the time. I would have ordered one from a bakery days in advance and rushed over at the last minute to pick it up before closing time on July 3. But then, of course, there wasn't a bakery in Pine Mountain, at least not then.

It was well after four and we were still at Diana's. I was getting uncomfortable. We need to hurry, I kept wanting to say. It's getting late. But I kept my mouth shut because they were having a ball. Time was the furthest thing from their minds. They were laughing at spilling the ingredients and horsing around, until even I got swept up in the hilarity of it all.

Around five, as I recall, we caravanned down the mountain in our SUVs. Mary Ann and I in one and Diana and her son, Matt, in the other. What, I wondered, would all the guests be thinking about their hostess showing up an hour late to her own party? Despite all the fun, I was anxious. But as we pulled in the driveway, Joe and some of their friends were scurrying around, laughing and carrying on while they casually went about setting up picnic tables and chairs in the front yard. No one seemed to have the slightest care about what time it was! And the party proceeded with great joviality.

Seconds flowed into minutes, minutes into hours, and hours into evening. We walked up to hear the music in the village. We came back to Mary Ann's, had hot drinks by the fire, and talked into the night. Then we slipped off to bed and night slipped into morning and morning into afternoon. Time felt like molasses and I couldn't remember when I'd been so relaxed.

PUT FIRST THINGS FIRST

While this was fine and good over a holiday weekend and I'm sure it played a large part in why we wanted to move to Pine Mountain, it was quite a different experience a year later when we finally got up here and needed to get settled in. We were still on L.A. time. Get unpacked. Get set up. Snap, snap, snap. But Pine Mountain just wouldn't move on our schedule. We intended to have the backyard fenced before we moved in. It was finished a month later. We needed some electrical changes made and expected to have them done the week we arrived. They were finished about four months later. We needed to add a garage and expected it to get done over the summer. But we weren't sure it would be up before the first snow. (It wasn't and still isn't.)

The person who was to paint our front hall didn't come the day he was scheduled to work. He called to say his son was ill and he had to leave town to take care of him. Several weeks later, he arranged for someone else to do the painting for us.

Our contractor was several hours late for an inspection. A friend had developed complications after surgery and needed someone to take him into town.

The woman we called to have some valances made for over the windows in our dining room was starting a Brownie troop and getting her twin daughters ready for school. So, she told us cheerily, she probably wouldn't be able to get to our project until around November 1. (It's May now, but two friends will be coming to start doing them today!)

The pet sitter we arranged to take care of Billy while we went to give our first out-of-town speech after moving canceled the night before we were to leave. Her daughter was having a baby two weeks early. Fortunately, the day of the speech just happened to be Take Your Dog to Work Day. Billy went with us and, although we were concerned about what people would think about having a dog in the session, they loved it . . . and him.

Had I been in L.A., I would have been irritated by all these inconveniences. I would have considered the attitude of these individuals toward time commitments to be unbusiness-like. Not that we're not supposed to have personal emergencies. Of course we do, but, I would have contended it's our responsibility as professionals to take care of such things after hours or in some way that doesn't interfere with business.

But up here, I just couldn't mind. First of all, everyone here is your neighbor, not just a name in the Yellow Pages. These are people, not just inspectors and seamstresses and painters and pet sitters. So instead of feeling irritated, I wanted to celebrate. What did a day or a week here and there matter really? We'll get it all done in time. Here is a whole community of people who are actually doing what I've been preaching, and seeking, for so many years. They are putting first things first in their lives. And gradually, so were we.

You, and only you, decide who puts what into your day. If you don't like what gets in, you can dump it out and say, "No more!" You can take charge and put first things first.

WHERE DOES THE TIME COME FROM?

The fall before we moved, I'd come up to Pine Mountain to stay over the weekend at the cabin of a friend. Early that Sunday morning, while cleaning up my breakfast dishes, I glanced out the garden window onto the neighbor's property. There he was, a middle-aged man on his deck, dusting the ledges around the windows of his house with a small, black bristle brush. He was taking his time, cleaning his windowsills with such care, making sure to get every bit of dirt that had collected in each crevice and cranny.

I watched him for some time while I busily finished up in the kitchen. I was working swiftly, eager to get on with relaxing and enjoying the National Forest. Why, I wondered, was this man spending his Sunday morning cleaning the outdoor windowsills of his house? Didn't he have anything more important to do? I couldn't remember ever having seen a man, or anyone for that matter, brushing their windowsills with such care. Hiring a service, yes. Quickly hosing down the deck or blowing the leaves off the front walk, yes, or maybe sweeping the porch. But dusting the window ledges? On a weekend getaway to a mountain cabin? I found it quite odd.

He was treating his quite ordinary house as if it were a collection of rare coins that he'd taken in a moment of leisure from their box on the shelf to polish until they were bright and shiny, taking the time to admire and treasure their beauty as he did so.

Caught up in his meticulous Sunday ritual, I stood for a moment with the dish towel in my hands, wondering what it would be like to have a life in which you had the time to dust your window ledges and, if you did, why you would.

Last Sunday, I thought fondly of this man and that day as I was dusting the windowsills of my front porch. I was taking the time, as I do every week now, to brush away each particle of dust, remove each spot of pine resin, and reach each cobweb. I was beaming with satisfaction at their shiny white surfaces and I understood at last why a man would be dusting his window ledges on a Sunday morning. Because he wanted to . . . and he had the time.

I marvel now at what I have the time to do. I sweep the deck. I clean the windows. I water my potted plants on the front porch. (Me, growing plants? Yes! For the first time in my life I've actually kept five potted plants alive for over a month!) I visit with neighbors on the way to pick up the mail. Paul and I socialize at the Club House on Friday nights. I go for hikes. Meet neighbors for Bar-B-Qs at a local outdoor restaurant. Sit on the porch reading a novel. (I hadn't read a novel in more than three years). I volunteer for a local art group. Host dinner parties and open houses. Help a friend open an inn. And dance in the street during village festivals!

Where does all this "free" time come from? Or perhaps a better question would be: What was I doing with my time before so that I never had any "free" time? I'm still getting my work done. If anything I'm more productive. But I'm not sitting in traffic for an hour every day to do business and personal errands. We go to L.A. to shop and do errands for one full day once every three weeks. I'm not watching so much television anymore. I feel too good to want to sit and veg out.

"I don't do anything anymore that I don't want to do," Eileen Applegarth, the widow and seamstress, had told me. Rosie Reuter, the mother of two teenage daughters who operates the cleaning service, had used those same words. So had our neighbor Mary Ann. And Scott Rosen, the Internet service provider. Their words played over and over in my mind. Gradually, with each passing day, I'm aware that I do fewer and fewer things I don't want to do.

There you have it. That's where the time goes! And there's where it comes from. It's as simple and as difficult as that. What I choose to do may be easy or hard, fun or challenging, but increasingly it's fulfilling. For after all, according to Csikszentmihalyi's research, the best moments of life are those when our minds and bodies are stretched to the limits in a voluntary effort to accomplish something we find worthwhile.

➥ Try This

Can you say, "I don't do anything anymore that I don't want to do?" Look at your day. Track how you're spending your time. Does it reflect what you want most in life? Your daily schedule is a snapshot of what you've chosen to be most important to you. Do you agree with your choices? If not, who's making them?

GET OFF SPEED

We're addicted to speed," says James Gleick, author of the book *Faster: The Acceleration of Just About Everything*. We like fast food, fast computers, sound bites, instant news, quick-cut videos, pagers and cell phones, microwaves, e-mail, Fed-Exing, Web surfing, channel surfing, and speed dialing. Face it, he points out, we're speedaholics. "We know that when we're multitasking, we don't do any one task as well as we'd like. We know that fast food is just a synonym for mediocre food," he says. "And yet, that's us standing in line at McDonald's and Burger King. No one is holding a gun to our heads."

We say we'd like to slow down, get away, and simplify our lives, but "Every time we curse the overflowing in-box and pass another chain e-mail joke along, we expose a disparity between how we feel and how we act . . ." Gleick writes. "We tell ourselves we're too busy to do X, but what we really mean is that we'd rather do Y. . . . We can't stop ourselves from going to the beach with a cell phone tucked in our bathing suits."

We don't want to hear this and we'll vehemently deny it. Why, it's just not so! I'd like to stop, but I can't. I don't have the time. I don't have the money. I'll lose my job. I won't be able to compete. All these excuses sound just like someone who can't quit smoking or drinking. But time-use studies at the University of Maryland by sociologist John Robinson confirm that Gleick is right: People who lead busy, overcrowded, and rushed lives have largely chosen them.

Are you addicted to speed? Is it and other addictions eating up your time, eroding the quality of your life, and preventing you from making room for what you're wanting most?

Was I addicted to speed? Am I in withdrawal, going through recovery? Perhaps. But it's not true that we can't stop ourselves. We can. As all practical dreamers know, we have a choice. We can use our time as we wish. We can opt for the quality of life we're seeking. We can take a stand. Eileen has. Rosie has. Scott has. Mary Ann has. And I have.

Have I stopped using my many speedy electronic "time-savers"? Absolutely not. I still use the microwave most every day, but I'm no longer doing six other things, including tapping my foot while I'm waiting for my two-minute bowl of oatmeal to warm. Instead, I take a deep breath and look out at the garden. I still watch television most nights, but I no longer watch anything that isn't worth giving 100 percent of my attention to. I don't read the paper anymore while watching television, and instead of waiting to hit the mute button during commercials if Paul or I want to have a conversation, we turn off the television. We still take the cell phone with us into L.A. (we can't get it here in Pine Mountain), but we use it for outgoing calls only. We never take it into restaurants, parties, or movie theaters.

Slower and one-at-a-time works better for me. I'm focusing more on whatever I'm doing and not doing anything else. So if I'm writing I'm writing, not taking phone calls. I'll return calls later. If I'm talking to a neighbor, I'm talking to a neighbor, not thinking about the calls I need to return. If I'm hiking, I take in the sights and sounds of the forest instead of talking business with Paul. Instead of rushing to answer our phone on two rings, as we've always thought was good business practice, we've set the voice mail system to pick up after three rings, so when we're home, we have plenty of time to get to the phone before it picks up.

In these and other ways, the simpler, more meaningful life I've been dreaming of and longing for is coming to life.

 **Try This**

Try going off the clock for an hour, an afternoon, or a day. Don't think of it as taking "time off," but as having "time on." Whatever you'd like to be doing—whether it's playing with your children, walking in the woods, drawing, writing, brainstorming new ideas with a business associate—set your life up so, at least for that period of time, you can do just that and absolutely nothing else. No cell phones, no pagers, no faxes, no interruptions. Set an alarm or arrange for someone to call or contact you when you must go on with other activities, so you won't have to be watching the clock.

Depth versus Breadth

"We're experiencing in our time a loss of depth," writes Sven Birkerts in *The Gutenberg Elegies.* "The knowing not of facts but of truths about human nature and the processes of life." In a world of multitasking and multimedia we can enjoy a breath of experience, but that experience is of necessity shallow. We wave to the neighbor and mumble, "Hello, how are you?" but we rarely converse without a scheduled appointment. I thought about how too often we only skim the surface of life one morning when my mother came to visit us from Kansas City.

I was taking her on a quick tour of the area before treating her to a pedicure at the hair salon in the village. As I pulled into the parking lot to show her the equestrian center, Rosie's truck passed us on the way out. "Hi," she hollered, stopping and rolling down the window to hail us. Happy to see her, I stopped, too. She introduced me to her daughter Melissa. I introduced her to my mother, expecting that we'd both then drive quickly on. But, instead, Rosie continued to chat, as if we all had plenty of time.

I was enjoying the comfortable, casual flow of the conversation, but too soon remembered IT WAS GETTING LATE! My enjoyment of the moment slipped into concern. We'd be late for our appointment! "I've got to go," I said to wrap up as politely as

I could, and we drove on, just making it by the appointed hour. At the salon, Karen was running a bit behind.

I thought of that moment often and wished I had it to do over again. Experience takes time. When we hurry through life, we rob ourselves of it. When we pack our day full to the brim, we lose the chance to savor each part of it. "Ideally," Birkerts writes, "I suppose, one could have the best of both worlds"—the breadth and novelty of flitting through infinite variety and the depth and satisfaction of settling in to savor the rich nectar of any one thing.

But the best of both worlds is exactly what's possible today if we choose to partake of it. We now have access to the wealth of a world of activities that would have been dizzying to our ancestors. But to have the best of both worlds, we can't become so fascinated with the world's abundant novelty that we forget to take time to engage the richness of the familiar. We need to remember to enjoy the beauty and the wonder of the person next door, the child in the bedroom next to ours, and the trees that are bending in the wind outside the window.

Is your life full, but shallow? Or is it deep, but dull with the sameness of worn-out routines? Do you sip at life or drink from it deeply? Can you take time for both, trying out lots of what's new and becoming more intimate with the familiar?

CUSTOM ROUTINES AND SCHEDULES

How do you ever get anything done up here?" a colleague asked after visiting our new home office. "It's too beautiful. Too relaxing. Too enjoyable up here." She had expressed my greatest fear. What would happen if I relaxed and allowed time to flow through my life with the simplicity and peace I remember from my childhood? How could I accomplish anything without the discipline of breaking my day into specific, structured goals with rigid action-steps and allocating them to a fixed time schedule with deadlines? Isn't that what the experts have said we must do if we want to accomplish our dreams?

I've always been a very disciplined person. Some people would say it's in my Capricornian nature. Capricorns just don't flow. But then, I've also been told I have an Aquarius moon, and that Aquarians love to go with the flow. Practical dreamers must learn to do both. I first discovered this when interviewing Torvill and Dean, the Olympic gold medal ice dancers. I asked Christopher and Jane how they had created such a unique, innovative, and unusually beautiful program. Skated to the music of Ravel's Bolero, it was like nothing anyone had seen before. Obviously this couple were extraordinary dreamers. They had imagined and conceived a stunning work of art. So I expected to hear about how they'd been inspired to transcend the ordinary. To my surprise Christopher answered my question with a single word, "Practice."

Practice? How could something so beautiful arise from something so mundane and routine as practice? Yet there it was—the practical side of the practical dreamer. There's the dream and then there's the practice. We practice in reality until we can mold time and space and material into the elegant shapes of our dream.

Torvill and Dean had learned that structuring time into routines and schedules and disciplining themselves to follow them provided a conduit through which the inspiration of their dreams could flow into reality. Most likely, not easily or even comfortably at first, but eventually. Dreams unfold on their own time table, but not without a considerable investment of our time. Much like planning a harvest, we plant our dreams moment by moment, then we tend the soil day by day. We push the plow and wait for the harvest, but meanwhile the seeds we've planted are dependent on our consistent care.

What comes more easily to you, following a structure, discipline, and routine, or going with the flow? How could you find a better balance between the two?

Charles and Elizabeth Handy faced a serious time crisis. After more than thirty years of a traditional marriage, two children, and several years of working as a "managing partner" to help her husband launch an independent career as a noted writer and speaker on management theory, Elizabeth was growing resentful. She had completed a hard-won degree in photography, but her career as a portrait photographer was essentially relegated to "hobby" status. That was not her dream. But she had no spare time.

"My work was swamping Elizabeth," Charles recalls in his book *The Hungry Spirit*. "She would say, 'You call me your manager and I'm your slave.'" But Charles specializes in creative approaches to the work-related issues of complex and changing times, so he felt he should apply his philosophy to his personal life as well. Together, he and Elizabeth decided to use their time in a unique and creative way that meets both their needs. They admit this solution might not work for anyone else in the world, but it doesn't need to. It only needs to work for them.

The Handys have divided the year into two equal parts, "his" and "hers," and now strictly enforce the times of the year when each can do his or her "own" work. Charles travels to give speeches only in the winter months (October through March). During this time Elizabeth accompanies him, handling his calendar, managing his calls, negotiating contracts, and making his appointments, as she has been doing since he left his job some fifteen years ago.

Elizabeth takes photographic assignments only in the summer months (April to September). During this time Charles helps her mount and organize exhibits and assists in managing the launch of her book *Behind the View: Portraits of a Norfolk Village*. "Successful marriages should be flexible enough to withstand changes in people's working lives," Charles contends, be it moving your office home or a spouse returning to the work force after raising a family.

The Handys believe "time can be a formidable foe, running away with itself . . . consuming you in the process. Unless you're very careful you use up all the time doing things you don't want to do." To rectify this situation the Handys have made many other changes in how they use their time. Some are simple: Charles no longer goes to business lunches, for example; if someone wants to meet with him, they come to breakfast at his home. But they also made more far-reaching decisions.

Ten years ago, the Handys looked at their appointment book and noted that they were working every Saturday, most Sundays, and some holidays. So they decided to award themselves overtime, in effect, and provide 115 days off for the 52 weekends and the holidays they've worked. They live and work 100 days each year in London, where Elizabeth runs the house while Charles works. Then they live 100 days in Norfolk, where Charles does the cooking and housework while Elizabeth takes photographs. The remainder of the year is filled with 70 days of travel and 90 days in Tuscany. Tuscany is purely vacation time. No work intrudes there, not even mail.

While they're away, they have printed up slips of paper that the cleaning lady sends to people wishing to contact them, explaining that the Handys are committed for the next six months and to write to them later if they wish. Most people think that to have such flexibility and choice the Handys must be independently wealthy. Actually, they live modestly, having bought their various homes "extremely cheaply" in various states of disrepair and then fixing them up. "Just as we sat down and said how many days is enough, we sat down and said how much money is enough?" Charles points out. They've decided upon £50,000 a year (that's $80,000 in U.S. dollars) and they work together to achieve that goal without compromising their schedule.

The Handys illustrate what practical dreamers know so well. If we keep using our time the way we've been doing it, our life will remain essentially as it has been. We can't change our life without changing how we use our time. If we want something to happen, we must make it a habit, a routine part of our day. Habits are those things we do without thinking about them. They're the things that always get done. They're the underlying core, not the exceptional diversions, of our lives.

➡ **Try This** ☆☆☆

Take a look at your habits. The things you do every day without thinking about them. Is living your dream a habit or a diversion? Can your dream pass the test of time—your time? Are you willing to do what it takes for as long as it takes? Have you structured your time in the service of your dream? Can you make living it a habit? What routines and schedules could you create that will allow your dream to flow into your daily reality?

"You've changed," my friend Ed Miller said with a twinkle in his eyes. "How?" I asked, curious about what he'd noticed. "You're always smiling," he replied.

REFERENCES

Faster: The Acceleration of Just About Everything. James Gleick. Pantheon Books. ISBN 0679408371.

Flow: The Psychology of Optimal Experience. Mihaly Csikszentmihalyi. HarperCollins 1991. ISBN 0-06-09043-2.

The Hungry Spirit: Beyond Capitalism: A Quest for Purpose in the Modern World. Charles Handy. Broadway Books. ISBN 0767901886.

Slowing Down the Speed of Life: How to Create a More Peaceful, Simpler Life from the Inside Out. Richard Carlson and Joseph V. Bailey. Harper San Francisco. ISBN 0062514547.

Time for Life: The Surprising Way Americans Use Their Time. Geoffrey Godbey and John P. Robinson. Penn State Press. ISBN 0271019700.

8

HAVING THE ENERGY

Most enjoyable activities . . . demand an effort
that initially one is reluctant to make.

MIHALY CSIKSZENTMIHALYI

She was animated and excited when she approached us during the break in our seminar to ask about what she needed to do to start a medical billing company. It was a business we knew quite well. We have featured it in all our editions of *Best Home Businesses* and served as series editors for *Making Money in a Health Service Business on Your Home-Based PC*. So we made several suggestions for where she might begin, a couple of books she could read, a professional organization she could join, where she could get training in medical terminology, and some of the best marketing methods.

As we talked, her smile slowly faded into a frown. The enthusiasm drained from her voice. I paused for a moment, then asked, "Is this the kind of information you were looking for?" "Well," she responded, "it seems like an awful lot of work. Just the thought of it makes me tired." She sighed as she spoke and then laughed, but I could see a wave of fatigue sweep through her body. "How did you pick this business?" I continued, wondering why learning more about how to pursue something she'd been so excited about could leave her so weary. "I heard that a medical billing service is an easy way to make some money from home," she replied, hopeful again for a moment that I would reassure her this was true.

Of course, I couldn't. Getting her company under way would probably require a considerable investment of energy, especially since she has no medical background. But I could see that, like so many of us, energy was the very thing she had far too little of. It's one reason we're looking for a better way to live and work. We're burned out. The number of people who call in sick for work due to stress has tripled over the last four years. Our lives are draining energy out of us, sapping our passion, our enthusiasm, and our excitement for life. We're either driving ourselves on fast-forward in a perpetual state of overwhelm or we're so burned out and exhausted that we drag ourselves limp and lifeless through the day, only half conscious of what's going on around us.

So we're faced with an intriguing paradox. To create the simpler, less stressful lives we're seeking we need to summon up a fresh supply of the very thing that's most in short supply in our lives. Crafting our dreams takes effort and that means energy. Energy to find a less stressful, more enjoyable career. Energy to start our own businesses with the flexible hours and added control. Energy to leave the congested, polluted megalopolises where we live for more restful environs. Energy to restructure our time, to generate needed income, to deepen or change our relationships and engage the support and help of others.

When the time comes to take action on our dreams, we're no longer just hopping between two worlds, one imaginary and the other real. We have to start living in two worlds, the one that once consumed us full-time and the other that's under construction. We're like the juggler balancing spinning plates on a stick, who must keep the first one going in one hand while getting another one going in the other hand. We have to keep our existing life from toppling over while we get a whole new one under way, even though balancing the existing one is exhausting enough!

CATCH-22

This was the dilemma I saw written on the face of the woman who was standing before me. No wonder she was looking for an easy way out! Just the prospect of an easy escape from the grind of her existing life had energized her, but the realization that it would be placing even more demands on her had quickly dispelled her joy. As she sighed repeatedly at ideas for researching her new business, I could see this dream would never pass the energy test. It wasn't inspiring or energizing her. It didn't have any juice. She wasn't eager to get to work on it. Unfortunately, the "easy" way is usually a Catch-22.

"You don't sound very excited about building this business," I decided to suggest. "Is there something you'd be more interested in working on?" She looked at me for a moment, clearly surprised. "Oh, there's lots of things I'd rather be doing. They're just not realistic." "Like what?" I asked. "What would you feel really most energized to start working on?" "Well, most of all," she responded, "I'd like to write. I've always wanted to write." Momentarily her eyes danced with energy again. "I thought if I could get this medical billing thing going, it would give me the chance to quit my job and move to Oregon and I'd have free time to write."

Now I understood. She thought by starting a medical billing company she would be able to do what she really wanted to do. Instead, it would be just another thing that would drain her energy away from what she most wanted to do. Writing for a living might not seem realistic. But chances are, because doing it would inspire and energize her, it would be more realistic than doing something that the mere prospect of preparing for exhausted her.

"From where does the strength come to finish the race?" the Olympic sprinter Eric Liddell asks in the movie *Chariots of Fire*. It's the question all practical dreamers must answer. Where do we find the energy to build our dream? Just as it's our job to find the time and make the money, so we must discover what we need to do to have the energy to build a new and better life.

How is your energy level? Do you bound out of bed in the morning? Or do you start the day dragging? Does the thought of adding additional effort to your day to build your dream leave you feeling weary?

SOMEDAY

Before we moved, each weekend visit to Pine Mountain gave us a sneak preview of what it would feel like to be uplifted, inspired, and energized just by waking up in the morning. Just by walking onto the porch. Just by looking out the window. Just by breathing the air, feeling the wind, and hearing the sounds around us. But we could never have imagined what it would actually feel like to live that way every day of our lives because we had never experienced it.

It took several months for us to leave the stress and exhaustion of our city life behind. We had no idea how stressed out we really were, but once we moved I did know something restorative was happening. On days when we had to go into the city for groceries and supplies, I'd come home exhausted from the pell-mell, push-shove, whoosh, clatter, bang I'd taken for granted only weeks before. Once I'd get home to Pine Mountain, no matter how late it was, I'd rush out onto the deck to drink in the mountain air. I'd throw myself into it, gulping and gasping for it just as a parched traveler in the desert coming upon an oasis might throw himself into the splendors of a waiting pool of water.

But gradually that began to change. Trips to the city became less stressful. They had less and less effect on us. I found myself strangely detached from the urban swirl around me. I let go of having to get everything done on our days in town. If we ran out of time, I'd just say, "Well, we'll get it next time." I'm no longer willing to fight the clock or the freeways. We can't predict the traffic congestion patterns in L.A., so when getting together with friends, we tell them we don't know for sure when we'll arrive. We can only hope they'll welcome us when we get there. If it gets too late, we'll reschedule for next time.

Here on the mountain, even during the most stressful of workdays, a few moments of sitting on the porch, glancing out the window, or walking to the post office restore my energy. I may head off to the village worrying and fretting about some business matter until a small cottontail rabbit bounds across my path and all my concerns dissolve instantly into delight.

Over and over again in many little ways, I'm realizing that this is how life can be. It can be a wellspring that feeds and heals, nourishes and restores us . . . if we can conjure up the energy to create such a life from the exhausting hubbub around us. It's no easy task, to be sure, but well worth the effort.

Can you imagine a life that nourishes and feeds you? A life that energizes you instead of draining you? Once you know it's possible, let your desire and hope for creating it spur you to find the energy you need to create it.

FIND THE SOURCE

When I was a little girl, one of my household jobs was to dry the dishes after dinner. Of course, as a ten-year-old I always had a hundred other things I would rather do, so I'd hurriedly wipe the towel over the dishes exactly as I'd been shown to do. When my father went to put them away, however, he'd say to me, "Sarah, these dishes aren't dry!" "Well, I dried them!" I'd respond defiantly. Night after night my dad would remind me, "You haven't dried the dishes until they're dry." The problem was, I didn't care if the dishes were dry or not. My energy was someplace else.

But to construct a new life, we've got to care. Caring is what gives us the energy to keep the platters spinning while we put up the walls for a new life. Caring counts for everything. Not long ago, I experienced just how much caring counts. We were taking the trash to the recycling center. I was so tired from working that I stayed in the car to let Paul carry the trash over to the bin by himself. Meanwhile, he left the back hatch open on the SUV, and Billy, our toy Manchester terrier, jumped out the back just as I heard the engine of a nearby parked car start up to leave. Suddenly, I had enough energy to do just about anything. I was Superwoman. "Billy!" I shouted, leaping from the car and sprinting like a gazelle to the rear of the car where I scooped the little dog into my arms at the speed of light.

Where did all that energy come from, when the moment before I'd had none? It came from the same place it does when, as children, we're too tired to dry the dishes until they're done, but moments later we can run like dynamos outside to play. It came from the same place as it does when, as teenagers, we're too tired to keep our eyes open while doing our homework, but become balls of fire the moment a friend calls to say, "Let's go to the mall!" It came from the same place that kept me busily dressing up our town house to show prospective buyers instead of enjoying a much-needed, relaxing Sunday afternoon.

"From where does the strength come to finish the race? It comes from within." It comes from caring . . . a lot! Usually it's easier to do something difficult we care about than to do something easy we don't care to do. Our energy wants to move. It has a mind of its own. It wants to go with the flow of our deepest desires. To stop the flow of where our energy wants to go is actually painful. It's why some people drink and others overeat or take drugs: to dull the pain of holding back and diverting our energy from where it wants to go. But when we go with the flow, life surges through us like a river tumbling toward the sea and can carry our dreams along with it.

Until we honor the flow, we will be tired and we will be weary, because we're fighting our very nature. Where is your energy? How much do you care about your dream? Is it where your energy wants to go?

GO WITH THE FLOW

"When the idea for my business came to me, everyone thought I was nuts," Stuart Wilde, the man who started Wild Earth Llama Adventures tours, wrote us. "They told me 'You can barely afford to feed yourself. How do you expect to feed a herd of llamas, let alone purchase them?'" To overcome all the negativity from family, friends, and colleagues, he wrapped himself in his own novel experience, living it out in his mind. To keep his dream alive while he figured out what he could do to actualize it, he visualized what he wanted to do. "I imagined it in every little detail over and over and over again to 'incorporate' (make part of the body) it into my life," he emphasized.

He spent more than two years putting it all down on paper, everything from a business plan to "to do" lists, from detailed Forest Service permit applications to in-depth questionnaires for liability insurance; even the text for a brochure he couldn't afford to print. "I took the dream as far as I could go without the actual funds to buy the llamas," he recalled. When he got frustrated with his lack of progress, he'd make more "to do" lists, start doing them, and "dream harder," until the day came when he met someone who believed in him, because he believed in himself. And, he adds, "Because I had everything ready to go except the checks to write." Wild Earth Llama Adventures was almost a turnkey operation by the time Wilde got the chance to buy his first llamas on credit.

More often than not, that's the kind of effort it takes to effect the kind of changes we want to make. There's no going through the motions. No swiping the towel over the dishes. But as Wilde has concluded, "If one is persistent and diligent in keeping one's dream alive, feeding it with thoughts and images and doing whatever it takes to manifest it, it will work out. Not by magic, but by keeping at it and earning it by working toward its creation."

Wilde's desire to conduct nature adventure tours was so strong that it supplied him with the energy to keep going until he could make it happen. When he went with the flow, it took him where he wanted to go. That's what dreams should do for us. To survive, they must pass the energy test. They must energize us. They must fuel us and serve as a surging source of reserve power we don't even know we have. They should burn like a fire in our bellies, for if they don't and the flame of our desire grows too weak or goes out, our dreams will most likely die.

Can your dream pass the energy test? Does it energize you? Are you eager to work toward it? Does it provide you with much of the very energy you need to pursue it?

CHARGE UP

"But I'm so tired," she said as I continued talking with the woman who wanted to be a writer. I could hear that, like many of us, she felt way too tired, overwhelmed, and worn out to start building a whole new life. Her dream to write in the Pacific Northwest had juice, but she had little to give to it. It alone could not ignite her dead battery. She was suffering from the most common ailment people complain about to their doctors: fatigue. We're a nation in a chronic state of fatigue. So, we sometimes need to stop the chronic drain on our energy and restore our charge before we can tap into the abundant energy of our dreams.

Practical dreamers know everything is created from energy, so they learn how to create the energy they need. Our desires for a better life can keep our dreams alive, but they can't keep us alive. That's not their job. That's our job. And we can't do that when we're beat. So, as practical dreamers, we must become energy managers, learning to pace ourselves to have the energy to do what's needed.

Take Off the Badge

Chellie Campbell did a lot of networking with other business owners to bring the bookkeeping business she'd purchased from her partners back from the brink of bankruptcy. In these meetings she noticed an interesting pattern. "I'd come to meetings with colleagues and everyone would be competing for who was the most exhausted, overworked, and stressed out. It was like a badge of honor," she remembers. She played along with this routine for a while, but as she tells the students in the popular Financial Stress Reduction courses she teaches in Los Angeles, "What we focus on expands. If we focus on how tired and exhausted we are, we just become all the more tired."

Now when Campbell goes to such meetings and people start trading stories of how tired and burned out they are, she pops in to point out how relaxed and rested she feels. Next thing she knows, everyone is talking about how energized and relaxed they are, too. "If you're really tired," Campbell says, "don't talk about it. Go to bed."

 **Try This**

Whenever you hear yourself saying "But I'm so tired," tell yourself, "I have plenty of energy." And to be sure you do, get plenty of sleep.

Sleep

One reason we're chronically fatigued in this country is that not only are we stressed out, we're also sleep-deprived. The National Commission of Sleep Disorders Research reports that most Americans get 20 percent less sleep today than we did 100 years ago. When there are not enough hours in the day, we take them from the night. But, the experts warn, we can't shortchange ourselves for more than one or two nights in a row without consequences. For some people, eight hours of sleep is a must; for others slightly less or slightly more is required. The goal is to get enough sleep each night to wake up feeling refreshed, but not so much that we feel sluggish.

 **Try This**

To find the optimal number of hours you need to sleep, notice how you feel each morning when you wake up and adjust your schedule to get the sleep you need. If you have trouble sleeping, try this:

Chase yourself out of the office at a reasonable hour. Good bosses make sure their employees go home. Insist that you leave ample time between work and sleep. Allow at least an hour or two to unwind from the workday before trying to sleep. Do relaxing, pleasurable activities before retiring.

Don't work in bed. Reserve your bed for sleeping and other pleasurable, relaxing activities.

Hang your work problems on the coatrack when you leave work. At the end of the day, as you close the door on work, imagine putting your concerns in a special box or basket where you can pick them up in the morning. Write out a to-do list or an issues-to-address list for yourself so you'll feel confident you won't forget about something important overnight.

Avoid stimulating food and beverages late in the day. Caffeine, sweets, and salty and fatty foods keep you wired.

Keep your bedroom restful. Philip Goldberg and Daniel Kaufman, the authors of Everybody's Guide to Natural Sleep, *recommend keeping the bedroom quiet, dark, and comfortably cool (between 64 and 66 degrees Fahrenheit).*

When Paul and I get tired during the day, we take a short nap. Many of the greatest minds throughout history have been inveterate nappers. Researchers have found that people who take at least a 30-minute nap daily are healthier and less stressed. This correlates with evidence that countries where the afternoon siesta is commonplace have a lower incidence of heart disease!

Take a Break

He sat on the side of the bed and cried tears of relief. It's a common experience when people come to visit Pine Mountain. The joy of respite. Not only are we stressed out and sleep-deprived, but we're also overworked. According to a report by the Community Research organization, in 1999 more than 80 percent of workers aged twenty-five to fifty-four consider themselves to be workaholics. But it's an illusion to think we get more done by overworking. Research shows that overworkers actually produce less in more time than their more rested colleagues.

Without respite there is no regeneration.

When we're overworked, we don't think at our best or make the best decisions. We need breaks, in the day, in the week and the year to relax and recharge. Some studies suggest short breaks each hour throughout the workday boost energy and productivity. Taking weekends off or at least taking off one day a week (but really taking off, not just working hard at something else) can create miracles; as can spending an hour, a day, a weekend, or a week in nature. Usually, the more we think we can't get away, the more we need to.

 **Try This**

To rebuild your energy, try this three-pronged recovery program:

1. Take multiple mini-breaks throughout the day.
   —Stop to take several long, deep breaths. Count to ten on the inhale and ten on the exhale.

—*Stand up and shake out the tension that's built up in your body. Tension stops the flow of your energy.*

—*Take lots of mental mini-vacations. Just close your eyes and imagine that you're in one of your favorite places.*

—*Put a bird feeder outside your window and watch the birds while enjoying a beverage of your choice; or get a fish tank and watch your fish swim while you take a break.*

—*Or take a pet break. Research shows that stroking or playing with a pet can reduce stress and even extend life, not to mention putting a little levity into the day. Petting an animal actually reduces blood pressure, as does watching fish swim around in an aquarium.*

2. *Take regular nature breaks. Research shows that being in a natural setting can dissolve stress and leave us relaxed and energized. Watching sunrises and sunsets is particularly relaxing. If you don't mind getting wet, standing in the rain is an unusually renewing experience. Whenever you feel uptight, go outside. Lie under a tree on the grass. Sit in the breeze on the porch. Walk in the park, or if you have water nearby, stroll by the river, lake, or ocean. Go to the nearest National Park forest, lake, or beach on weekends or for a vacation.*

   Geologist Dr. Roger Ulrich has documented that even viewing scenes of nature reduces muscle tension, blood pressure, and heart rate in stressed individuals and helps them recover from stressful events, including surgery, more quickly. Environmental psychologist Stephen Kaplan found we can also get the stress-reducing advantages of nature simply by spending a few moments looking out the window or walking through a garden.

3. *Take at least one rejuvenating vacation a year. Not all vacations are rejuvenating. Identify where you can go to totally relax and recharge. Travel light so you won't wear yourself out packing and arranging to get away. Don't fill your vacation with exhausting activities. Leave your cell phone and laptop at home. Try doing absolutely nothing for a while, or at least do only activities that leave you relaxed, inspired, and energized. To keep costs down add a holiday onto the end of a*

business trip, use frequent-flyer miles, or stay at youth hostels or college and university student facilities (see References).

STOP UP THE DRAINS

Once we're rested, recharged, and have begun restoring our stamina, we need to take a good look at our lives and identify the biggest drains on our energy, so we can figure out how to eliminate or alter them. Otherwise, we'll quickly get burned out again. Sometimes it's people who are draining our energy. We may have to change how and if we relate to certain people. Sometimes it's our work, and we have to change what we do or how we do it before we can get on with our dreams. Sometimes it's where we live or how we live that's consuming us, and we'll need to change that before we'll have the energy to move on with our lives.

For me it was traveling. We used to travel extensively in our work. At first it was exciting. I loved the thrill of flying off to new places and meeting new people. But over time it became a major drain. Packing and preparing to leave while keeping up my regular work schedule left me exhausted before I even got out the door. Then there was the agony of waiting to catch a plane in those cacophonous, crowded airports, being herded down tight, crowded aisles and jostled by irritable passengers, squeezing into sardine-tight seats in stuffy, noisy cabins, and then waiting in long lines for taxis or rental cars so I could lug my luggage into one more hotel room.

Then there was coming back to huge piles of mail and phone calls that had to be returned. There was unpacking, taking clothes to the dry cleaner, writing thank-you notes from the trip, following up on problems that developed while we were away . . . all while picking back up my normal schedule. Well, it had to go. Only when I started to cut back on travel did I have the energy to start planning and creating a new life, one with even less travel!

What are the energy drains in your life? How can you plug the holes and accumulate the energy you need to pursue your dreams? Monitor your energy level throughout the day. When do you feel tired, hassled, bummed out, pooped, discouraged? What drags you down? When are you excited, energized, invigorated, and optimistic? What gives you a boost? Note what you're doing. Who's around? What's happening? What are you saying to yourself? What time of day is it? How could you start eliminating the things that drag you down? How can you put more boosters into your day?

➡ **Try This** ☆☆☆

Give up your alarm clock. According to Rob Krakovitz, the author of High Energy, *the sound of an alarm clock starts our day by throwing our bodies into distress. It blares us into a hyperalert state and puts our system into panic. Krakovitz maintains that if we go to bed early enough, we can program our natural internal alarm to wake us up without all the commotion. Paul and I can attest to this. Awakening to our natural alarm clock works wonders. It helps us ease our way into the day gently, naturally, and quickly, feeling refreshed and energized.*

GET IN CONDITION

When you first meet Linda Miller, the woman who started the Pine Mountain Day Spa, the first thing you notice is her high state of energy. People rarely mention Linda without adding a comment about what a ball of fire she is. So when Miller decided to open a B & B in Pine Mountain, everyone's response was, "Well, if anyone can do it, Linda can." Although lots of people had wanted to open one, there'd never been a B & B in Pine Mountain. "It can't be done," folks would say. "The county won't allow it." "The CC&R's (Covenants, Codes and Restrictions) prohibit it." "The residents won't like it." "The merchants will oppose it."

With all that opposition, everyone else who'd come up with an idea for a B & B decided to fold and give it up. "You can't have a B & B in Pine Mountain," they'd tell you. Then Linda came along. She researched property lots, zoning restrictions, county requirements, and the CC&R's and concluded there was no reason she couldn't have a B & B on the property she wanted to buy. Of course, she didn't have the full amount of money she needed to purchase the property, but that didn't stop her, either.

She had only a two-month window to secure the property she had in mind. It was one of very few that could legally be used for a B & B. In that two-month period, Linda talked to 283 residents, lined up support from the local merchants, allied with the local restaurants, secured investors, prepared a presentation for the Club's Environmental Committee that would have to approve the land use, and proved to the county clerk that she could have a B & B on that property.

When the county clerk told Miller the area wasn't zoned for a B & B, she sent him back to review the regulations again. She'd done her homework. He called back to apologize. He'd been wrong, and he and his wife, who loves B & Bs, volunteered to be among Miller's first guests. Meanwhile, Linda was busy enlisting more community support, because B & B experts had advised she would need $40,000 to $50,000 per room for renovation. But she had only $50,000 for her entire four-room establishment.

To stay in budget, Miller enlisted the support of dozens of people in the community from caterers to local restaurateurs. Neighbors donated furniture, contributed antique silverware, offered to provide hors d'oeuvres, greet guests, and be guest breakfast chefs. Four friends volunteered to decorate each of the rooms along a particular nature theme. These decorating divas completed their rooms for under $2,000 each. Paul and I donated draperies, provided business consultation, and lined up publicity for the story behind the B & B. We all piled into Linda's van to go shopping for bargains.

Where does Linda get the energy to do all this, while she's running her day spa and raising a family? Well, she credits the positive people she surrounds herself with. "They give me energy," she explains. "We network, share ideas, and support one another. Their excitement excites me." But she cautions, "I've learned we also have to shield ourselves from negative people who drain our energy and bring us down."

Like Linda, most practical dreamers seem to have boundless energy because they do more than just stop the energy drains in their lives. They've learned how to get charged up and in condition. They put taking care of themselves at the top, not the bottom, of their "to do" lists. They know everyone and everything in our lives benefits when we put our own energy fitness first. Fortunately, there are many ways we can build up and protect our energy reserves.

Create a Supportive Environment

A supportive work environment can help us relax, boost our energy, and concentrate on our goals. We need to design and furnish our work and living spaces so they are places where we like to be, places that nourish instead of fatigue or distract us. We can select colors, lighting, soundproofing, windows, plants, artwork, music, and other accessories that have energizing, relaxing, and restorative qualities. Such touches need not be expensive. For example, when Justen McCormack needed to give her home a new look to support her new life, she gave the whole house a makeover on a shoestring budget.

She cut up an old floral print bedspread to make framed tapestries for her living room and used what was left over to create a runner for the dining room table and new covers on the nearby bar stools. These simple changes gave the entire area a fresh and coordinated look. Moving on to her bedroom, she replaced outdated pictures with collages of clippings from magazines and photos of herself and her daughter and hung stylish hats from her closet along the walls. She framed greeting cards to turn her daughter's room into a "Secret Garden" and lined the walls with a white picket fence and gate. The wood fencing cost all of $10 and could have decorated five rooms.

Anthony Lawlor, award-winning architect and author of *The Temple in the House*, suggests we can also create a special area or room in our home or office for inspiration and relaxation. Setting aside a "sacred" place, he writes, may be as simple as creating a shelf in the corner of a room or setting aside a special room for quiet reflection, relaxation, or meditation.

Meditate

If there's one thing we can do to recharge and energize ourselves on a regular basis, it's taking twenty minutes out of the day for silent meditation. A large body of scientific research now demonstrates that daily meditation is one of the best, most reliable ways to condition our mind to function in a perpetually relaxed and energized state. Actually, the research is startling. It shows that meditating regularly lowers levels of stress hormones and plasma cortisol and reduces cardiovascular risk. As a result, it's been proven to reduce stress, improve ability to learn, prevent insomnia, enhance relationships and job performance, improve memory, normalize blood pressure, slow down the aging process, and leave us feeling happier throughout the course of the day. It's like a prescription for health, wealth, and happiness. And all this in only twenty minutes a day!

Personally, I still have difficulty finding time to meditate, so I've incorporated it throughout my day. When my computer is slow in pulling up a Web site or transferring a file, I meditate now instead of growing impatient. I meditate to music while doing Chi Kong exercises in the evening. I meditate on the wind or the shafts of light on the trees as I walk to the post office or while hiking in the forest.

Be Realistic

According to research by Joseph Procaccini of Loyola College in Baltimore, unrealistic expectations are the real culprit behind much of today's burnout. Burnout occurs when the demands we put on ourselves outweigh our energy supply. Unrealistic demands slow us down and sabotage our performance. While high expectations are a good way to motivate ourselves to go beyond unnecessary limits, success requires a delicate balance between the energy we have available and the demands we place on ourselves. When energy and demand are equal, we perform at our peak. If we don't believe in our ultimate success, however, we tend to make unreasonable demands on ourselves in order to compensate, and ultimately our performance suffers. On the other hand, when we believe fully in our ultimate success, we instill in ourselves the confidence to work at a sensible pace, and our performance improves.

Poet and publisher Rusty Berkus of Red Rose Press is an excellent example of this point. Rusty's staff members were pushing her to take on major speaking engagements to help sell her poetry books. She refused to bend to the pressure, however, because she had never spoken before large audiences and public speaking made her anxious. She did believe in her ability to learn, though, and knew that in order to become an accomplished speaker, she needed to begin with smaller, more informal audiences where she could make mistakes and learn without risking her reputation. That's what she did. She now speaks successfully to increasingly larger audiences. Recently she's been appearing on radio and television shows, but all because she proceeded at a manageable pace.

Are you placing unrealistic demands on yourself, trying to be the perfect superwoman or superman, all things to all people? Give yourself the time and space to create at a realistic pace. Don't compare yourself to others, simply ask, am I doing my best at what I can do right now without jeopardizing my health and well-being or giving up on my dreams?

Eat Right

Good nutrition can also help boost energy and reduce stress. Judith Wurtman, a researcher at the Massachusetts Institute of Technology, has found that certain foods pick us up while others help us to relax. In her book *Managing Your Mind and Mood through Food*, Wurtman recommends that we can boost energy with a diet of protein-rich foods like fish, chicken, and lean beef, low-fat dairy products, dried peas and beans, grains, seeds, and nuts. Also, she suggests that we leave out or minimize energy drainers like alcohol, sugar, salt, coffee, and junk food, which seem to charge you up but actually stress you out. To feel more relaxed, she recommends that we eat complex carbohydrates like breads, muffins, pasta, cereals, potatoes, and grains.

Dr. Charles Tkacz of New York's Nassau Mental Health Center stresses the importance of the B vitamins in managing stress, while Dr. Robert Haskell of San Francisco recommends vitamin C as a stress reducer. Whole grains and leafy green vegetables are high in B vitamins. Foods rich in vitamin C include sweet red and green peppers, brussels sprouts, strawberries, cauliflower, and salmon.

How do you feel about your diet? Are the foods you eat providing you with the energy you need throughout the day? Or do they leave you feeling hyped up or sluggish? Are you satisfied after your meals? Do your meals enable you to maintain a healthy weight? Or do they leave you feeling overstuffed or quickly craving more again?

Paul and I have spent years searching for the right balance and combination of foods that allow us to both enjoy our meals and eat healthfully. Paul now follows the Blood Type diet developed by Dr. Peter J. D'Adamo (see References). He feels satisfied, alert, and energized when he eats according to his blood type. I've followed the Zone diet developed by Barry Sears (see References) for the past seven years. I feel energized and satisfied on this diet. I don't gain weight, and never feel hungry between meals.

We both also screen our food choices for low acidity as described by Dr. Theodore A. Baroody (see References), because high-acid foods tend to put more stress on our bodies. We believe everyone has his or her own unique dietary needs: there is no one-size-fits-all diet. Each of us has to find the particular combination of foods we need to achieve and maintain optimal health.

➡ Try This

To boost energy throughout the day, keep healthy, high-energy snacks on hand like pumpkin seeds, almonds, carrots, hard-boiled eggs, grapes, and whole-grain bread. Or try one of our Energy Meals-in-a-Drink™. Each of these drinks has been created according to Eat Right for Your Type. *They are also roughly balanced in carbohydrates, fats, and proteins for optimal energy according to the Zone diet, and they've been screened for low acidity.*

ENERGY MEALS-IN-A-DRINK™

TYPE "A"

4½ OZ. TOFU (NORI LITE EXTRA FIRM)
I HEAPING TABLESPOON SOY PROTEIN POWDER (JARROW ISO-RICH SOY)
½ CUP NONFAT SOY DRINK

Liquefy in a blender (such as a VitaMix), mixer, or food processor; then add:

¾ CUP FROZEN SWEET CHERRIES
I LARGE CHILLED APPLE
I½ TABLESPOONS FLAXSEEDS OR ½ TABLESPOON FLAXSEED OIL
I TEASPOON MAPLE SYRUP (OR RICE SYRUP OR STEVIA) TO TASTE
CINNAMON OR GROUND CLOVE TO TASTE

Then liquefy all the ingredients together.

TYPE "AB"

4½ oz. TOFU (NORI LITE EXTRA FIRM)
I HEAPING TABLESPOON SOY PROTEIN POWDER (JARROW ISO-RICH
SOY)
½ CUP NONFAT SOY DRINK

*Liquefy in a blender (such as a VitaMix), mixer, or food processor;
then add:*

½ CUP FROZEN RED GRAPES
½ CUP FROZEN PINEAPPLE
½ CUP FROZEN SWEET PITTED CHERRIES
6 WALNUTS
I TEASPOON MAPLE SYRUP (OR RICE SYRUP OR STEVIA) TO TASTE
CINNAMON TO TASTE

Then liquefy all the ingredients together.

TYPE "B"

2 SCOOPS PROTEIN POWDER (DESIGNER BRAND FRENCH VANILLA)
I TABLESPOON LECITHIN
2 TABLESPOONS PAPAYA CONCENTRATE
1½ TABLESPOONS FLAXSEED OR ½ TABLESPOON FLAXSEED OIL
½ CUP NONFAT SOY DRINK
I LARGE FROZEN BANANA (CUT INTO PIECES)
½ CUP FROZEN GRAPES
⅓ CUP FROZEN RASPBERRIES AND/OR FROZEN SWEET CHERRIES
OPTIONAL: ⅛ TEASPOON GROUND CLOVE

*Liquefy in a heavy-duty blender (such as a VitaMix), mixer, or food
processor.*

TYPE "O"

4½ OZ. TOFU (NORI LITE EXTRA FIRM)
1 HEAPING TABLESPOON SOY PROTEIN POWDER (JARROW ISO-RICH
  SOY)
½ CUP NONFAT SOY DRINK

Liquefy in a heavy-duty blender (such as a VitaMix), mixer, or food processor; then add:

4 PRUNES (REALLY SWEET PLUMS WHEN AVAILABLE)
6 WALNUTS
1 LARGE FROZEN BANANA (CUT INTO PIECES)

Then liquefy all the ingredients together.

EXERCISE

There's ample evidence to prove that nothing boosts energy and increases stamina like doing some type of regular aerobic exercise (swimming, running, cycling, dancing). To get the beneficial results, we need to do at least twenty to thirty minutes every other day. But this isn't difficult if we choose an activity we enjoy doing. Paul and I have tried many different forms of exercise, from swimming to jogging to biking. The type of exercise we can enjoy and work into our schedule changes from year to year as our lives change. Now that we live in Pine Mountain we're doing a lot of hiking, but when time or weather doesn't permit that, we use the exercise equipment in our bedroom. I have a step machine. Paul has a Health Rider. We both use a set of hand weights and do twenty minutes of Chi Kong before going to bed.

 **Try This**

Bring yourself back to life in seconds with one of these Instant Energy Builders:

Put on some lively, exhilarating music. Sing along. You won't feel sluggish for long, especially if you get up and dance or just move around to the music.

Give yourself a sixty-second round of vigorous applause. Stand up. Take a bow. Whistle and stomp your feet.

Count from one to ten as loud as you can.

FOCUS THE FLOW

Four years after moving to Pine Mountain, Jeannie Quintana and her husband, Ron, had a dream. Having always loved music and enjoyed a lifetime of concerts and festivals, they wanted to create a music and arts festival in Pine Mountain. They saw it becoming an annual event where people of all ages could come to the forest from surrounding areas to enjoy and celebrate music and art. Over an eight-month period, Jeannie and Ron learned everything they could about producing a music festival. They rallied community support and selected eight musical groups including the El Tejon high school band to which some of the festival proceeds would be donated to help further the music program there. They organized a T-shirt contest in which local children competed to create the logo for the festival. They signed up thirty artisans to display and sell their work and dozens of local advertisers for the program guide.

Creating the festival of "Music in the Forest" required a tremendous amount of energy. Ron and Jeannie worked seven days a week every week for eight months. For Jeannie the energy came through her daily morning ritual, a personal energy-building ceremony she's done every day for the past five years. She gets up each morning around 5:30 or 6:00 A.M., fills the eleven bird feeders on her deck, and sits down with her coffee to meditate and commune with nature. There she finds the joy that will propel her through the day.

She meditates and prays, and mentally organizes her day, often casting aside whatever plans she'd made from the previous day so she can go with the flow of what seems to be the best thing to do on that particular day. "It's a joyful, cozy, welcoming experience," she explains. "Making the time and the space for deep thinking is important to me; a space where you know you can go that means something personal to you and provides you with energy you need." Around 8:00 A.M. Ron joins her and they spend time together in the Jacuzzi, sharing and coordinating their day.

This morning ritual helped them through both the excitement and the challenges of launching a first-time-ever music festival. They encountered one unexpected roadblock after another, and at one point they were even threatened with a restraining order to block the festival. At the same time there was a tremendous groundswell of support from the community. Soon, "The festival had a life all its own and I had a tiger by the tail," Jeannie remembers. That made doing her ritual with "purpose and conscience" all the more important. Her purpose became how she could best be of service to the community through this festival and she found that "You have to surrender to the energy of your dream and do whatever your duties are for creating it as they arise."

On August 22, music filled the village and rang through the pines as 600 to 1,000 people enjoyed the first annual Music in the Forest, Music and Art Festival. Several months later, a steady flow of donations are still coming in for next year's festival.

Find a Balance

As the artists and architects of our dreams we must find ways to pace ourselves so we can go the distance. Many of us think that to fulfill our desires we have to constantly push and drive our way to success. But then, instead of enjoying the quality of life we're working to achieve, we end up feeling overwhelmed, exhausted, and burned out from trying to achieve it. We end up frantically seeking simplicity, driving ourselves for the chance to relax, and trapping ourselves in a conundrum of hassles.

On the other hand, others of us never seem to get our dreams off the ground because we're so tentative, waiting and wishing and hoping that something will happen to change our lives. So, while some of us are expending too much energy, others of us aren't expending enough energy. What we need is to find a balance between pushing and waiting. We need to learn when to put the pedal to the metal and when to coast.

How about you? Do you have the pedal to the metal most of the time? Or are you waiting impatiently for something to happen?

There are times when we must push and times when we must wait. Those of us who tend to push, push, push must learn to pause, to let up and pace ourselves. At first this feels uncomfortable and risky. We fear we'll miss out or lose out on something if we stop pushing. But if we allow ourselves to pause, we learn that life goes on even when we relax and loosen up. We learn that, should we miss something, it will either come back around or something else just as good or better will present itself if we keep an eye out for it. We also learn that when we pause, we see opportunities we miss by constantly driving ahead. And best of all, when we pause, we give ourselves a chance to relax, recharge, and come back to our goals renewed and energized.

Those of us who tend to wait must learn to charge up, take initiative, and do something spontaneous. Again, doing this feels impulsive and dangerous at first. We fear we'll make a mistake or take a wrong turn. But then we learn that mistakes often open un-expected doors by showing us what we need to do instead. And wrong turns often lead to new and better paths. Of course, we also learn that much more comes to those who initiate than to those who only wait. And best of all, taking action will inspire and energize us to do even more.

Notice when you push and when you wait. Notice how you decide when to do which. Is there an ebb and flow? Is now a time you need to push? Or have you been pushing too long? Is now a time you need to wait? Or have you been waiting too long?

 **Try This**

Without reflection, there is no inspiration. To become better acquainted with what is and isn't working in your life, find times for solitude and reflection. Start a journal to record your thoughts, observations, and insights about yourself, your life, and your dreams.

Concentrate

Concentration is focused energy—the ability to direct our energy toward accomplishing the task at hand. But how can we concen-trate when we're surrounded by so many distractions and pres-sures? How can we respond readily to the many things that are pertinent to our goals and ignore all else? Practical dreamers learn how.

First, because they're following an inner compass, they know what they want to do and what it takes to do it. They aren't asking themselves, "Do I really want to do this now or should I wait un-til later?" They aren't wondering, "Should I go in this direction or some other one?" What they do may not always be the right thing, but if it's not, by taking action they soon discover what is.

Second, at key and decisive moments, their goal becomes the

sole focus of their efforts. They are not multitasking. That means they have the phones covered, someone else is watching the kids, there's a do-not-disturb sign on the door. For me, focusing has meant no longer taking phone calls while I'm writing. It has meant dropping certain writing projects so I can concentrate on the most important ones and still have time to develop a new dream that's taking form. It's meant turning down out-of-town speeches and even some L.A. speeches. With too much on my plate, I can't concentrate fully on any one thing.

Third, they stay in the moment. Once the preparation, practice, study, strategy, and so on are behind them, they give 100 percent of their energy and attention to what they're doing second by second, step by step. They're not looking back at what they did the last time. Nor are they looking ahead at what might happen next time. They're not thinking about how they're doing or if they're doing it right. They're focused on doing the best they can do in the moment.

When 1984 Olympic gold medal gymnast Tim Daggett fell from the horizontal bar in training and ruptured a spinal disc less than a year before the qualifying tournament for the 1988 Olympics in Seoul, I asked him if he thought he would be able to recover in time to compete. He told me, "There are a multitude of things I can do to qualify for the Olympic Games while I'm recovering. There are also things I have no control over at all . . . and if I dwell on those points or worry about them then I'm taking away from the time I could be spending on the things I can do to get to the Olympics."

That's what we must and can do as practical dreamers. We can set up our lives to concentrate fully on *what we can do*, and stop focusing on those things over which we have no control.

Stop Worrying

Worry is one of the biggest drains on our energy. It saps our enthusiasm and confidence faster than any other activity. Mark

Twain once claimed he had many worries, most of which never happened. Isn't that the truth? Still, a nationwide survey found that 42 percent of those interviewed report worrying a lot, spending at least 25 percent of their day worrying.

Alan Loy McGinnis, the author of the book *The Power of Optimism*, defines worry as the misuse of our imagination. Instead of using the imagination to project positive outcomes, the worrier imagines dreaded disasters and defeats. Optimists, on the other hand, use their imagination to rehearse success. And indeed we find that most practical dreamers do this routinely. According to Robert Ornstein and David Sobel, the authors of the book *Healthy Pleasures*, not only do optimists imagine a rosy future, they remember their successes much better than they recall their failures. They dwell on the pleasant. They skip over, although they don't ignore, their shortcomings. They *anticipate* success. They don't hope for it; they expect it.

Research now confirms that optimists are more successful in all areas of life. They excel in school, have a better love life, make more money, have better health, and may even live longer! Dr. Michael Scheier of Carnegie-Mellon University in Pittsburgh has found that optimists also do better in the face of stress. They take action sooner; break big problems into smaller, more manageable ones; stick to their goals longer; and believe others can help. Optimists also report less fatigue, depression, dizziness, muscle soreness, and coughs than pessimists when facing the same stressful events.

➡ Try This

When worries arise, ask yourself, "How likely is this to happen? What's the worst thing that could happen if it did? Can I live with that?" Then think of what you can do to ensure the best possible outcome and imagine it going well.

THE DARK NIGHT OF THE SOUL

I'm too far along to turn back," she told me, "but this has become a nightmare." She'd quit her job and used her savings to start a small gift basket business. It was her dream come true and it got off to a grand start, a large order, hundreds of centerpieces for a corporate awards banquet. She purchased the materials and began creating the ornate baskets stuffed with goodies that would serve as the centerpieces. As the event approached, however, she began to feel concerned that the event coordinator hadn't called with delivery instructions and wasn't returning her calls. "He's probably really busy," she had told herself, and proceeded with making the baskets. When all the baskets were finished, she left a message saying they were done and asking for the time and precise location where she should deliver them.

"I can still hear his voice ringing in my ears," she continued. There had been a mistake. They wouldn't be needing the baskets after all. The president of the company had decided to hire his wife to create the centerpieces. "I'm sorry. Hope this hasn't inconvenienced you." Being new to the business and eager for opportunities, she hadn't gotten a written contract, nor had she asked for a deposit up front. She was out the hefty costs of her materials, which she'd charged on a credit card. And since her time had been tied up on this huge project, she hadn't brought in any other business.

In their birth throes some dreams become a living nightmare. Like when Daggett was injured and the local merchant threatened to sue Jeannie Quintana, this woman's dream had turned ugly. It's at times like these that we must truly master our energy. It's tempting to panic. To sink into depression. To flail about recklessly; or rant and rave. Cry. Take a stiff drink. Climb in bed and throw the covers over our heads. Any of which are quite normal, of course, but we can't allow our energy to spiral out of control for long. If we still want our dream, we can't lose our focus.

"You do all you can do," Jeannie Quintana told us, "and then you let go." That's what she did. That's what Tim Daggett did. And that's what this woman would have to do. Tim didn't make it to the Seoul Olympics. That dream was not to be. But Jeannie's dream was born into this world in glorious colors. When a dream takes us into the dark night of the soul, we can't always choose the outcome, but we can choose our responses to it. The woman with the gift basket business could have folded up shop, swallowed her losses, and taken another job. Instead, she decided to marshal her pride and her energy and concentrate on finding a way to carry on.

She borrowed some money from her family to pay the rent and the minimum balance on the credit card and began a campaign to sell the hundreds of baskets she had on hand. She decided to donate one to every business meeting, nonprofit event, and charity fund-raiser on the calendar that month. Not only did that provide her with lots of valuable publicity, it resulted in a rush order from an organization that needed most of her inventory immediately. Her dream was alive and well again!

LET GO AND MOVE ON

It was more than ten years later and the ex-pro football player being interviewed on the radio was still lamenting a pass he hadn't caught. "I think about it every day," he said, his voice filled with pain. "I let the team down. I let the coach down. I let myself down." How sad, I thought. Could that one pass, that one game, possibly have been worth so many years of regret?

While it's difficult to have the faith to keep a dream alive, it's far more difficult to have the faith to believe that the death of a dream can ultimately be for the best, or at least OK. As all practical dreamers know, not all dreams come true. But again we must manage our energy, grieve, let go, and move on. It hurts because we cared. We had to care. We can never create masterpieces unless we care.

But there are many lessons to be learned from a dream that is not to be. And it's part of our job as practical dreamers to learn those lessons. One such lesson helped Tim Daggett to know he was a winner whether he went to the Olympics or not. "Everybody in the world isn't going to be an Olympic champion," Tim told me, "but the feelings and memories I'll have from just trying are good enough for me."

Just as life abounds around a fallen tree upon the forest floor, fallen dreams can bear great fruit. Some will serve as doorways to future dreams. Others, as Jim Morris knows so well, will return to be reborn another day and another time. Morris's dream of pitching for the major leagues died when he was twenty-three, after three years on a minor league team. He was benched by a series of surgeries to his shoulder and elbow. From that day forward, he couldn't watch a major league baseball game. Someone he knew might be playing and that would be too painful.

But Morris moved on with his life. He went to college, got married, had a family, and settled into teaching high school physics and chemistry in Big Lake, a small town in West Texas. There he also coached the school's baseball team. The year Morris turned thirty-five, his team had a chance to go to the playoffs for the first time in several years. So he pulled them together and delivered a stirring pep talk. "Go for your dreams. Go past your dreams," he was saying when a couple of the students called out, "But what about *your* dream?" They knew he'd given up on his dream, not because he'd told them so but because they could tell from the way he pitched at batting practice, so fast they could barely catch or hit the balls.

The team offered him a dare. If they made the playoffs, he'd try out for the major leagues. Not wanting to set a bad example, he accepted the dare, and when his team went to the playoffs, he had to deliver on his promise. Without having played baseball in twelve years, Morris headed off to Brownwood, Texas, to try out for the Tampa Bay Devil Rays. Because his wife had to work that day, he had his three small children with him, one in a stroller.

After two hours of waiting and watching and almost turning around to go home, there were chortles and snickers when he took the mound. Who was this old guy? But to everyone's amazement his pitches were clocked at 98 miles per hour. Disbelieving, the scouts called for another radar gun. He threw twelve consecutive 98 mph pitches. Even then they made him come back a week later to be sure it wasn't some kind of fluke. But one month later he was throwing those 98 mph pitches in the minor leagues and now for the Tampa Bay Devil Rays. A reborn dream come true!

When it comes to pursuing our highest desires, even dead ends need not be the end. We never know where our dreams will go, we just have to keep following the thread.

REFERENCES

A Call for Connection: Solutions for Creating a Whole New Culture. Gail Bernice Holland. New World Library. ISBN 157731039X.

Alkalize or Die. Dr. Theodore A. Baroody. Eclectic Press. ISBN 0-9619595-3-3.

The Complete Guide to Prayer-Walking: A Simple Path to Body-and-Soul Fitness. Linus Mundy. Crossroad Publishing Co. ISBN 0824515463.

Eat Right for Your Type. Dr. Peter J. D'Adamo, with Catherine Whitney. ISBN 0-399-14255-x.

Enter the Zone. Barry Sears, Ph.D., with Bill Lawren. ISBN 0-06-039150-2.

Feeding the Body Nourishing the Soul: Essentials of Eating for Physical, Emotional, and Spiritual Well-Being. Deborah Kesten and Herbert Benson. Conari Press. ISBN 1573240680.

Feng Shui: The Book of Cures: 150 Simple Solutions for Health and Happiness in Your Home or Office. Nancilee Wydra. Contemporary Books. ISBN 0-8092-3168-9.

Food & Mood: The Complete Guide to Eating Well and Feeling Your Best. Elizabeth Somer. Henry Holt. ISBN 0805062009.

Healing Environments, Your Guide to Indoor Well Being. Carol Venolia. Celestial Arts. ISBN 0-89-87-497-2.

A Home for the Soul, A Guide for Dwelling with Spirit and Imagination. Anthony Lawlor. Clarkston Potter Publishing. ISBN 0-517-70400-5.

The Hostel Handbook for the USA and Canada. Jim Williams. ISBN 0966730518.

Learning to Use What You Already Know. Stephen A. Stumpf, and Joel R. Deluca. Berrett-Koehler Publishers. ISBN 1-881052-55-9.

The Long Road Turns to Joy: A Guide to Walking Meditation. Thich Nhat Hanh, and Robert Aitken. Parallax Press. ISBN 093807783X.

Open Road's America's Cheap Sleeps. Tracy Whitcombe, Open Road Publishing. ISBN 1883323819.

Power of Optimism: Becoming a Tough-Minded Optimist. Alan Loy and Dr. McGinnis. $59.95, Audio Cassette, Nightingale-Conant Corporation; ISBN 9992472197.

Sacred Space. Denise Linn. Ballantine Books. ISBN 0-345-39769-X.

Secrets of Self Employment: Surviving and Thriving on the Ups and Downs of Being Your Own Boss. Sarah and Paul Edwards. Tarcher/Putnam. ISBN 0-87477-837-9.

Travel That Can Change Your Life. Jeffrey A. Kottler, Ph.D. Jossey-Bass. ISBN 0-7879-0941-6.

Vacations That Can Change Your Life: Adventures, Retreats and Workshops for the Mind, Body and Spirit. Ellen Lederman. Sourcebooks. ISBN 1-57071-124-0.

➡ PART II: REMEMBER THIS

Anytime you have difficulty taking the action you need to take to follow your highest desires, be it difficulty with finding the money, making the time, or having the energy, turn here to this section and remember . . .

Following the Thread

Dreams are built from remnants of reality. Sometimes we let go of our dreams because we can't see them as realities. We look at the reality around us and it is so different from our dreams—our real dreams—that they seem impossible, so we settle for less than the magnificence we imagine. Yet every dream, even the most magnificent, is built on the platform of reality from the real life materials we have at hand.

Are you watching or playing the game? "You know we can't get out of life alive!" motivational speaker Les Brown has been quoted as saying. "We can either die in the bleachers or die on the field. We might as well come down on the field and go for it." Chances are, if you're reading this book you're out on the field or at least want to be. Whenever you follow a dream, you are no longer watching life go by. You're on the field with the balls whizzing by, winning and losing and going back for another inning. So keep that in mind and cheer yourself on. Hold yourself in the kind of esteem you would afford to any player who stays in the game and plays with all his or her heart. And, if you're holding back, take Les Brown's advice and go for it!

Don't let your music go unsung. Unless we start singing our tune, the world will never hear it. As Rabindranath Tagore has said, "I have spent my days stringing and unstringing my instrument while the song I came to sing is still unsung." Too often we plan and talk about what we are going to do. Then we plan and talk about what we're going to do some more. Sometimes we think we need to take one more course, get one more degree, have just a bit more money set aside, and so forth . . . meanwhile our life goes by like a moment in time. We all have great ideas dancing in our heads to tunes we hear only in our dreams. What a loss to all if we're the only ones who ever hear these melodies. It's time to start singing.

Take action. It is great to dream. Dreams show us the way. They keep us on track and inspire us to continue. But dreaming is a doorway, not a destination. Only action transforms dreams into realities. Planning, too, is important, but planning only shows us a possible path for us to take. We go nowhere until we act on our plans. Sometimes we dream and plan and dream and plan and think we're making progress. But only when we begin to act on our plans will our dreams and plans become realities.

Walk your talk. "I'm not interested in people's claims—only in what they do," said Alfred Stieflitz. "The act comes first and then the word." We don't know who Alfred Stieflitz is, but he sure hit on a key issue here. (If you know who he is, please, let us know.) Most people aren't so interested in what you say you want to do as in what you have done or are doing. Good intentions are important, but good action is better. So let's not talk so much about what we want to do, but instead start taking whatever steps we can right now to do what we most want to achieve.

Catalyze your intention. Whatever your aspirations, take some action each day no matter how small in that direction. Even if you don't know what you need to do (as is often the case), make your best guess and act on it. Often by taking even one small step, we gain a better sense of what needs to come next. As singer Kenny James told us, "Success is like standing in a grocery line. If you stay in line and keep moving forward, your turn will come."

Trust your intuition. We all get that feeling in our stomach, or hear that little voice in our head, telling us not to proceed or to go for it. Often we ignore this inner wisdom, because it doesn't appear to jive with the facts, the practicalities, or what we want. But how often have you later thought, "If only I'd listened to my hunches"? Your hunches may seem impractical and unjustified. They may seem to come out of nowhere. Yet they can provide you with clues for when to look beyond what appears to be practical, factual, or desirable to deeper, less obvious truths.

Learn from your instincts. Our intuition is an instinctual guidance system. Much like a powerful computer, it collects, synthesizes, and integrates vastly more sensory, emotional, and cognitive "data" than we can process consciously. Then, going beyond the capabilities of even the most powerful of computers, it draws conclusions and makes judgments based on its vast databank of conscious and unconscious experiences. Often we don't trust our instincts because we fear they could be wrong. Well, they can be, just like the conclusions of our logical, rational mind can be wrong. But if we rely on and trust our intuition, it, too, learns from experience. The more we trust ourselves, the more trustworthy we become. So heed your inner voice. Let it protect and guide you. Let it teach you.

Look first within. We know much more than we might think. We're so accustomed to looking outside for the answers. We're encouraged to turn to the experts. As a result, we may miss our personal truth. Of course, there are times when we can and should rely on the wisdom of others, but if we are to become wise ourselves, we must find our own answers. We must listen to our own counsel, experiment with it, and learn what works for us.

Be your own teacher. Every day our lives are filled with a myriad of experiences, some pleasant, some not so pleasant. If we think of ourselves as our own teacher, these experiences can become lessons of great value. A good teacher is not one who has all the answers, but one who helps his or her students discover the answers in what their lives present to them. A good teacher poses questions, presents options, and designs experiences from which one can learn. So, present yourself with questions each day that your mind can address, that is, What would I need to do to accomplish this? Why does that keep happening? and so forth. Take a moment at the close of each day to garner the lessons embedded in the experiences of the day.

Be an options thinker. How many people have concluded they can't garden because despite following the directions on the package, the azaleas died? How many of us have tried to start a business following a formula and decided we aren't suited to be our own boss because the business doesn't "take off"? A formula is a procedure or blueprint for what someone else has found to work for them. In many situations procedures come in quite handy, that is, assembling your child's first bicycle, installing a new software program, changing the oil in your car. But in other situations, like planting a garden, creating a work of art, writing a play, or creating the life you're yearning for, procedures just won't cut it. For such things, you can follow a procedure to the letter and still not get the result you want. To create the life you want, you must become an options thinker. Define your desired outcomes, set goals, experiment, and explore to generate options for achieving them. Then select one, try it out, and watch the results.

Experiment. Creating a life suited to your own unique set of desires and needs is an experiment—an act undertaken to discover something unknown. There's no predetermined right or wrong way to do things. You get to discover what works, and if you keep exploring the possibilities you can find the most amazing, even unimagined success. This sense of exploration can be exhilarating, if you undertake the quest with a sense of adventure. Exploration is at the heart of creation.

Think of yourself as an explorer. Unlike other creatures, we come into this life with only a scant blueprint. We must learn how to live, how to support ourselves, how to hunt and gather the experiences of life we seek. This is true now more than ever, in that there is no one clear path for most of us. Instead, there are many possible paths, and we must choose among the forks in the road and often even create new paths where there have been none. But as modern-day explorer Douchan Gersi has said "There are so many places I would not have gone, so many people I would not have seen and met, so many expeditions I would not have led, if I had only known in advance what I was to experience." As modern-day explorers, we find ourselves venturing into new places and if we have the courage to proceed, we, too, will find many treasures we would otherwise have missed.

Expect the hurdles. When hurdlers go out on the track, they don't moan and groan when they see hurdles laid out along the track. Of course there are hurdles. That's what the sport is about. So hurdlers prepare to take the hurdles in stride and so must we. Creating a life we desire is like running the hurdles. There will be obstacles, even unexpected ones. It's inevitable. But much of the misery we experience comes from thinking we'll be sprinting only to find a track full of hurdles. If we expect the hurdles and think of them as part of the challenge, part of the chance we get to perfect our skills and abilities, then we'll greet them in a much better frame of mind. As Albert Schweitzer said, "Anyone who proposes to do good must not expect people to roll stones out of his way, but must accept his lot calmly, even if they roll a few more upon it."

Do you feel lost sometimes? Good! As author Sue Bender says, "When you're lost, you start to look around and to listen." When we focus single-mindedly on where we're headed we can sometimes overlook important signs along the way. So we need to focus, yes, but we need not worry if we periodically feel lost. It means we're taking note of the changes swirling around us and within us, and as Shakespeare said, "By indirections [we can] find directions out."

Don't panic. Often it's when you're most lost in the struggle that you find your way. According to complexity theory, one of the newest approaches to science and management, creative thinking is only possible at the interstices between order and chaos. In fact, if you think about it, you'll probably recall that many of your breakthrough ideas and solutions have come at some of the most chaotic times. So, next time you start to feel like everything is getting completely out of hand and falling apart, don't panic. Remember, such times provide the best opportunities for creative thinking and problem-solving.

Follow the yellow brick road. When I was a young child, my father used to read *The Wizard of Oz* to me. I don't know what I was learning from this story, but whatever it was I must have needed to know it, because I begged him constantly to read it again and again. As I think now about this story, I realize it's a perfect tale for those of us who are seeking to create a new and better way of living and working. Like Dorothy, we suddenly find ourselves in a strange land, often swept there by forces out of our control. While we may find the new land exciting and interesting . . . we want to go home. We want security and recognition and certainty. Instead we feel beleaguered by demons like cash flow and escalating expenses and rising taxes, needy parents, and demanding kids. So, in search of the Wizard to help us find the comfort and security we crave, we must follow the yellow brick road, the unfolding possibilities each day presents. But the road is winding, and we can't see where it's going. We have to trust and follow the road. That requires us to use the three things Dorothy's companions were seeking: courage, brains, and heart. So, each day, let us summon our courage, use our brains, and listen to our hearts along our own yellow brick road.

Going through the labyrinth. Anytime we have a dream and set a goal to manifest it, we will be tested. It's a test of will, a test to see if we're committed, a test to determine how much we really want to attain this goal. In many ways, this is good. We might prefer our wish to be the world's command and that what we dream will manifest itself easily and quickly. But we can only know if we truly want to manifest a particular dream by discovering its reality. This is the labyrinth we often find ourselves in when we set out toward our dream.

As we're tested by the realities of achieving a goal, we may discover that our true dream is somewhat or even totally different than we'd thought. We can only find our true mettle and our true dream by calling upon ourselves to show it, develop it, and to grow from who we are to who we can become.

Face reality; it's when we're not looking that we trip over it. Usually, when we hear someone tell us to face reality, we think they mean giving up on our goals and dreams. So we may try to ignore unpleasant realities, hoping they'll go away. But actually, by looking reality right in the face you have the chance to alter it to fit your desires. When you look it right in the eye, you can take hold of it and dance it in the direction you want to go.

Facing reality only hurts a little while, but not nearly as much as ignoring it. Facing the truth of a situation may feel uncomfortable. Maybe your bank balance is down, or your job is changing. Perhaps someone you've been counting on isn't following through on what you agreed to. It's tempting to dismiss such things as aberrations or insignificant details. "Nothing to worry about." Indeed, worrying about them probably won't serve you. But taking immediate action will. Adjusting your budget or talking to your associate, for example, could prevent things from deteriorating, while ignoring them almost ensures that they will. As a Native American Indian teacher once said, "Sometimes a truth has to hurt a little bit to be remembered." So when you are feeling the pain of truth's burn, keep in mind that, much like the aches and pains of working out, facing the truth is a side effect of getting and staying fit.

Finding Money, Having Time

Take a stand. Are you trapped in your life and can't get out? Do you ever wonder how your life got like it is? It's easy to get trapped into agreements you wish you hadn't made and into doing things you wish you weren't doing. Take a stand for what's most important to you. Take the position, "I am going to do things differently from now on," and then just do that. Whenever you hear yourself saying, "I don't want to do so and so, but I have to . . ." stop and ask yourself, "Who says?" Whenever you hear yourself saying, "I would like to do so and so but I can't," ask yourself, "What prevents me from doing that?" These two questions will ferret out the reasons you're using to keep doing what you don't want to do. Take a look at the reasons you're giving yourself and rethink your possibilities.

Mind the details. Success, it has been said, is in the details, but which ones? If we attend to all the details of life we'd never get anything done and we'd drive ourselves crazy. The truth of that saying lies in giving the important things in life the full attention they require. Why waste time, money, and energy cutting corners that lessen the impact or even negate the value of what you're doing? Honor your intentions by attending to the final touches that say you truly care about what you're doing and where you're going in life.

Develop a stomach for success. We all have dreams. Yet realizing them often comes with unexpected challenges. We're called upon to be and do more than we expected. We're presented with both more of the things we welcome and more of the things we don't. Success may bring more money and more opportunity, but it may also bring more difficult choices and additional work and responsibilities. In this way, success makes us strong. So let's welcome the challenge.

"Don't Worry, Make Money," says the popular book title by Richard Carlson. As a multimillionaire once told us over lunch, "Financial success is all a matter of zeros." Instead of worrying about hundred-dollar concerns, he had graduated to worrying about tens or hundreds of thousand-dollar concerns. Too often we think, "If only I had more money . . . Oh, then what I could do!" But where does such thinking get us? It leaves us to a life sentence of dreaming and wishing. So, instead of worrying about the zeros you don't have, multiply the ones you do have.

Throw your money in the direction you want to go. We all have limited budgets. Instead of thinking about how much money you wish you had and all the things you would do if you did, think about what you can do today with whatever money or resources you have right now. Regardless of how limited your resources, invest the assets you have at hand in getting where you want to go. You'll be surprised at how quickly dreams can become realities.

Accept less to have more. We can never accomplish more in life if we can't accept ourselves as OK not yet having it. Too often if we face facts and admit that we don't have what we want, we feel so bad about ourselves that we can't proceed with confidence. Or, not wanting to feel bad about ourselves, we pretend we don't care about whatever it is we want. In fact, sometimes we even put people down or make fun of those who have accomplished the things we want, just so we can feel better about not having them. Instead, if we can look at others who have what we want and think, "Hey, I am so glad to see that what I want is possible. That's for me," then we can be inspired. Then who knows what we might do!

Get clear on money. For some people making money is the central focus of their lives. For others, time is money. For some, having time is more important than money. They'll forgo many of life's extras to have free time to do with as they wish. For some, money is a means to an end, while others view it as their reward for a service well done. Some consider it to be the root of all evil; others say it is a necessary evil, a means to an end. Our society abounds with views about money. So you can think about money any way you want, or not at all, for that matter. But how you think, or don't think, about money can affect how much you have of it and the overall quality of your life. The key is to realize that we can each decide what role money will play in our lives. Once you do that, you'll no longer be working for money; money will be working for you.

Turn the "No's" you get into "Hows." Twenty-six-year-old Nicole Dionne was working in the sound design industry when she found the twenty-page improvement plan she'd written for her employer discarded and dusty on a pile of papers. There and then she decided to leave her job and start her own sound company, Primal Scream, providing music for commercials and movie trailers. She developed a business plan and negotiated a $30,000 bank loan. Three months later she'd paid off the loan and she now has a 4,000-square-foot studio and nine employees. And she won two Cleo Awards—the Academy Awards of the advertising industry!

When asked by the Los Angeles *Times* to write about how she did this, Dionne explained, "I think the more you spend time

complaining about the answer 'no,' the less time you have to figure out another option. When I heard 'No,' I immediately started
figuring how to turn it into a 'How.' "

First you support your dream; then it will support you. Creating
a dream is like raising a child: you have to support it until it can
support itself. There is usually not an immediate source of steady
income for or from a newborn dream. It's more likely to be an immediate source of steady expenses. The expenses need not be
high. Making whatever investment you can is what's important.

"Track your success, not your failures." As Vice President Al
Gore has said, "We get what we measure." It's important to track
how you're spending your time and money, what's working in
your life and what's not. Too often, though, people spend more
time worrying about the money they don't have, than they do in
planning for the money they'd like to have and tracking from
whence came the money they do have. But if you track your success, your results can be your guide. So ask yourself, which of
your activities are bringing you more of what you want and focus
your energy there.

What are you up to? It's so easy to get caught up in making
money that we can forget what our life is about. "Money," the
Japanese saying goes, "is your reward for having done a good
job." So, if we focus on doing a good job—a really good job—
often money issues take care of themselves. Keep your focus
today on what you're up to accomplishing through your work.
Then let the results be your guide.

Take heart by looking at past and future impossible dreams.
Sometimes building a new life for ourselves seems like an endlessly long and dark night packed into an uncomfortably tight
budget on rough economic seas with no window from which to

view the future. At such times we can take heart from our ancestors' struggles for a better life by considering how much of what we take for granted today would have seemed impossible to them. Think also about how, because of your current struggles, your children and your children's children will take for granted the very things you're striving for. They'll be off pursuing other seemingly impossible dreams that their heirs will come to take for granted, too.

Invest the effort to make your own breaks. An actress once told me, "I cannot act until someone hires me to act." Many of us feel this way. Yet it is not true. Consider Roy Lopresti. He wanted to build an airplane, but he didn't have the money required to build it himself. Most people would have done what so many others advised him to do, to "get on with something more practical." But, no, he had no intention of just talking and dreaming about the airplane he wanted to build, so he created a model of it. He laid out the specifications. He developed a detailed business plan that showed what he could do and began traveling coast to coast to sell an investor on his dream. After some considerable effort, he found that investor and he built his airplanes. He left his first trade show with a long list of orders he returned home to fill.

Where does the time go? There are only so many hours, so many days, so many weeks, so many months, and so many years in a lifetime. They fly by at an accelerating pace. Often it's said we must make every moment count. Usually this is interpreted to mean we must knuckle down and work harder and harder. But perhaps making every moment count means thinking more about what is most important to us and putting first things first. Perhaps it means devoting as much of each day as possible to what really matters to us. As the teacher Marva Collins tells her students, "This day has been given to you fresh and clear to either use or throw away." What a gift. Enjoy it.

Pass the test of time. We need not dread the passage of time. Time need not be our enemy. We can think of it as a resource and a teacher instead of a taskmaster against whom we must constantly race to keep pace with. "Time is a filter, like a fine mesh screen that day by day, year by year, filters out the muck of our insecurities and self-doubt. Time is a purification system that makes us wiser, freer, and better. Are those the characteristics of an enemy?" asks the copy of a *Vanity Fair* advertisement. Make time your friend and embrace its lessons and its gifts.

Don't be a slave to time. It's easy to get caught up in the pressures of deadlines and time schedules. Before long you can feel driven by the clock. Free yourself from time pressures by keeping in mind that you're the boss in your life. You get to decide what goes into your day. If your days have become too full, you've taken too much onto your plate. You're stuffing too much into the drawer called your life. It's time to take a stand. Make time work for you. Decide what's most important and put those things first.

Get firm. Say "No" or "Later" to less important things. Don't agree to do more than you can comfortably fit into your day. The more respect you have for your time, the more people will have respect for you. As long as you're still breathing, you have all the time in the world. In fact, that's all you have. It's your most important resource. You use it or lose it. So go ahead, have the time of your life!

Initiate, don't wait. Waiting is about anticipating the results of your labors, allowing them to take root, grow, and bear fruit. After the planting, we wait for the harvest. But there will be no harvest unless we first do the planting. Too often we wait for "something to happen" and wonder why nothing comes about. The results will be much better if we plant something every day by initiating some activity that could lead to the results we aspire to. If you keep taking regular action directed toward your most important goals, waiting for the results will certainly be more interesting and infinitely more fruitful.

Honor the details. Do you sometimes feel like your days are filled with bothersome details and other administrivia? Do you wish you could get on to the more important things? Helen Keller had a unique perspective on the pesky particulars that invariably fill our days. She said, "I long to accomplish a great and noble task, but it is my chief duty to accomplish small tasks as if they were great and noble." Perhaps the greatest and most noble of accomplishments are but a collection of seemingly insignificant ones done day by day with the greatest of respect and care.

Ask and you shall receive, but don't expect overnight delivery. No matter how hard you work, or how well you do, some things aren't going to happen today. That doesn't mean they won't happen or can't happen. Success has a schedule of its own. We can be masters of our own fate, but not always on our own time table. Often those who reach the summits in life are those who are willing to proceed onward long after others have abandoned the journey.

Energy

Tap the source. The results are dramatic when you use your talents and assets to pursue your deepest desires in ways that meet the needs of others and the world. Your desires provide you with the energy you need to apply your talents artfully and arduously, and as you pump energy into your life, it's returned to you in the form of money, satisfaction, and other rewards that literally "feed" you on every level: physically, emotionally, and spiritually.

Focus your energy by setting an intention for each day. Focus is one of the most important elements of success. From a general perspective, focusing means defining the type of life you want to live and not scattering your energy by trying to be all things to all people. In a more specific sense, focus means providing a direction for your day. As we head into the day, we are a ball of energy. Some mornings our ball of energy is large, blazing, and bright; other mornings it is smaller, slower, and dimmer, but energy it is nonetheless. If we do not focus that energy, it will find a myriad of more or less random activities to seep into and we will disperse the day away, responding first to this, then to that, attracted here, and then there. But if we set an intention for the day, our energy can become directed and laserlike in focus. What is your intention today?

Break goals into bite-sized pieces. The secret of getting started each day is breaking complex, overwhelming tasks into small, manageable tasks, and then starting on the first one, said Mark Twain. Remember this advice whenever you begin to feel overwhelmed by all you have to do. There are times to think big, to look at the big picture, but when you begin feeling overwhelmed you're trying to attend to too much at once. Being overwhelmed is like gulping your food. You get the hiccups. You get indigestion. Instead, when you're feeling too pressed, it's time to narrow your focus so you can take just one simple step at a time.

Start each day with an attitude of hopeful anticipation. The way you begin your day often sets the course for the day and your experience of it. While we can't ever be entirely in charge of what happens on a given day, we can always be in charge of how we think, feel, and respond to whatever occurs. One of the best things about creating a life in which you have more flexibility and control is that on any given day, literally anything can happen. Any day can be your big break or an unexpected opportunity. Starting your day with an attitude of hopeful anticipation sets the stage for recognizing whatever opportunities the day may bring.

Play heads-up ball. When I was growing up, my brother played Little League baseball. His coach was G. T. Rhodas, and G. T.

was a wise man. We learned from him that baseball is a lot like life; you've got to play heads-up ball—all the time. During a baseball game, depending on the position you play, there are many slow times, punctuated by sudden demands to act quickly and skillfully. One of G. T.'s biggest chores was to get the kids on the field to pay attention to what was going on during every moment of the game, even at times when it didn't seem like there was anything going on to pay attention to.

Well, that's precisely how it is in creating our own lives. We're going along doing our thing, then suddenly life throws a wild pitch or hits a line drive our way and we have to be ready to respond instantly. We have to be playing heads-up ball or we miss the opportunities or, worse yet, get hit in the head. We can't be looking at our shoelaces. We have to be on our toes and keep our eye on the ball. But if we pay attention to what's happening on the field, if we read between the lines, we'll be better prepared to duck, take, bunt, or swing away at the situations life presents.

Who says, "Easy does it"? Humankind is often at its best under two circumstances: when we face a crisis and when we voluntarily take on a challenge. Obviously we don't want to go around creating crises for ourselves just so we can be at our best. But we can give meaning to our lives by taking on a challenge. We can go beyond our comfort zones, stretch ourselves, and strive to surpass what we and others expect. We can approach our lives in the spirit expressed by President John Kennedy in the early sixties when he said, "We choose to go to the moon in this decade, not because it is easy, but because it is hard."

Make your struggle a good one. Sometimes we think what we want most is a stress-free life, but in fact, what we really need is an opportunity to strive and struggle for a worthwhile goal that we have freely chosen. Through such struggle, we transverse the gap between what we are and what we can become. We "fulfill" ourselves. Twice recently I have been reminded that a certain amount of tension between our reality and our desires is a healthy state for one's work and one's life. It gives us meaning and purpose. At first I resisted. "No," I thought, "I'm tired of struggling. I want things to come effortlessly." But then I remembered the most joyful times of my life and, indeed, they were all times when I was giving my all for a worthwhile goal. Not needless, routine, and meaningless struggle, but struggle that accomplishes something larger and more important than ourselves.

From darkness comes the light. Martin Luther King said, "Only when it's dark enough do we see the stars." What path has no shadows? We cannot fear adversity, nor can we despair of its arrival. Often it's how we find our way, for in darkness we must seek and in seeking we find insight, clarity, and wisdom. So take heart and know an honorable journey is well worth whatever struggles it presents.

When times are tough, remember your time will come. It's not unusual to experience a round of disappointments when you start to follow a dream. In fact, at one time or another it may even seem like everything is going down the tubes. The best antidote we know for such times is to decide that they're a sign that something better is coming your way. Call it mind games if you will, but it works. Anticipating something better right around the corner lifts your spirits so you can see new options, stay focused, and get to work doing whatever you need to do to make sure good things will materialize in the days and weeks ahead.

Discover what you want enough to persist through whatever arises. "Nothing in the world can take the place of persistence. Talent will not; nothing is more common than unsuccessful people with talent. Genius will not; unrewarded genius is almost a proverb. Education will not; the world is full of educated derelicts. Persistence and determination alone are omnipotent," said Thomas Watson, founder of IBM. So why is persistence so difficult for all us talented, educated geniuses? Is it that we are lazy laggards, softies who can't take the heat? No. We don't persist because we don't know what we want enough to persist. We get buffeted by circumstance, going first this way and then that. Or we don't claim the power of our innate talent, genius, and knowledge because we don't believe we can achieve what we seek, no matter how much we persist. So if we are to persist, we must listen to our hearts and believe in our abilities to follow wherever it leads.

Make yourself strong. "From where does the strength come to finish the race?" Eric Liddell poses in the movie *Chariots of Fire.* "From within." Sometimes we think we can't stand things another minute. Like a runner in a race, our lungs are bursting. We cannot catch our breath. Our muscles are strained to the limits. Then there comes a second wind, and we surge on. And, thus, we grow stronger. So to that voice within that cries out, "I can't go on," affirm with a certain voice, "I can."

We have strength within we never knew we had. Canadian Olympic medalist Elvis Stojko won his silver medal despite the fact that he was recovering from the flu and had a high fever during the week before his performance. Stojko went into the final round of competition with a torn groin muscle. How he completed seven triple jumps without a single error amazed the figure skating world and Stojko himself. He had to be assisted in walking to the scoring area and could not skate to the podium to receive his silver medal. Of the feat Stojko said, "I've never been so focused in my life. I heard nothing. I saw nothing. I don't even know what marks I got."

When asked why he did it he told reporters, "You've worked countless hours and sacrificed so much. I didn't want to look back and say I could have done it. I wanted to know I gave everything that I could possibly give." When asked to comment on his feelings about having to settle for a silver medal instead of the gold he could have attained if he'd been able to do a planned quadruple jump, he said, "It's a matter of dealing with what you have and not what you want."

Seize the moment. When we had the chance to see the New York stage production of Andrew Lloyd Webber's musical *Cats*, we had a surprise in store. As we took our seats and looked through the program guide, we were dismayed to discover that the three lead characters of the large cast would be played that evening by stand-ins. Our passing thought was how unfortunate it was that we would not get to see the best. Then the lights darkened and the spectacular staging of the evening began around us. As we walked back to our hotel, still under the musical's magical spell, we were commenting on the two show-stopping, breathtaking, goosebump-producing performances of the night. Who were those performers? we mused. Perusing the program guide, sure enough, they were Heidi Stallings and John Paul Christensen—the stand-ins!

We have all heard the saying "The more you give the more you get." Yesterday, I saw this principle in action. At the closing session of a four-day conference, the leader thanked all those who had helped with the event. The audience responded in appreciative applause to each name, yet what was most noteworthy was that the applause, hoots, and hollers exploded in direct proportion to how much of themselves each of these individuals had given to the group. The more a person had invested of themselves in our well-being, the more they had extended themselves, the more raucous the appreciation. This applies directly to creating our dreams. If we want to receive rich rewards from our efforts, we can never simply go through the motions, doing as little as possible to meet our obligations. We must invest our bodies, minds, and souls in giving our best to each client and customer.

Put yourself fully into what you do. Some of us step timidly into our work with soft, hesitant strides; others jump in with full-bodied gusto, giving our all and literally breathing life into our intentions. The difference is dramatic and readily apparent to others. When we enter wholeheartedly into what we do, we have an impact on everyone we contact. They sit up and take notice. When we simply go through the motions, we're easily overlooked. The effect of our work fades quickly into the background, unnoticed. To have an impact on the world, you must enter robustly into what you do, give it your all and in so doing, the enjoyable results will provide you with still more energy to put back enthusiastically into your work.

You can stand the heat. "A clay pot in the sun will always be a clay pot," said Mildred Struven. "It must go through the white heat of the furnace to become porcelain." She could just as easily have been talking about creating the life we yearn for. Think of the times on your journey that have been the most difficult and how you feel about having survived those times. Ultimately, the heat of tough times makes us stronger, more confident, and more competent. It hones us for still more challenging activities. Many people pay good money to have tough experiences. They go on wilderness adventures, do bungee jumping, parachute from airplanes, walk over hot coals. They return from such endeavors feeling stronger and more confident. "If I can do that, then I can do anything." Well, when following our hearts, we don't have to pay to have such experiences unless we want to have them just for the fun of it. Creating a dream leads us on many harrowing adventures and takes us out on a limb many times a day. We may feel like we're walking on hot coals or diving out of an airplane, but if we continue we'll have the joy that only accomplishing a dream can bring.

You're doing fine; keep practicing. When I was growing up everyone had to take gym classes. I never did very well in gym because we weren't taught how to do the sport of the month; we were just given a chance to try it out and then were graded on how well we did. Since I had never played basketball before, I didn't do very well on the free throw test. Since I had never climbed a rope before, I didn't do very well on the rope-climbing test. So I concluded that I was no good at sports.

There is a sad life lesson in this story. It's a lesson many of us learn somewhere in life and it's a lesson that prevents us from fulfilling our highest desires. The conclusion I reached was that you're either good at something or you're not. What I missed is that we can *learn* to make free throws or climb ropes. In fact, only later did I discover that those who do well at making free throws or climbing ropes have usually not only done it before, but spent many hours practicing it. And so it is with creating the life we desire. We're all practicing our livelihood and the longer we do it, the more we learn and the more we learn, the better we get.

So if you're not achieving your goals as yet, remind yourself that as long as you're learning from what you are doing, you're doing fine. Like all the girls in my gym class, we each have a learning curve. Some of us start from ground zero, as I did with basketball, so it takes us a bit longer to get the ball in the hoop. Others of us have had a lot of practice already. We need to start from wherever we are and move ahead, continuing to practice getting the ball into the hoop until we can get it there most of the time.

Through achievement comes understanding. "You have to move through the darkness of your pain alone," said the Indian teacher Agnes Whistling Elk, "so you can emerge on the other side through the effort of your own individual will. From your extraordinary isolation of will, you feel the first taste of true achievement." We do feel alone sometimes as practical dreamers, but from the knowing silence of night comes the wisdom of day. Once the sun rises, knowing we can come through the night on our own, we find the meaning of all the pain in the joy of our achievement.

Embrace mistakes. Don't dismiss them as unimportant, unchangeable, or something you can't handle. Don't berate or blame yourself, someone else, or fate. Don't blame, period. Don't make excuses, feel sorry for yourself, or give up. Don't use your mistakes as evidence that you can't succeed. Don't worry endlessly about where you went wrong. When you make a mistake, compliment yourself for your courage and ingenuity in trying what you did. Remain confident in your ability to excel. Resolve not to repeat the same mistake. Take responsibility, do necessary damage control, and make it right, if you can. Apologize if others have been adversely affected. Learn everything you can from it and immediately try again to do it differently from then on with the confidence of knowing you won't ever have to make that mistake again.

Move on. There are important lessons to be learned when things don't go as planned. We must look for those lessons and then shift our focus back to the road we're on. We can't undo what's done, but we can redo it. So as the head of Northern American Aviation said in the HBO mini-series *From the Earth to the Moon,* "You've gotta let go of the 'what if's'. . . they'll kill ya." Imagining what could have been is only useful when it helps us toward what can be.

Do you ever feel like giving up? Most practical dreamers feel like quitting from time to time. It's a natural response to an extended or particularly difficult challenge. At such times, it's easy to feel like, "Hey, who needs this?" or "I can't stand another minute of this." What marathon runner hasn't felt like that at some point in the race? Ironically, creating a simpler, more balanced life can itself feel like running a marathon at times. So feeling like quitting need not be considered negative. It doesn't mean you're a weak-willed pessimist. It doesn't even mean you don't like what you're creating. The impulse to quit is like a self-test mechanism. It gives you a chance to check out your motivation. It reminds you that you really are your own boss in life. You can quit any dream. You have freedom of choice. You can shape your life.

When we truly realize that we have a choice, if we can continually reconnect with what originally motivated us to do what we're doing, we can recharge our commitment with resolve. If we can't connect with our resolve day after day, it's a sign we need to make a change. It's time for a course correction. We must either redirect life so we can feel motivated and energized to pursue it once again or head off in a new direction our energy wants to go in.

Greet challenge with confidence. You're already an old hand at handling challenges. Any new endeavor can seem arduous, terrifying, and even impossible. But all through life, from our first day of school to our first date to our first job, with time, the terrifying becomes commonplace; the arduous becomes second nature; and the impossible becomes routine. In fact, often even the most difficult of accomplishments gradually pass almost unnoticed into our repertoire. With mastery, great challenges become mundane and we quickly seek new ones. So greet today's challenge as another stranger who, if you wish, will soon become an old friend.

SATISFACTION— ENJOYING YOURSELF

How much joy can you stand?
SUZANNE FALTER-BARNS

Writer Suzanne Falter-Barns saw the couple standing in an elevator. They were obviously in love. When the three of them struck up a conversation, Falter-Barns asked the couple, "How is it you can be so in love?" "Oh, some days are ecstatic," the woman replied, "and other days we'd like to kill each other, but how much joy can you stand?" The comment inspired Falter-Barns to write a book about the fears that stop people from pursuing their dreams. But when she discussed this comment on our radio show, I thought of something else. I wondered about the fears that prevent us from enjoying ourselves when our dreams come true.

A chain of pictures and feelings flashed through my mind. . . . The way I'd felt when I left my government job to go out on my own—like "Queen for a Day"! I could get up when I wanted. Watch a soap opera if I wanted. Pick up my son after school and, if I wanted, stand on the sidelines to watch him play soccer.

. . . The ecstasy I'd felt on our first drive through Topanga Canyon when looking for a home in California. The pines. The jagged rocks. The jaw-dropping beauty. And the realization that PEOPLE LIVE HERE!

. . . A large room in Atlanta, Georgia, packed with close to a thousand people listening to us talk about starting their own businesses. The crowd leaving with armfuls of our books. Happy, excited people, eager to begin a new life.

. . . The green room before our first appearance on the *Today* show. A moment in time so long awaited. So long prepared for. Here at last. Blood pumping through my heart in anticipation.

. . . Our first night in Pine Mountain, holding each other in the dark, enveloped in the crisp, fresh air from the open window. The first morning light streaking through the pines into the room to the call of the ducks.

Fleeting moments in time, the savory morsels of dreams fulfilled. All gone too quickly. Like a meal gobbled down without time to taste its flavors. Or dipping your toe in an icy lake only to pull it out in fear of its bracing welcome. So many moments, gone as quickly as they came . . . until . . .

The joy of my newfound freedom from a harried job had dissolved too quickly into the fear of not having enough business. The joy of possibly living in the Topanga mountains near the sea had dissolved into disbelief that this could be for me. The joy of my long-awaited career success had dissolved quickly into concern about what would happen next. But not this time, I thought. This time, I wanted to savor living in Pine Mountain for a long time to come. While years ago after finally quitting my job I literally couldn't sit still for five minutes to just savor the pleasure of being my own boss, this time I wanted to sit in silence for hours, doing little more than breathing in the teeming wildlife around me.

Why is it we have such a dreadful time enjoying ourselves? I don't mean the way we've learned to party ourselves into frenzied celebration. Most of us have done that. We've got that down. It's one of the few acceptable outlets for joy in our culture, but often we're barely conscious during such festivities. Our emotions and feelings are numbed by the noise and activity swirling around us, washed down and drowned in an endless stream of wine or a few six-packs of beer, deadened by an onslaught of salty snacks, stringy pizza, greasy burgers, French fries, and potato chips with dip. In fact, sometimes we actually abuse ourselves in the name of enjoyment, bludgeoning ourselves mercilessly in an effort to feel good.

No, I mean, why is it so hard for us to just sit still for a while and feel content and fulfilled? Why do we have to have just one more bite and one more dessert until we feel so stuffed that we suffer through our joy? Has satisfaction been a dirty word? Yes, *Entrepreneur* magazine concluded when year after year Gayle Sato Stodder would interview successful entrepreneurs to determine if they felt satisfied with their success. "It was as if I'd inquired about a criminal activity or the prospect of death," she wrote.

But times have changed. Changed for me and changed for many of us. This past year when Stodder dared to ask once again if the most successful among us were satisfied with their lives, she found a new attitude toward satisfaction. Greg Giaforte, co-founder of a New Jersey software company, for example, told Stodder about how he once fretted into the night about his competition and worried by day about missing opportunities. Now, having sold his company, moved his family to Bozeman, Montana, and started a smaller company, he limits his business travel.

He takes time to enjoy the satisfaction of using his skills to do worthwhile work, being with his family, fishing and flying, and having enough money to support a life he can enjoy. He and his wife sat down and decided to draw a line, identify a point where they had enough to pause and take a breath, and make satisfaction a top priority in their life.

Where do you draw the line? When do you allow yourself to take a breath and enjoy the fruits of your life, meager or lush as they may be?

It seems many of us are ready to pause for contentment, even if briefly. We're ready to say, "Yes, this is enough for the moment, let me enjoy it!" This new attitude says it's OK to feel great, even if we haven't done everything or accomplished everything or gotten everything we could. Eight years ago, for example, Tracy Porter and her husband moved to rural Wisconsin to be closer to nature. They started their own business, Tracy Porter—The Home Collection, designing and licensing upscale home furnishings. It's been a difficult experience, Porter told Stodder, but "being satisfied means many things . . . It means that every day we're on an amazing journey. It means we're laughing no matter what is going on."

Maybe we're realizing it's not possible or even necessary to be the Energizer rabbit. It's not nature's way to only produce. There's an inhale and pause before the next exhale. There's a lull even in the midst of a storm. It's the nature of things, to feel desire, take action to fulfill it, and then feel satisfaction.

How much do you have to accomplish or need to achieve before you pause and enjoy yourself?

Satisfaction is the opposite of obsession. Obsession is like a record player stuck on a scratch; it prevents us from moving on. When we're obsessed with fulfilling a desire, we're no longer freed by our dreams but enslaved to them. Satisfaction, on the other hand, offers the freedom to pursue and enjoy whatever you're doing, both while you're doing it and once it's completed. Satisfaction is a pit stop, not a finish line. It's part of the game, not the end; it's like the completion of an inning or a quarter. It allows us to continually refresh, reflect, recharge, and refuel. The practical dreamer knows that without satisfaction, no matter how magnificent a dream may appear, there is only exhaustion.

This section is about how we can breathe in as well as out. It's about how to stop pursuing long enough to enjoy the pursuit. It's about allowing ourselves time to appreciate this moment before rushing on to the next. It's about giving ourselves time for gratitude. It's about pausing long enough to allow the quiet, still waters within us to flow on their own into a new desire, a desire we might never have imagined in the whirl of dreaming and doing. In this way, success never becomes a burden, but is instead always an intriguing doorway between what is and what could be.

9

FEELING FULFILLED

> *The moment of victory is far too short*
> *to live for that and nothing else.*
>
> MARTINA NAVRATILOVA

Max Carey's life had been the epitome of the American success story. Always a top student, he set NCAA records as a defensive back on the Columbia University football team. After graduating from Columbia he became a Navy pilot, earned Top Gun certification, and flew more than 100 combat missions off aircraft carriers over Vietnam. After completing his military service, he joined a major corporation and climbed from entry-level salesman to national marketing manager in only five years. In 1981, he left corporate life to start his own business. But while pursuing the American dream, Carey had no idea he was creating a set of habits that would one day become his undoing.

His intention was to start a business, be successful, get rich, have a great family and a great life. Instead, within a year he was in dire straits. "All of a sudden, me being the superman, me doing it all, me running it all, me driving it all wasn't working. For the first time in my life," he recalls, "I was failing." His staff plummeted from six people to one. The gas and water were turned off in his home. His car was repossessed. "I was in trouble, so with my typical Superman resolve, I started to sell harder and work

harder. I did everything in the business because it was only me."
Over the next year, he was beginning to pull the business back up,
when one day he just started to shut down.

Carey found himself breaking into tears against his will. At
first he pushed these episodes aside, but they happened again and
again until finally tears started running down his face in the middle of a business meeting. He was scared to death. "I was afraid I
was having a breakdown. I saw the possibility of losing everything
I had." The new employees he'd recruited to come on board to
work with a fearless and invincible leader were concerned. His
wife who had loved and trusted him to always be there to lead saw
his distress and became frightened, too.

Carey was in such distress that he decided to consult an old
friend who was a psychologist. "You're not losing your mind," his
friend told him. "Your body is telling you that the way you've
lived, the way you've driven yourself, and the way you've motivated yourself is no longer working. You are totally and completely depleted, physically, psychologically, and emotionally, and
you're going to have to make some changes."

Carey had peaked out. Over time he'd become so driven, so
one-dimensional in the pursuit of his dreams, that he'd lost the
richness and the fullness of the other sides of life. He was suffering from what he now calls the "Superman Complex," thinking
he should and could do everything. He was so ready to learn and
to heal that he hung on every word of his friend's advice.

"You've been through massive stress throughout your life," his
friend explained. "You've separated your world into that which
you believe you should be and that which you really are inside.
You've built a brick wall between the two, adding new bricks with
each year to keep them apart so you can be the high-achieving,
tough macho guy you think you should be. But it's taking more
and more of your energy to hold the wall up. Every day before
you start to do whatever's important to you, you're at least 50 percent depleted from trying to balance who you've become with
who you really are inside."

Carey felt a great sense of relief as his friend described what was happening to him. "We are led to believe," he points out in his book *The Superman Complex*, "that there is a certain model you need to achieve to be successful. It's the American dream: If you work hard, if you sacrifice, discipline yourself and focus, if you are willing to give up other luxuries in life and just get the job done, then you will be successful. That's been our definition of success."

In talking more with his friend, Carey discovered he had become addicted to achievement, addicted to his next success. "I wasn't even through with one success before I was no longer satisfied and was looking on to the next. There's nothing wrong with achievement," he emphasizes. "My goals today are higher than they've ever been. But it's a question of balance. It's a matter of what's motivating you, what achievements you're working toward and how you reward yourself for your achievements."

The biggest fear Carey had in making the changes he knew he needed to make was that he would be found out. "Maybe," he thought, "I'm not strong enough to be the person I've become." But his friend helped him to see that within our weaknesses lie our strengths. Once he discovered the impact of the Superman Complex on his life, he was able to take a good look at himself. Admitting he couldn't do it all himself and didn't have to helped him make the necessary changes in his life to have the peace and balance he'd missed for so long. Now, he's back and he's thriving. His relationships with his wife, his three children, and his employees are thriving. The company, CRD of Atlanta, Georgia, is back, too, and it's thriving. He's learned that, as singer James Taylor says, "The secret to life is enjoying the passage of time."

Carey has also learned that, as Mother Teresa taught, "To keep a lamp burning we have to keep putting oil in it." Having the time to feel the satisfaction of living is as much a part of the oil that keeps us going as are food, water, and sleep. We need to breathe, to feel, and to live consciously, or we get lost, swallowed up in the pursuit of the dream. It sweeps us off our feet and carries us away.

Have you been swallowed whole by your dream?

GET OUT OF THE WHALE'S STOMACH

Carey's story illustrates so graphically how, as in the tale of Jonah and the whale, our dream can swallow us whole if we don't pause to experience the best of what our lives have to offer. When we get lost in the dream, we lose ourselves, and when that happens, not only does the dream collapse, but we collapse. We become the character in the novel instead of ourselves. Our life becomes about the play. We're the corporate manager, the media personality, the mother, the community leader, an actor on the stage we've created instead of a living, breathing human being.

Carey's story could as easily be about a stay-at-home mom who lives twenty-four hours a day for her children or an environmentalist who has become obsessed with his cause. If what we're seeking prevents us from living, we've been eaten by our dream and must climb out from the belly of the whale and take our lives back.

Moving to Pine Mountain, I hoped, would be my way out of the whale's belly. What's yours?

Here now I'm in Pine Mountain—living my dream! It does feel like a living dream. I often get a feeling of déjà vu, like right now as I'm sitting at my computer, looking out on a stand of ancient ponderosa trees and the small pond where the ducks are making V-shaped trails across the surface of the water. There's a stellar blue jay foraging on our lawn, and the air is alive with a chorus of other birds. It feels so familiar here because I'd been imagining it for so long, living in my novel experience of it.

Stepping into the reality of my dream has been like returning home. I felt comfortable immediately. But the real thing is even better than I imagined. So . . . we're happy. The kind of glowing happy you feel when the world is young. The kind of happy you feel when you fall in love for the first time. Or when you wake up on Christmas morning as a child, eager and ready to discover what you'll find as you unwrap the day.

The kind of happy of a child at play, running in the wind, catching fireflies at dusk, making angels in the snow, weaving clover chains under a shady tree, frolicking in a sudden rain shower on a hot summer afternoon. So happy you're afraid to feel that happy, afraid it will end if you get caught feeling that way. But it's so delicious you throw caution to the wind and dare to let it fill you until you simply fall on your knees in gratitude and wish only to share it with everyone and everything.

I've felt this delicious feeling before, the feeling of living your dream . . . but only for a brief interlude before rushing on to something new. How long would it take this time, I wondered, for all this beauty, all this joy to fade into the background? Would I bring my harried, hassled life here? Would the whale pursue me and swallow me whole once again? I knew it would come for me, but could this time be different? Like Max Carey, must I always dash on to something new? What would life be like if it were savored extendedly? What would emerge on the other side? How much joy can I stand? And for how long?

We do change when we move to a new place. Environments do affect us and determine our behavior to some extent. So it's much easier to change who we are and what we do when we change where we live, but our personal habits and our career and family demands come along with us. So, as the saying goes, wherever you go, there you are. Until *we* change who we are and what motivates us, the same things that made the whale so attractive to us will continue to keep us under its influence. Am I ready to climb from the belly?

We each have our reasons for why we have to remain in the belly of the whale. What are yours? Do any of these sound familiar? Or do you have your own?

Stolen Bliss

"All good things come to an end," they say. If we really enjoy something, we fear it will just be taken away from us. But if we pretend we don't care, or if we just don't notice how well things are going, or maybe if we even mess things up a little so we can't enjoy them too much, then perhaps nothing will be able to steal our happiness. Even if all good things should come to an end, by not caring, we think perhaps we'll be cushioned from the pain of disappointment.

In reality, life changes whether we're happy or not. Things come and things go, however we feel about them. By not caring, we may not feel the pain of loss as much, should it come, but nor do we feel as much of the joy.

Empty Gas Tank

A few years ago, best-selling fiction writer Dean Koontz told us he writes every day, 365 days a year. If he ever stopped writing for even a day, he said he feared his creativity would dry up and he wouldn't be able to write anymore. Hopefully, he's gotten beyond that fear and now allows himself to savor a few days off here and there, or even a few weeks. But Koontz's fear is not unusual. Many of us fear that if we take our foot off the gas pedal for even a moment, we'll run out of gas and all our success will disappear. Only by pressing forward continually, we think, can we keep the good times rolling.

In reality, our talent is our talent. We don't lose it when we sleep and we won't lose it when we enjoy ourselves either. Actually, we're more likely to lose it if we don't take any breaks.

Undeserving

Perhaps we believe we don't deserve so much joy. Maybe no matter how hard we worked we don't think we've worked hard enough. Considering all the things we've done in our lives, how, we wonder, could we possibly deserve such blessings? "There's no rest for the wicked," you know.

Fact is, as long as we obtain our happiness through legal, moral, and ethical means that do no harm to others, we deserve whatever rewards we've created in our lives and we can feel grateful for the opportunity to enjoy them.

⟶ Try This ✩✩

Take a few minutes each night to list at least five things about your day for which you are grateful. Gratitude frees us to enjoy our good fortune with dignity and humility.

Bogeyman

Sometimes we can't shake the feeling that when things get too good something awful lies right around the corner. To really enjoy life for more than a passing, spontaneous moment, it seems to some, is tempting fate and attracting the next catastrophe. But if we keep our shoulder to the grindstone, then fate might pass us by and deliver its disasters elsewhere.

The reality is, bad things can happen whether our lives are going well or not; so we might as well enjoy ourselves before and even after misfortune could befall us.

Ripped Britches

If we really enjoyed ourselves, might we not get too big for our britches? Wouldn't feeling satisfied and content make it look like we're stuck-up, snooty, conceited, cocky, superior, and swelled-headed? It would be embarrassing. Wouldn't it be better to just play down our good fortune?

Actually, it's usually people who aren't happy who get too big for their britches. They feel unimportant so they puff themselves up to look important. Happy people are usually the first to celebrate and enjoy other people's happiness.

No Company

We all know misery loves company. If we were really happy, might we end up all alone? How much of our time with friends, colleagues, and family is spent sharing the ain't-it-awful's of life? If our happiness is more than a passing fancy, would our friends feel resentful and jealous?

In reality, there are people who are addicted to being miserable and they usually do hang out with others who are miserable; but are these the kind of people we want to hang out with? Good company enjoys the good along with the difficult.

 **Try This**

Spend time each day sharing and enjoying positive experiences with friends, colleagues, and family and inviting them to share and enjoy theirs with you.

Eternal Slobhood

If we were to really enjoy our lives, wouldn't we get so self-satisfied that we'd just turn into fat, lazy couch potatoes? "If I stop to relax," we think, "I might never start again." In other words, we fear that we're reluctant workers in the factory of life and that if we ever took a day off, we'd never come back to the factory. Chances are, if we've been driving ourselves relentlessly for too long, that could be exactly how we feel.

But in reality, if we go with the flow, in time we will move naturally from the joys of satisfaction to a desire for something new. Filling up doesn't keep us from getting hungry again. We will dream and do again in good time.

Junk Food Junkie

Some things we think will make us happy are like junk food. Instead of satisfying us, they leave us wanting more. Fame and fortune are two examples. We think they will make us happy, but like potato chips, they usually leave us all the more hungry. We can eat the whole bag and still yearn for another because they just don't fill us up.

Actually, true happiness lies in attaining the meat and potatoes of life, those things that are intrinsically fulfilling, like friendship, contribution, love, and the creation of something worthwhile.

Drama Freak

"If I get myself straightened out," she asked me in our counseling session, clearly concerned about something she needed to know, "will my life be as boring as yours?" Her question startled me. I had never found my life boring. But I had eliminated most of the needless drama of trauma from my life, filling it instead with things I find interesting and challenging. But she, like some people, had been in love with the drama of the pursuit, the chase, the endless quest for the new, the novel, the dangerously bizarre and wild.

If, in fact, someone finds the continual pursuit of the dramatic to be truly enjoyable, that's great. More often, however, as this woman came to realize, it's a continually frustrating, lonely, and empty experience. She had to learn how to replace the excitement of her trauma drama with the perhaps less dramatic but more fulfilling excitement of living an enjoyable life.

The Finish Line

Often we don't think we can take the time to enjoy ourselves because there's so much more to do. "I'd feel too guilty," we say. We think celebration is for the finish line, but in life we never really get to the finish line. We may accomplish this goal here or that goal there, but until we die, we're never really done.

The only people who don't have too much to do are bored teenagers. There will always be too much for us to do whether we stop to enjoy ourselves or not. If we wait until we're done, until everything is complete and perfect, we'll go to the grave waiting. As businessman Greg Giaforte told us, you have to draw your own finish line so you can celebrate, enjoy, and then when you're ready, move on to another race.

What are you waiting to finish before allowing yourself to get some satisfaction?

Starving Children

"But how can I feel good when there are so many miserable people and so many awful things going on in the world?" Guilt about having a good life often spurs us to make even the best life as miserable as possible, or at least just miserable enough to keep us from being truly happy.

In fact, the happier we truly are the more likely our happiness will flow into helping others who are less fortunate. Those who are always busy dreaming and doing don't have much happiness to spare. Nor do they have much time or energy left over to share. But happy people always seem to have lots to share and they love to spread their happiness around. It brings them even greater joy.

Idle Hands

Since we were children we've been admonished to keep busy. "Idle hands do mischief make." So we've learned that at least we've got to look busy. Otherwise, we'll get reprimanded, or worse, be given additional, usually unwelcomed, tasks to do. But if we look like we're working hard (which is hard enough in and of itself), those who would intervene in the flow of our lives will hopefully leave us be.

In fact, overworked hands make plenty of mischief in the form of mistakes, misjudgments, and missed opportunities, whereas the calm hand charts and steers a steady course.

DARE TO ENJOY, MAKE IT A PRIORITY

Perhaps it's the Puritan heritage of this country or maybe it's the American work ethic. Whatever it is, we have plenty of opportunities to fear actually enjoying ourselves. Contentment, gratification, happiness, satisfaction are all words that make us somewhat uncomfortable. We're never quite sure if we should be experiencing them and if so, for how long it's safe to do it. As the national weight statistics will attest, we have a hard time pushing away from the dinner table in this country and saying, "This is enough." Drawing the line takes courage.

Like everything else in life, whether we take time to feel satisfied is up to us. It's a choice we make. It's just another thing that's competing for space in our twenty-four-hour day. But satisfaction isn't much of a squeaky wheel. It's not clamoring for its place on our calendar. No deadlines press us to push all else aside to include it. Rarely is there anyone else demanding that we make room for it. Usually we're the only ones who can take a stand on its behalf. We have to make satisfaction a priority, just like other important aspects of life, or it will end up at the bottom of the "to do" list. Or may not even make the list. Often, maintaining and furthering a dream requires as much or more time and energy as creating it.

But we have the choice to stop and enjoy life anytime we want. We don't have to set aside an afternoon, evening, weekend, or weeklong vacation to feel fulfilled—although that's great, too. We don't need to hold our breath until we have time to come up for air on a few big occasions. We can enjoy hundreds and hundreds of tiny moments of fulfillment throughout the day from dawn to dusk by simply adding them onto each of the day's many cycles of dreaming and doing. It's our choice.

Try This

To practice putting satisfaction into your day moment by moment, begin by enjoying each bite of your meals. Instead of gulping them down while standing at the fridge, watching television, or working at your desk, find a quiet place to eat, sit down and savor each bite, concentrate on your desire for each one. Notice the aroma, taste, and texture of it as you put it into your mouth. Notice how satisfying it is, or isn't. Skip foods that aren't satisfying. Notice how good it feels to savor your meal.

LET LIFE IN

Making satisfaction a priority in life played an important role in Greg Giaforte's decision to move his family from New Jersey to Montana. He started a new, smaller company there, Right Now Web, producing software for technical support and customer service on the Internet. In Montana, he says, he can't numb himself to life the way he did in New Jersey, so it's easier now for him to let life in.

We can't feel satisfaction when we're closed down to life; yet so much about our fast-paced urban lives invites us to close down. I first noticed how true this is while I was walking home from the post office one day after we moved to Pine Mountain. "Why do I feel so much better here?" I was wondering as I took in the open, expansive blue sky and rolling pine-covered mountains that surrounded and dwarfed me. Here, I realized, I don't need to close down. I don't need to shield myself from the ruckus of the sounds and sights around me. In Santa Monica, without knowing it, I had become like a horse with blinders, narrowing my focus to only those things that I had to let in to go about my business.

Here, on the other hand, nature never lets me forget that there's more to life than me. Everything around invites me to experience life. It says, "LOOK, SEE, HEAR, FEEL." "Let me in!" say the mountains and the trees, the sun and breeze. "Notice me! I'm here. Don't look away. Don't shut down."

I walk out to get the paper and there it is. I look up from my computer, I glance out the kitchen window, I take the trash out onto the porch, and there it is. Everywhere I look, everywhere I turn, there's nature in its naked beauty. It surrounds me and won't allow me to turn it into background. It refuses to go unnoticed. Here it remains, as it once was everywhere, predominant. Not just during earthquakes, tornadoes, or hurricanes, but every day, every minute, always a presence, never letting me forget to breathe and let life in.

Without effort, the joy of life comes tumbling in, catching me unexpectedly again and again. Walking through the living room, intent upon my goal, working at my desk, putting the salmon in the microwave to defrost for dinner, I'm accosted by the pleasure of a breeze, or a shaft of sunlight, or the call of a nearby dove, the glimpse of a flock of red-wing blackbirds gliding across the meadow. And suddenly joy comes to me unasked, unsought, a surprise guest who drops by often just to say hello.

It feels good and I want more. I'm consciously stopping to let life in and taking time to savor the moment. Paul and I have located favorite spots around the house, both inside and out, where we can take special pleasure: around the hearth of the fireplace on our deck, under the rafters of a cozy room on the second floor, on a cushy leather couch in our office, on an old carved log overlooking the pond, alongside a stream down the street, or in our favorite meadow down the way.

Satisfaction needs fertile ground to put its roots down into the fabric of your life.

➡ **Try This** ☆☆☆

Take a joy break. Once you make satisfaction a priority, try taking frequent breaks of even a second or two anytime day or night to savor the moment. Notice what gives you joy in the moment. Is it the color of the print on your office wall? Is it the softness of the rug beneath your feet? Is it the light coming through your bedroom window? Is it the laughter of your children playing down the hall? Is it a hug from a friend or a kiss from a loved one? Fill your home, your office, and your life with things that call out to remind you regularly to savor and enjoy the dream-in-the-making that is your life.

FERTILE SOIL

Often we cut corners when building our dream. We forget the little details that symbolize what the dream is all about. Grace, for example, always wanted to work with children, so finally she garnered the courage to create her dream. She saved enough money to leave her job as a customer service rep, moved to a lower-cost area of her community, and took a job teaching art for a small government-funded not-for-profit school. Financially her income fell by nearly half, but psychically her income more than doubled. She felt so nourished by her work that she was willing to work long hours and forgo the many perks a bigger salary had provided. Gone were the weekly manicures and pedicures, the dinners out, the trips to the lake on weekends, the antiquing sprees with friends. In fact, she sold most of her furniture and traded in her car for a used model. But she was happy, at first.

She hadn't anticipated the long-term effects of the impoverished neighborhood where she worked or the sparse, utilitarian furnishings of her pared down studio apartment. "It's just a place to sleep," she told us. But soon she was dragging her way through the day, feeling as harried and drained as she had felt in her corporate job. The kids were as demanding as they were rewarding, and as the year sped by, she felt she had less and less to give them. Unintentionally, in the name of frugality, she'd planted her dream in barren soil and it was drying up before her eyes. She desperately needed to enrich the soil around her dream and fortunately, as Robbie Bogue has demonstrated, she wouldn't have to spend a fortune to do so.

Bogue was working as a sales executive for one of the largest printing companies in the nation when, as he puts it, "I was canned along with the president and fifteen other people in a corporate takeover." He began sending out résumés in search of another position, but in the back of his mind, a dream was beginning to take form. He was thinking about opening his own marketing company.

When one interview led to a job offer, Bogue realized if he was ever going to give going out on his own a try, the time was now. "If I hadn't given it a try then, I would never have known if I could have done it," he recalls. So he turned down the job offer and a week later, to his surprise, his potential employer called and asked to become his first customer! So Bogue got busy setting up his business.

Having been accustomed to the perks of an executive suite, he knew that the physical setting of his home office would be important to his success, so he made every effort to plant his dream in a pleasant and peaceful atmosphere. Bogue enjoys what he calls a "boutique" lifestyle. Every morning he gets dressed professionally for work and goes to his office, 100 feet away in a converted detached garage off the backyard of his home. It's a lovely, shaded walk down a stone pathway. The walkway is canopied by an ancient live oak tree so large and lush that Bogue and his clients don't even get wet walking to the office on a rainy day. "I don't drive a Mercedes," Bogue says. "I spend my money on art."

His office is decorated with art he has collected. Music from his jazz collection can be heard in the background while he works. He has chosen comfortable seating beside large windows that look onto the lush tree-shaded patio. The relaxing sounds of a small waterfall in the backyard adds to the office ambience, as does the gurgling fish tank he's turned into a novel coffee table.

Not only do these special touches help Bogue to be more creative, they also make it easier to get to work in the morning. He always looks forward to the short walk to his garage-based office and he never has trouble motivating himself to get to work on Mondays. Bogue lives in the heart of the suburbs, but his home and office are as tranquil and pleasant as any remote locale. He's demonstrated that if we make the effort, we can fill our life and work with things that feed our dreams and remind us to savor the choices we've made.

Grace discovered this as well. Enjoying her work had been her dream and she wasn't willing to lose it to the poverty of the environment around her. She began adding personal touches to her home, including family mementos from her parents' attic and artwork from the children in her classes. She enlisted their help to build a fountain in the entryway of the school. Together, they planted a garden around the fountain, including a weeping willow tree. Over the year she decorated the hallways and classrooms with art from the children's class projects. Soon, both her home and the school were nurturing her well-being and feeding her dreams beyond what she could have imagined.

She began hosting art showings at the school for fund-raising events. Donors, moved by the love and caring they saw, increased their contributions, providing the school with new funds to create an even more inspiring environment for the school, the children, and the community.

A nurtured dream soon has glorious children of its own. Are you nurturing your dream? Is it planted in fertile soil? Does it call out to be saved? Are its roots growing into the fabric of your life? What new dreams will come from savoring the fulfillment of the life you're creating?

I awoke to the dawn's first light, arose quietly, and walked softly to our deck. This time, as the sun crept through the Jeffrey pines and inched its way down the mountainside to the meadow, I sat in silence, breathing in the teeming wildlife around me. I was happy, really happy . . . awaiting a new day.

REFERENCES

How Much Joy Can You Stand? How to Push Past Your Fears and Create Your Dreams. Suzanne Falter-Barns. Beyond Dreams Publishing. ISBN 1-58270-003-6.

The Superman Complex: Achieving the Balance That Leads to True Success. Max Carey. Longstreet Inc. ISBN 1-56352-516-x.

10

APPRECIATING THE PROCESS

Our natures lie in motion . . .
without which we die.

BLAISE PASCAL

Tomorrow's dreams are born on the shoulders of today's.
As we bask in the enjoyment of having fulfilled our desires,
we soon see new opportunities and become dissatisfied with
things we once overlooked or found tolerable. We begin considering new possibilities that might not have seemed possible or
even desirable before. New desires begin to stir within us and the
creative cycle begins again—unless . . .

He grew up on the wrong side of the tracks, the son of the
black sheep in a prominent family. They, the rest of the family,
lived in East Haven, on tree-lined boulevards with manicured
lawns in stately homes with circular drives. Every year since he
could remember, he and his family would be invited to visit their
well-to-do relatives for special holiday festivities. He would leave
the 900-square-foot, rented frame house where he lived with his
parents and older sister and travel across town. There the streets
had curbings and sidewalks. The houses never seemed to need a
new coat of paint and there were no old couches, mattresses, or
cars on cinder blocks in the front yards.

He always looked forward to those holidays because in his

imagination he was never going to visit; he was going home where he belonged. He decided, at quite a young age, that there had been some grand mistake in the scheme of things. Somehow he had been delivered to the wrong parents in the wrong house. When he grew up, he would say to himself every day, he would take his rightful place and live on a boulevard in East Haven. He would have the marbled entry hallway, the wide spiral staircase, the lush carpeted rooms, the glittering chandeliers, the verandas and gardens that left him wide-eyed with delight on every holiday.

More than twenty years had passed since I'd seen him, but I knew he'd achieved that dream years ago. He lived on the boulevard, next door, in fact, to one of the homes he'd visited as a child. While most of the prominent families had long since moved from the area, there was still a sense of gentility about the aging neighborhood that had for so long been the focus of his dreams. Now, as he recognized me across the room, his face lit with a wide smile. He rushed to greet me with a round of hardy bellowing "Hellos," arm pumping mine a little too long and a little too hard. "Sarah, so good to see ya! Let me get you a beer," he offered eagerly, his speech slurred, his eyes glassy, his face red and puffy.

His wife had left him a year before, I learned, taking the kids with her. "Still working at the same damned place I have been for thirty years," he groaned. But, he explained quickly, the smile once again spreading across his face, he was redecorating the house again this year. He went on to tell me about the dramatic changes he was making in the carpeting, the railing on the staircase, the new stereo sound system. "I'm doing it all myself. It's still a work in progress," he declared with a pride that oozed from every pore. "You should come by sometime," he added.

I wanted to be happy for him. But I couldn't. Despite all the show, he was not a happy person. He seemed to think he was, but instead, he was stuck in yesterday's dream, living a life he'd imagined more than forty years before. In reality, he was an alcoholic, financially secure, but alone and overworked; afraid to let his dream move on to whatever else it might become. Where, I wondered, would the desires of the forty-nine-year-old man he was today lead him if he would step outside of the world he'd created as the five-year-old boy he had been? It appeared no one would ever know. I could only imagine.

Sometimes when we've wanted a dream very much and worked very hard for many years to attain it, we become overidentified with it and can't let our life go on without it. The irony is we think we're happy, because, after all, we're living our dream! It's what we always wanted. How could we not be content? But, if we're paying attention, there are signs that let us know when we're stuck in an outdated dream.

Are you stuck in a dream of the person you used to be? Do any of these sound familiar?

– Does it take a lot of energy to project the happiness and contentment you want to convey to the world?

– Are you exhausted after telling people about yourself and your life?

– Are you doing more drinking, smoking, binge eating, or any other addictive behavior?

– Do things that once left you feeling fulfilled seem more like responsibilities than opportunities? Do you drag your way through them?

– Are you sighing a lot throughout the day? Do you hear yourself complaining or whining about things you used to look forward to?

DREAMS MOVE ON

Like children, all dreams move on. They grow up. They mature. They have children of their own. It's the nature of life. Desire, action, satisfaction. Practical dreamers love this creative process even more than any particular dream because they love life and this is life, the endless rhythmic cycle of the inhale and the exhale, the inspiration and the manifestation.

Like artists, practical dreamers love coming up with new ideas and new possibilities they can create. They love rolling up their sleeves and getting into the process of creating them. They love the satisfaction of having completed what they set out to do. They love to savor their creations. They like looking at them, exploring and admiring them. They even love sending their creations home with new buyers who they hope will cherish and adore them (although saying goodbye to one's creations isn't always easy either for them). They even enjoy the lull between dreams as a time to relax and restore their creative energy.

In an ideal world, the creative cycle of desire moving into action, followed by the respite of satisfaction would flow effortlessly from one phase to another. Just as we are feeling fully satisfied we would move easily and naturally on to new desires and new dreams. But the process doesn't always flow so easily. Sometimes a dream may end before we are ready to move on, or we may be ready to move on but can find no new dream to take on.

I'm Not Done

Her heart felt like it was being ripped from her body. "I'd had disappointments before," she told us, "but it was never this bad. Before there was always hope for the next time. I was so happy—happy beyond words. But now I have to say good-bye to all I've worked for." The dream she'd been living and savoring had come to an abrupt and premature end.

Since the first time Julia sang in church as a child, she'd dreamed of becoming a professional singer. She sang the lead roles in all the high school musicals, won a role in summer theater productions, and starred in her college arts program. After graduation came a few minor productions, a few horrifically disappointing auditions, and finally her big break. She toured for a year with a traveling company. She was living her dream and it was even better than she'd imagined . . . until she developed a growth on one of her vocal cords.

At first she thought it was just a temporary interruption in her career, but soon it became clear that she would not be able to sing again professionally. Her vocal cord would recover, but she would have a limited range of vocalization and speak with a slightly deep and raspy voice. "Oh, how I wanted it to go on," she remembers, tears still pooling in her eyes as she spoke of that time in her life. "I wanted to cling to that dream. I wanted to throw my arms around it and hold on for dear life. I wanted to scream and beg and throw myself before the forces that be in anguish. Please, please, please. I'm not done. There's so much more. I haven't finished. Please, please keep this dream alive!"

But it was not to be. Her plate at the banquet had been snatched away before she'd finished enjoying its delights. Every dream has its own life span. Some are short. Others are long. Some are like a fine meal that leaves us feeling satisfied for a long time. Others are like a quick snack that leaves us feeling hungry again almost immediately. The most difficult dreams, however, are usually those like Julia's that get snatched from us before we've had the time to fully savor them, time to roll around and wallow in them and just soak them up. The most difficult dreams are those that end before we can heave that mighty sigh of satisfaction that says, "AHHHHHH, yes, that was great!"—the sigh that leaves us ready to rise from the table feeling better than ever and ready to get on with the rest of life.

Often, when faced with the premature death of a dream, instead of facing the fact that it's over and time to move on, we simply pretend it hasn't ended. Julia couldn't do that because she couldn't sing no matter how hard she tried. She couldn't pretend her life hadn't changed. But Barbara could. Also a singer in the same touring company, Barbara finished the tour and planned to go on with her career. She'd hoped the experience would lead to bigger and better things. Instead, she couldn't find anything that would live up to the success she'd had while touring with the company. She ended up eking out a living in smoky rundown bars in truck stops where the crowds talk raucously throughout her sets. Although her heart was breaking, she pretended she didn't care, preferring to imagine herself still as the traveling diva she'd been and hoped to be again.

I believe that's what my friend from so long ago has been doing as well. Living in the shell of a dream, pretending things are as they were. Unfortunately, or actually fortunately, as long as we're still sane, reality eventually wins such flights of fancy. The question is how long it takes us to recognize what's happening and what we're going to do about it.

Many things can suddenly make our dream obsolete: illness, divorce, the death of loved ones, the economy, technology, or just the ways things are. The recession, for example, wiped out Arielle Ford's thriving public relations business. The Tax Reform Act eliminated the need for the specialized type of tax accounting Payne Harrison provided, drying up all the demand for his business. The oil embargo sent Mark Victor Hanson's prefab housing business down the tubes overnight. Illness ended J. B. Morningstarr's career as a highly paid engineer. It prevented Deb Holmes from continuing her beloved work as a forest ranger. It stopped interior designer J. T. Taylor from doing the work she loved. Actress Sandy McKnight's agent died and the steady stream of roles she'd enjoyed dried up almost overnight in spite of her new agent's efforts.

When life snatches our dream before we're complete, it's a lot like being left by a lover. Or falling down in the middle of a performance. We have to get back up and ask ourselves, "Now what?" That's what the writers and directors of highly acclaimed television shows have to do every time one of their critically acclaimed television shows gets canceled—which is all too often. They've conceived a masterpiece. They've created it and it's impacting people's lives for the better, stopping them in their tracks, waking them up and showing them a side of life and themselves they've never seen before, delighting or disgusting them or perhaps a bit of both, but certainly entertaining them. Praise pours in from the critics. Fans fall in love with what's unfolding each week. But if ratings aren't good enough with the right target group of people, even brilliance isn't enough to save some of the best of shows. They're yanked from the air and the dream is over.

But practical dreamers invariably come back again. They're ready to do the next show, create the next work of art, find the next lover, give the next performance. When Stephen Bochco stumbled with *Cop Rock*, he came back with *Murder One* and *Brooklyn South*. When those were canceled, he came back again with *City of Angels*. After *Thirtysomething*, Edward Zwick came back with *Once and Again*. In this same vein, Arielle Ford rebuilt her PR business after becoming an author herself, writing books like *Hot Chocolate for the Mystical Soul*. To keep from sinking into despair while looking for another job, Payne Harrison wrote a novel based on his passion for the Air Force. That book, *Storming Intrepid*, was published and Harrison became a novelist! Mark Victor Hanson came back as a motivational speaker and is now the world-renowned co-author with Jack Canfield of the *Chicken Soup for the Soul* series.

After moving home with her parents, Deb Holmes healed her body and in the process became an artist and poet. In her efforts to recover from her illness, J. B. Morningstarr experimented with making healthy desserts she could eat on her newly restricted diet. The results led to a new career in her own business, Healthy Chocolates. She now works from home at her own pace instead of putting in long, grueling hours in a facility that was making her ill.

J. T. Taylor shifted her work from decorating to another life-long passion. She works with other decorators as a collector of rare and fine artwork. Sandy McKnight began offering voice coaching and now conducts the popular Theatre of Life training program, helping individuals and corporate staff "find their

voice" through drama. Changing careers also enabled McKnight
to leave Los Angeles and move to a ranch outside Santa Fe, an
area of the country that feeds her creativity and speaks more directly to her heart and soul.

Each of these new dreams was born on the shoulders of past
ones and could not have been anticipated until the previous
dream had been snatched away. If we listen, if we wait, our
dreams, even those that are snatched from us before they're finished, will produce another generation of children all their own.

*How many times do we need to go through this cycle before we learn
there is always, always another dream if we will but welcome it? What
have your faded dreams bequeathed to you? What heirlooms have they
left for you? What new seeds have they sown in your heart and soul?*

WAIT UNTIL DINNER

I've never been good at waiting. When I was a child I was usually hungry well before my mother had dinner on the table.
"Wait until dinner," she'd admonish me when I'd beg for a snack.
"You don't want to spoil your meal." With much moaning and
groaning, I'd have to wait. Even to this day, I'm often hungry before the "dinner hour." But now, of course, I don't have a mother
to make me wait, so sometimes I don't. I grab something from the
fridge and gobble it down while standing at the door, only to regret it later when I'm not hungry for what should have been a satisfying dinner.

So it is with dreaming the next dream. Sometimes we're hungry before dinner, ready to move on to a new dream when there's
nothing on the table yet. We're such a purposive species that we
may soon feel pressed to get going somewhere even when there's
nowhere we really want to go.

Our neighbor and photographer Mary Ann Halpin was ready
for a new dream. She had been for some time. In 1997, she completed a dream that had been five years in the making. Her first

coffee table art book, *Pregnant Goddesshood: A Celebration of Life,* was published. The story of that book is featured in Arielle Ford's book *More Hot Chocolate for the Mystical Soul,* and it was a magical journey from which Mary Ann learned a lot about waiting and trusting her creative muse. But it was two years later and that trust was being tested.

The photo book had begun with Mary Ann's concern about how self-conscious and dissatisfied so many women are with their bodies. While photographing a pregnant client, she noticed that this woman was refreshingly comfortable and at ease with her body. Some time later, she mentioned this observation and her interest in body image to her friend Cassandra, who was pregnant, too. In the conversation, Mary Ann also mentioned that she wanted to do a photo book about women on skid row, so her friend suggested the name of an editor who might be interested in the book.

When Mary Ann called, the editor listened politely to the idea but explained that while she wouldn't be interested in a book about women on skid row, she would be interested in the book Mary Ann was doing on pregnant women. Disappointed, Mary Ann explained that she wasn't doing a book on pregnant women, but the editor was sure Cassandra had told her about such a book and urged Mary Ann to call back if she decided to do one.

A week passed, Mary Ann remembers, before a voice went off in her head saying, "If you don't do this pregnancy book, someone else will." She called the editor back and the book was born. "Sometimes," she told us in reflecting on the experience, "if you don't listen to your creative muse, it goes to someone else who will listen for you. Thank goodness Cassandra was listening." And since the book came out Mary Ann has been listening, too. But as the lull following publication stretched from days into weeks, weeks into months, and months into years, it was difficult to keep waiting for the voice of her muse to return. Like so many of us, her need for accomplishment kept pressing her to do *something* productive.

"I've felt scattered at times," she admits, but "we can't force the creative process." Instead of being impatient or starting something just to have something new, she's spent her time feeling grateful for the success she's had and trusting that the next inspiration will come. She continued running her studio and spent lots of time cleaning, redecorating, and just enjoying her home in Pine Mountain. "When I don't know what to do next, I do what inspires me. If that's a false start, I do the next thing that inspires me. I'm confident that if I keep hopping from one inspiration to the next, I'll eventually get across the river and discover where I'm going."

For a time she created a workshop for actors with a life coach. It was a great success, but doing the workshops didn't ignite the fire in the belly she'd hoped for. She organized a group for artists in Pine Mountain, in which she still participates with Jeannie Quintana. But again there was no burning flame to take off running with. She worked up a few new ideas for photo books. Again, nothing stuck. No magic. No fire. Until . . . eventually hopping from inspiration to inspiration led to an intriguing and serendipitous new dream.

When Linda Miller decided to open the first B & B in Pine Mountain, Mary Ann, Jeannie Quintana, and Eileen Applegarth (who were enjoying their own lull following the music festival), and another friend, Laurel Quinn, came up with the idea to help Linda decorate the rooms. They each "adopted" one of the four bedrooms. Mary Ann chose to create the Forest Room and, as part of the design for the room, she had an inspiration. She would photograph local children with various objects from nature relating to the themes of the rooms like apples, trees, flowers, and the like. She also wanted to interview the children on digital video talking about their feelings about nature and their life in Pine Mountain.

"I don't know yet why I'm doing this," Halpin admits. "I don't know where it's leading, but I know that I'm inspired and I'm trusting my inspiration." There's fire in this desire and it's taking on a life of its own. It might lead to a new photo book or a documentary about what a community of friends can do when they share a dream. Regardless of where it may lead, Mary Ann knows there's something on the table now that she can sink her teeth into because "It's happening effortlessly and that's what I love. I love to follow my energy."

 **Try This**

Are you willing to wait and allow your natural creative desire to speak to you? Are you listening or doing all the talking? If this is difficult for you, try going fishing or bird-watching. From these activities we can learn much about patience and waiting in silent anticipation. Or just sit down, close your eyes, and listen. But have a pad of paper and pencil nearby, because ideas may come fast and furiously.

LOOK AND LISTEN

My new dream started two summers ago, a full year before we visited Pine Mountain for the first time. Paul and I had gone to do a workshop in San Diego and while participating in the program, I had my first inkling that a new desire might be growing in my heart. Little did I know at the time that it would change the course of my life.

On the final day of the workshop a scene flashed into my mind, a scene I'd never imagined before. I was a very old woman, sitting in a circle teaching half a dozen or so other people who had come a long way to see me. I felt like it was a glimpse into the future. "That's how you're going to support yourself in your old age," I thought to myself. "What?" I interrupted that thought abruptly. This image didn't fit with my plans. Paul and I expected to live out our old age updating our books. With that reminder, the image of the old lady flew from my mind as quickly as it had come.

But it didn't stay away for long. It kept drifting back over the weeks and months that followed. As it returned again and again like an itch that demands to be scratched, I could no longer dismiss it. I grew curious about what it might mean. What was I doing in this dream? Where was I living that involved people coming from a distance? What was I teaching that drew them there? But nothing came to mind. I didn't understand this image, but I was inexplicably attracted to it, so much so that by the end of the year I told Paul about it while we were on vacation and taking a quiet afternoon to discuss our intentions for the new year.

"I think we should consider doing something new," I suggested because I couldn't see how the life we were living at the time would ever lead us to the scene I kept imagining. Paul was intrigued, but not terribly interested in heading off in some new as-yet-unseen direction. We had a lot of work on our plate. A lot of responsibilities. We were living in our dream home in a dream location, doing the work of dreams. Why would we break up a winning hand? Our future seemed pretty much on track.

About that time, a friend approached us about doing a seminar on finding your perfect work, the subject of one of our books. "Oh!" I thought. "This is it! We're going to be doing a seminar!" But, no, that didn't work out. Not long after that, a colleague suggested the three of us do workshops for professionals on getting business, the topic of another one of our books. "Oh! This it is!" I thought immediately. "This is what we're going to be doing next!" But, no, although the initial workshops went well, they weren't something we'd be doing on an ongoing basis.

Then came our July 4 visit to Pine Mountain. I immediately knew we'd be doing workshops there. This is the place people will be coming, I heard myself saying. During the entire fall that followed, while we were busily trying to sell our town home, I kept coming up with workshop outlines. They would usually come to me late at night, especially whenever I stayed overnight in Pine Mountain. I'd leap out of bed and grab my journal and start scribbling ideas down that were pouring through my mind. I probably generated a dozen different programs.

But none of them held my enthusiasm enough to convince Paul to join me in doing them once we moved to Pine Mountain. As he kept pointing out, we had plenty to do to keep up with the full-time careers we were pursuing. But in November we traveled to Beaver Creek, Colorado, to speak to the national Association of Bridal Consultants. As we wove our way down the Vail mountainsides to leave, I thought about how similar Pine Mountain was to the Rocky Mountains and suddenly another image flashed in my mind. "Paul," I said, "I think we should establish the Pine Mountain Institute." His response was even more surprising than the idea itself. "Yes," he said matter-of-factly, "I think we should."

Over the next six months we had a variety of ideas for what the Pine Mountain Institute could be, but by the time we moved we still had no idea what it would be. Nonetheless, not long after we moved we registered the Pine Mountain Institute as a DBA and created business cards for our new venture. We were ready to begin . . . what?

FINISH THE TERM

The image of myself as an old lady teaching a circle of people in Pine Mountain was growing stronger, but I still had no clue as to what she was teaching, who the people were, or why they were coming. Like Mary Ann, I was finding it difficult to keep following the thread of this embryonic desire that seemed to be leading nowhere. Then I remembered an embarrassing lesson I'd learned during my last semester of graduate school.

I'd been supervising two senior undergraduates who, like myself, would be graduating that spring. But it was only April and they were growing complacent, slacking off on the job, not turning in their assignments, coming in late. In their minds, they were done with school. That dream was over. Soon they'd have their college degrees. They were ready to start new jobs in June. I was growing impatient with them. I wanted them to shape up so I could wrap up my own semester and focus on opening my private practice right after graduation. I wasn't really all that interested in supervising them anymore, but it was part of my practicum and they had to finish so I could finish.

Finally, I brought the issue up to my supervisor. He pointed out that what they were experiencing was exactly what I was experiencing. It was a normal reaction to ending one phase of our lives and beginning another. We were all ready to move on, but we couldn't because we had to finish the semester in order to graduate. "You're divesting in your role as students, but to complete that role you have to play the part to the best of your ability for another two months, until you've finished the term and can move on." We could make that a difficult, unpleasant experience, he emphasized, or we could continue doing a good job and enjoy our last two months as college students. I remember laughing at how easily I'd seen their problem without seeing my own.

I sat down with the students the next day and gave them the same pep talk my supervisor had given me. They shaped up just as soon as I did and we enjoyed working together those last two months. Part of our time went into developing a list of things we needed to do to wrap up, like winding up work with clients we needed to say good-bye to and refer elsewhere, and finally planning a grand graduation party.

What do you need to finish? We can't turn our backs on the past if we want to move on. What do you need to put in order, wrap up, and say good-bye to so you can dream on?

SO THIS IS WHAT'S BEEN GOING ON!

Once we thought about it, Paul and I could see we had a lot from the past to wind up before we could move on. We had a dream under way that had yet to come to term. It wasn't graduation time yet. The best thing I could do to invent my future was to take care of the present. We got busy wrapping up pending writing contracts. We discontinued some responsibilities. Finished two partially completed new book proposals. Completed the process of moving in and allowed ourselves more time to savor the joy of our new environs. The moment we did that the earth started to move for the Pine Mountain Institute. A seemingly unrelated series of events occurred, all within a few weeks:

– I came across a new statistic that reminded me that most small business owners and professionals don't take vacations. This is despite the fact that they're working longer hours and feeling more pressed than ever because changes in the economy and technology are turning their industries upside down.

– My friend Dean Allen, who's a psychologist, called to remind me he was still looking for a place within easy driving distance of the city where he could bring some of his clients for a retreat. He wanted to know if he could come up to check out doing a workshop here in Pine Mountain.

– The Pine Mountain Environment Committee approved Linda and Ed's B & B, so soon there would be an ideal place for people to stay while attending seminars and workshops up here.

– While speaking at the California Governor's Conference on Women, I heard the latest poll on telecommuting. It found that two thirds of the *Fortune* 1,000 companies now have programs that allow employees to work from home. Half of those programs were started in the last two years in an effort to compete in the tight labor market.

– Several people called Paul for help in making strategic decisions in their businesses, reminding me once again what a gifted strategist Paul is and has been over the years since I met him when he was working as a successful political consultant.

This confluence of events worked like a bank of floodlights. Suddenly I understood the purpose of the Pine Mountain Institute. It's difficult to have perspective under pressure and hard to make creative decisions while multitasking our way through hectic, overscheduled workdays. But Pine Mountain has an unusually tranquil yet energizing beauty. There are many places in the surrounding National Forest that people find to be especially healing and transformative, places some people would call power centers. The Shumash Indians, who still have a reservation nearby, call Pine Mountain the center of the universe. It's an ideal place for harried professionals and small business owners and others in transition to get away, relax, recharge, and reconnect with their creativity.

The Pine Mountain Institute can facilitate such experiences. Through small semi-private Creative Strategy Retreats small business owners and professionals could get away to a vacation-like setting and get the help they need to develop strategies for handling the complex changes they're facing and take their businesses in more rewarding directions.

Through the Institute we could also offer seminars for people who want to live in the mountains and telecommute via modem, fax, and telephone to jobs in L.A. or elsewhere (the first one will be held in just a few weeks). And we can facilitate other professionals, like my friend Dean, who want a nearby place to get their clients and customers away from the madding crowd so they can learn or heal. In the process, all those who come here experience a way of life they may have thought was no longer possible.

Are the events of your life suggesting a possible new direction for you to pursue? What path are they pointing you toward?

As in our case, the new desires that finally reignite a practical dreamer's fires most often grow naturally from what they've already been working toward. At first glance these new desires may appear to be a radical departure, but a closer examination usually reveals that we're weaving loose threads from other periods of our lives together with a new interest that has emerged from the satisfaction of having attained our most recent dreams. Long-abandoned talents and past passions are usually called back into service, along with dream fragments from other times in our lives.

While we may not know just where our new desires will take us, once we recognize them they often seem so obvious that we wonder why we didn't think of them sooner. Those who know Paul and me, for example, would agree that building the Institute is a natural outgrowth of our collective experiences over a lifetime. It's clearly a child of what we've been working toward for years.

 **Try This**

Draw a spiral that represents your lifetime. Place the significant events of your life along it. The center is your birth with your life flowing out from that center in ever-widening circles. What patterns do you see over the course of your life? What has changed? What has endured? Where is your life taking you now that your entire life up to this point has been preparing you for?

There's one way I can always tell when I'm about to start on the road to a new dream: all of a sudden my heart sings. My eyes fill with tears of joy and I want to leap to my feet and dance to its wild, pulsating beat. It's as if this were always meant to be and my body and soul says, "Yes, at last!"

And so it is that we're each walking once again with a foot in two worlds . . . but this time there's a difference.

WELCOME MIRACLES

In some miraculous way none of us could have planned or imagined, my dreams and Paul's and the dreams of our new friends were merging into a collective community dream. In pursuing our individual desires for more balanced and peaceful lives, we've come together in a place where the best of the past meets the best of tomorrow. We're not only creating more fulfilling lives for ourselves, we're beginning to work together to share the magic of this world with others who are also hungering for it.

Now, that's some magic trick! A constellation of forces have drawn together here a cadre of practical dreamers whose diverse paths have crossed in this particular place at this particular time to create something that's taking on a life of its own. Something we can now only glimpse as we begin individually and collectively:

. . . feeling a desire growing within us,

. . . yearning for it even when we don't know its precise form,

. . . imagining all it could be,

. . . believing in it fully,

. . . committing to fulfilling our desire,

. . . following the thread of that desire until we find the money, make the time, and have the energy to create it,

. . . and feeling satisfied and fulfilled in the creative process that is unfolding into whatever comes next.

Wherever you are in your journey, join with us in this collective dream to find balance and peace in these times of complexity. Let's remember the best of what has been and let's bring it back into our lives. Let's bring the best of both worlds into our homes, our offices, and our communities and let's enjoy the possibilities we can create together.

To join in this dream and share your dreams-in-progress, visit us at www.practicaldreamer.net

REFERENCES

Hot Chocolate for the Mystical Soul. Arielle Ford. Plume. ISBN 0452279259.

More Hot Chocolate for the Mystical Soul. Arielle Ford. Plume. ISBN 0452280699.

To learn more about Pine Mountain, visit www.PineMountain-Institute.com.

➡ PART III: REMEMBER THIS ✩✩

Anytime you have difficulty allowing yourself to fully savor and enjoy achieving your dreams and fulfilling your highest desires, or anytime you feel pressed to rush on and skip the joy of living instead of appreciating the creative process or feel stuck and unable to move on to new dreams, turn here to this section and remember . . .

Carry out your life with love. It seems that if you do whatever you do with love, as an expression of yourself, your life and your work are not only infinitely more enjoyable and meaningful, but the result is also infinitely more enjoyable and meaningful to everyone else you interact with.

If you're going to do it—enjoy it. Surveys show it's not success that makes someone a happy person. It's their attitude day in and day out. Many happy people have yet to attain the success they desire. Likewise, some people aren't all that happy even after they've achieved the success they sought. Whether you're as successful in creating your dream as you want to be or not, following that dream requires doing a variety of tasks you may just as soon not do. These tasks are part and parcel of creating a dream; so since you'll have to do them, why not just enjoy them?

Pay attention to what you tell yourself. Your inner dialogue has great power. "At the very instant you think, 'I'm happy,'" for example, Deepak Chopra tells us, "a chemical messenger translates your emotions . . . [so] that literally every cell in your body learns of your happiness and joins in." You can think of the voice of your self-talk as your inner coach or mentor. It's telling you what you think of yourself and how you think you're doing. If you call yourself a "dummy" or an "idiot" when you make a mistake, does that inspire and motivate you to do better? Or, do the cells of your body cringe and shrink a little, diminished in shame? Whatever situations you encounter, think of what you can say to yourself that will inspire you, help you to draw upon your strengths and rise above or address your weaknesses. The right words can do just that.

Laugh a lot. It's good for you. Scientific studies show that laughter boosts the immune system by flooding our bodies with chemical substances called endorphins, which give us a natural high. We need to take what we're doing seriously, but why not lighten up on yourself and laugh at life's absurdities? If lightheartedness doesn't come easily to you (it doesn't for many), take up with some lighthearted friends. Let their mood rub off on you. If you find yourself among gloomy people, don't catch their mood. Smile instead. It will shield you from their gloom and doom and may give them a lift, too.

Celebrate! Don't wait until you've finished. Don't wait until you've reached your goals. Put a little celebration into every day. Celebrate each step you take toward success. Acknowledging and enjoying the little steps will fuel your enthusiasm to carry on and reinforce your commitment and resolve. It makes the journey as fun and rewarding as reaching the destination. Make a special point to celebrate having done the important things you find difficult or unpleasant. Your celebrations need not be expensive. They can be as simple as calling a friend to share what you've accomplished, or taking a walk in the sunset.

Are you having fun? If not, why not? It's often said that life is about the journey and not the destination. For those of us who are toiling to achieve or preserve our dreams, concentrating on the journey may feel like a life sentence to drudgery and endless setbacks. You may wonder if the journey is the prize, then why am I doing this? Think for a moment about how you view your journey. Yes, it may be long. Yes, it may be filled with unexpected and unwanted challenges, even setbacks. But can't we have fun along the way? Virtually any path in life will be fraught with some toil. So why not whistle while we work? Why not dance a bit along the road?

Cultivate an attitude of gratitude. One of the best ways to accept the blessings large and small that we receive in our lives is to cultivate an attitude of gratitude. It feels great to be grateful. We get to acknowledge and enjoy our good fortune while honoring the contributions of others and the powers that be. Gratitude is a good response to difficult times, too, because it can put even the worst of things into perspective and enable us to take heart.

Congratulate yourself. Have you taken note of how far you've come? How much you've accomplished? It may seem as if you've achieved little because chances are your eyes are on the road ahead and all you can see is how much further you have to go. But think back to a few years ago, before you set your current goals, to the time when you decided to take your life on the course you're traveling now. Look back and you may be amazed to find how far you've come.

Balance intention with flow. What is a person to do? On the one hand, the wisdom of the day urges us to visualize our goals and pursue them relentlessly with laserlike concentration. On the other hand, we're advised to go with the flow, don't push the river, let your dreams unfold. Surely, constant pushing and driving can be self-defeating, yet always going with the flow may not take you anywhere you want to go. It seems that, as in so much of life, the issue is balance. We must balance intention with flow. Like breathing in and breathing out, our workday can be a process of giving out and taking in.

Pace yourself. Exhaustion and impatience arise most often when we've been pushing too hard or slacking off too much. Like the ancient yin and yang, we need to find a balance between driving and pushing to achieve preconceived goals while remaining open and receptive to new possibilities. When you feel exhausted, sit back a bit, breathe in, imagine your desired outcomes, and leave space for a clearer route to emerge. When you feel impatient and dissatisfied with your progress, rev up, become more focused, and take action to direct the course of your life.

Find a balance. A review of the history of work over the past few centuries shows that long hours have been the norm for men, women, and even children. The idea that we can and should have balance in our lives is relatively recent. This is just one more way we are pioneers, and as pioneers, sometimes we get where we're headed and sometimes we get lost along the way. The key is to keep sight of the goal and to continually self-correct. That means we must stay aware of how we're spending our time and schedule in rest, relaxation, respite, and renewal, as well as time for family and friends. Fortunately, as long as we're still alive, it's never too late to start balancing any given day with time for ourselves, our work, and our loved ones.

Go at your own speed. Are you a tortoise or a hare? We all know how important it is to get our lives up to speed, but actually, working up to speed is quite individual. Everyone has a pace at which they function most comfortably and productively. The idea that working faster and harder is always better is not only a myth but can actually be a detriment. It's equally mythical to assume that slow and steady wins the race for everyone.

Usually, we're most effective working at our individual pace. Some of us seem to be set on fast-forward. We talk fast, move fast, and work fast. Others of us seem to operate in slow motion. We take our time forming our thoughts and carrying out whatever activities we undertake.

Neither is intrinsically superior, although our culture seems to prefer speed and certainly some areas of life demand haste while others require care and caution. The key is to know yourself, how you function best, your personal clock from which you produce the best results and feel most comfortable, including knowing which activities you can breeze through and which ones you need to reserve more time to undertake. Then, give yourself the time and space you need to live at a pace that allows you to get the results you want and enjoy yourself in the process.

Does your life feed you? Of course, we all need to put food on the table, but today it's possible for our work to feed us not only physically, but also psychically. Our work supports us physically by providing food, shelter, and clothing, but as the old saying goes, we do not live on bread alone. So much more is possible from our work now. It can be a source of inspiration. It can be a way to make a contribution. It can leave us excited and energized. If, try as you might, you never or only rarely derive such psychic sustenance from your work, if you can honestly say, "I just do this for the money," then you owe it to yourself to refocus your work in ways that will feed your body, mind, and soul.

Get away. Have you ever returned from a vacation more exhausted than before you left? Sometimes when we take off in hopes of getting some R&R, we don't get the rejuvenating effect we seek from our vacations because . . .

We take our work on vacation with us, cellular phone, laptop, stacks of backed-up reading material, and all. We call in every day for our messages, talk to our clients, solve work problems, read contracts on the airplane, etc. Then we wonder why we don't feel refreshed when we get back. If you truly want some R&R, really GET AWAY. You will be more refreshed from a short trip during which you really get completely away from work, than a longer trip during which you are trying to work on the road.

Also we may not take the right kind of vacation. If you need to relax and get away from the pressure of a fast-paced, high-pressure life, don't go on a fast-paced, time-pressed vacation where you pack multiple activities into every moment. In other words, avoid the "It's-Wednesday-I-must-be-in-Paris" syndrome. On the other hand, if your work is exhaustingly sedentary or routine, a dose of fast-paced stimulation, variety, and excitement may be just what you need to come back refreshed and energized.

We may also mistake fulfilling family obligations for taking a vacation. While visiting relatives or sharing interesting activities with our children can be enjoyable, sometimes they're also just plain hard work. So unless your family getaways will also meet your own needs for relaxation or a fulfilling change of pace, separate the two so you can enjoy both types of getaways to the fullest. You may need to take two shorter vacations, for example, a long weekend with the kids at Grandma's and another long weekend where you get away for yourself without family obligations.

Step away. Sometimes we lose touch with the sense of what fulfills us. To reconnect with what's fulfilling to us, we need to step outside our daily lives and experience nature, reflect on our childhood or other times in life when we felt most alive, or spend time with others who are doing what energizes and enlivens them. Then you can feel fulfilled again and begin to reorient your life to reflect more of the essence of who you truly are.

Stay healthy; stay connected. A study at Carnegie-Mellon University in Pittsburgh found that people who have an active support network of friends, family, and colleagues are more resistant to disease, probably due to a more highly activated immune system. After eliminating other factors like age and whether people exercise regularly, researchers found that only 35 percent of people with six or more cohesive social relationships came down with a cold, while 62 percent of people with three or fewer such relationships got a cold!

So if you want to stay healthy, it's important not to become isolated. Take the initiative to get to know people, see them often and engage in the kind of activities that draw you together and lead to deeper friendships. Become an active volunteer for a social cause or get involved in a shared interest group like a hiking club or volleyball team. Team up with others to do interesting or challenging projects.

Foster your adventurous spirit. Research shows that people who consider themselves to have an adventurous spirit create more quality ideas. Anyone who willingly sets out to create a better life must be at least a little adventurous at heart. But once we achieve our dreams, it's easy to settle into a comfortable routine, relieved that the stress of pioneering is behind us. So if you need some new ideas, if you want to increase your creativity, take an adventure break. Explore some area of the city or countryside you haven't seen. Take a stimulating, challenging course or seminar of some kind. Undertake a physical challenge like hang gliding or bungee jumping. Find out what gives your brainpower a boost.

Where is the joy? As I turned the last page of the book I had been reading, I was wishing it would not end. There I found a note from the author. "It has been a joy," she wrote, "to share my thoughts with you on these pages. Please write to me." My day had been a grueling one and my mind flashed on the long days and nights of writing, the lonely grind of meeting pressing deadlines, the sometimes tortuous struggle to capture my thoughts in ways that make sense. "What happened to the joy?" I asked myself.

How easy it is for the joy to slip out of whatever we're doing.

Yet in an instant, those five words —"It has been a joy" —brought it all back, the flood of memories over a lifetime of wanting to write, to express my feelings, to share my experiences, to ignite possibilities and imagination through words.

So where is the joy? If you are living a life you love, it's always right there, covered perhaps at times by a blanket of pressures and demands. But always there for you, fueling your resolve, waiting silently for the moment when you remember to throw back the covers and let it run rampant again in your life.

Is your body telling you something? Illness is one of the common reasons people choose to change where and how they work and live. They recognize their illness as a wake-up call. Whether they're twenty or over sixty-five, growing numbers of people are noticing that their work, or their lifestyle, is making them ill and they're doing something about it. Sometimes we don't see the changes we need to make in our lives, so our bodies have to point them out to us. What messages is your body sending? The sooner you listen, the less likely it is you have to get ill to make needed changes.

Relax. You don't have to fix everything. Are you a fixer? Fixers can't stand to have a problem for more than a minute. They rush in to figure everything out and take care of everything and everybody. Of course, being able to fix things is useful, but doing it constantly is exhausting and not always productive. Sometimes we learn more and get better results if we just relax, observe what's happening, and allow things to work out based on what we learn.

Of course, for a dyed-in-the-wool fixer, that's tough. We fixers fear our problems will get worse if we don't nip them in the bud immediately. To ignore a problem, we fear, will do us in. And, sometimes that's true. We can't ignore our problems and hope they'll go away. We shouldn't let problems grow out of hand. But, have you ever noticed that often the quick 'n' easy, forced solutions to get a problem out of our hair don't seem to stick? Sometimes we don't even follow through on our handy get-it-over-with neat-and-tidy solutions, so the same problems keep coming back to plague us again and again.

Instead of finding the instant-fix solution that takes care of the moment, why not take the time to get beneath the surface of the problem and understand how it developed in the first place? This way you'll not only solve the problem for the time being, but you'll also know how to prevent it from happening again in the future.

"We need to stop asking about the meaning of life but think instead of ourselves as those who are being questioned by life, daily and hourly." As I read these words by noted philosopher and German psychiatrist Viktor Frankl, author of *Man's Search for Meaning*, I was reminded of a story about *Today* show weatherman Willard Scott. A few years ago, Scott had the opportunity to develop his own television show. As you might imagine, he was excited. It was his big break. Well, the show was a flop and that sent Scott into a relentless quest to figure out what had gone wrong. Day in and day out he racked his brain trying to figure out why his show didn't make it. Finally, he realized that there are some things you can never figure out, but simply have to accept and move on. And so it seems Frankl was saying, We must stop asking about the meaning of life and why things happen to us as they do, and instead find what meaning we can in whatever life has presented us with. Does this mean that we must "accept our lot," so to speak? No, it means we can make of things what we will.

Appreciate the growth of winter. We all have slow times, dark times, lonely and difficult times. These times are the winters of life. While it seems that such times slow us down, halt our progress, and threaten to defeat us, so much can grow beneath the surface of slow times. The key is not to get panicked by the harshness of these times but to allow ourselves to survive them with the courage and determination to proceed one step and one day at a time. As Amanda McBroom wrote in her song *The Rose*, "Just remember in the winter, far beneath the bitter snow, lies the seed that with the sun's love in spring becomes the rose." When you face tough times, remind yourself, "I'm growing roses."

Enjoy your prosperity. Often we think achieving prosperity means financial prosperity. But increasingly, prosperity has come to mean more than having lots of money. Today, many people would trade in a portion of their income to have more time, or to work at something they find meaningful, or to live somewhere that fulfills them. "True prosperity," says Shakti Gawain, author of *Creating True Prosperity*, "is the experience of having plenty of what we truly need and want in life." In this sense, each of us has some degree of prosperity already. We must simply take a moment to think about what we truly need and want and use the enjoyment of that which we have to spur us on to create plenty more of what is most important to us.

Is your life like a trip across Kansas? I grew up in Kansas City. When I was a little girl, each summer my family vacationed in Colorado or New Mexico. That meant we had to make the long and desolate eight-hour drive across Kansas. I remember vividly how ardently we watched the horizon for the first signs of the Rocky Mountains, because in our minds, our vacation did not begin until we got to Denver. I think many of us live our lives like that, waiting for Denver. We have a goal in mind for the great things that lie ahead, and we press onward with our eyes locked on that goal. In so doing, we fail to appreciate the beauty of the prairies of life. We miss the interesting experiences of the journey. Why not enjoy the entire trip? Why wait for life to begin someday? Why not start now, enjoying the best of what we have, whether we're in the desert, the meadows, or the forested mountaintops of life?

Accept your imperfections and proceed. It is thought by some that perfectionism keeps us from achieving our goals and becoming all that we can be, but the desire for perfection comes naturally to us. We seek perfection. We're drawn to it. We seek what we sense is possible from us and for us. And this is good. What stands in our way is not our quest for perfection, but our inability to accept our imperfection. As we strive for perfection, we are tempted to see ourselves negatively as perfection shines the light of truth on all our flaws. We see these imperfections and become disheartened. Instead, we must think of ourselves as a work in progress, an unfinished masterpiece. We can enjoy and take pleasure in whatever progress we've made, be it considerable or modest. We can stand in our strength and our imperfections and head on in our quest to become even more of what we know we can be.

Find happiness indirectly. Our U.S. constitution states that we each have the right to the pursuit of happiness. While it's vital that a free society allow us each to pursue our heart's desires, the more you make the pursuit of happiness your goal in life, the more it eludes you. Happiness is more an outcome or a by-product of other pursuits than something you can pursue directly. If we accomplish an important goal, we feel happy. If we do good work, we feel happy. If we bring joy to someone else's life, we feel happy. If we do something we enjoy, we feel happy. So we achieve happiness through the pursuit of other things and use its presence or absence as a gauge of whether what we're devoting our lives to is leading us in a desired direction.

Be a good sport. Having spent an entire year of weekends taking our dog Billy to dog shows, we were inspired by how much Billy enjoys being in the show whether he wins or loses. To Billy, he's always the winner. Watching him has been a valuable lesson: to be the proud winner in life even when you don't come out on top. It's never fun to lose to others who gain what we had hoped for. Instead of closing the door on future opportunities by bad-mouthing, blaming, or expressing your disappointment or anger, leave the door open and the welcome mat out. Wish those involved the best of success and offer to serve them in any way you can in the future and you'll always be a winner.

Beat burnout. Burnout is endemic in times like these when everything is becoming more complex and the pace of change is accelerating. When life begins to feel like a revolving door that's going faster and faster, trapping you in its endless rotation of hectic days, you're well on the road to burnout. While you may not always be able to stop the whirlwind of life swirling around you, you need not get caught up in it, at least, not constantly. You can step back, you can reflect, you can observe from a quiet place within. You can refuse to let pandemonium engulf you. You can slow down and deepen your breathing. You can remember who you are and what is important to you. Then, refreshed and reconnected to your purpose, you can step back into the bracing, exhilarating, ever-changing, thundering river that is life.

Be patient. Why are we so impatient? Is it merely because we're eager? Or is it because we don't really believe we can have what we want? If we knew for certain that we could have it and that it would continue, would we be content to simply enjoy the process? Or do we need our impatience to propel us forward because we don't know what the future will bring? Are we impatient because the present is unfulfilling? Or is it that we are simply so fixated on what could be? Impatience can be our enemy if it causes us to cut corners or miss the beauty of the moment. Or it can be our friend if it inspires us to use what is best about the moment to achieve an even better future.

Share your success. It's contagious. Each success, large or small, is a victory. Have you ever noticed how success rubs off on those you share it with? Just watching a victorious team or performer fills the audience with awe and energy. We go home from a winning performance feeling inspired and catalyzed. Sharing our successes is one of the best gifts we can give each other. And, we can bask, if only momentarily, in the glow and warmth of well-deserved congratulations. What successes can you share today? Pass them around.

Take a breather. As Sidney Lewis said, "The time to relax is when you don't have the time." The more pressured and tense you feel, the more important it is to breathe, to take one's space and time, to focus your energy with calm intent. If your intent never waivers, there is no room for fear. And, if you remember to breathe, really breathe (as in letting your stomach relax as you pull the air into your lungs), you'll have more energy, more strength, and more peace of mind no matter what is going on around you.

Step back a moment. Sometimes we get so entangled in the details of pursuing our goals and dreams, so locked into our problems and daily demands, that we lose our vision. We get lost in a fog of impossibility. We lose our vantage point and can no longer see the road ahead. That's when we must step back. We must step away for a moment to gain perspective, clear our head, and take the broader view that will enable us to return to our day with renewed clarity and confidence.

Cherish the gift of this day. As the future unfolds, we never know what will happen in our lives, so we must cherish each moment. We are blessed to be the artists of each of the days of our lives. We hold the brush in our hands. The events life presents are our watercolors. And our most treasured possession is our canvas, the twenty-four hours that lie ahead of us every morning of every day.

LIVING IN SYNC

> *There's nothing permanent*
> *except change.*
> HERACLITUS

We went into Santa Monica last week to do some errands and discovered it's changed. The streets we were so familiar with only months ago have been rerouted with a series of detours designed to handle the growing traffic congestion. Unfortunately, they've only made it worse. But when we got back to Pine Mountain late that night, we noticed that it, too, had changed. As usual, during the new moon, it was pitch-dark, but to our surprise, the ladle of the Big Dipper had slipped beneath the northern mountainside. All we can see of it now is the handle. It's a sign, our neighbor Joe pointed out the next day, that fall is here.

There are other signs of change now, too. The kaleidoscope of green in the meadow below us is turning to shades of tan. The pines are shedding their needles like gales of falling snow. The poplars are turning a brilliant yellow. The baby deer that often walks through our yard with its mother has lost its spots. Two red-tail hawks have taken up residence in the ponderosa pines on each side of our house, so the stellar blue jays and the squirrels no longer come to our feeders during the day. It's nippy now in the morning and we need our jackets to walk up to get the mail. The petunias on the porch are still as resplendent as ever, but we know they won't be with us for long.

Ed is about to finish putting in our generator. Ben and Marie, the previous owners of our house, weren't living here full-time, so they didn't need a generator. But since we'll be living and working here all year long, we'll be needing electricity when the winter storms take out the power. Ed's ordering a set of studded tires for us, too. Matt is resurfacing our deck for winter and plans for the garage will get under way soon. I've ordered in coats and sweaters and mufflers and mittens. I've unpacked Billy's parka and Linda is helping me pick out snow boots.

Meanwhile Jeannie and Ron have moved to a bigger house up the way from us. It sits in the trees above a year-round spring. The Reuters, Rosie and Roland, lost Prairie Dancer, their nineteen-year-old black-and-white paint to colic. Their daughters were inconsolable. Justen and Mike have separated, but Justen won't be leaving the mountain. Stephanie is close to completing her children's book and Rob is spending more time hiking with his daughter instead of touring. Scott just purchased a quarter horse so he can go riding with his nine-year-old daughter, Valerie. Eileen's two-year-old granddaughter has come to visit, and tomorrow Mary Ann will begin photographing and interviewing Pine Mountain children for her project. A card company has expressed interest in creating a line of greeting cards featuring her work.

Escrow on the B & B will close the same day we'll be sending this book to our publisher. We look forward to seeing the glow of the lights from its windows flickering through the pines across the highway from us. The Institute is under way. Tomorrow, Paul will be working with a new client who's coming up from L.A. to find a strategy for changing the direction of her company and her life. Next month Dr. Dean Allen will be here to work with several clients.

And yesterday a peculiar thing happened on the way to the post office. It was almost 4:00 P.M., so I glanced at my wrist to check the time, hoping Judith, the postmistress, wouldn't have closed up yet. To my surprise, I wasn't wearing my watch! As Winifred Gallagher illustrates so poignantly in *The Power of Place*, where and how we live go a long way in determining who we are and who we become. By spring, Linda Miller tells me, I'll be a mountain woman, and Paul and I will have turned to new pages in our dreams.

My life here is as different from the one I'd been living as that one was from the small-town, midwestern world where I grew up. It's a novel blend of both worlds, the past and the present, a mixture of the magic of nature with the magic of our high-tech, high-touch times. It's a harbinger of a new trend: the nearby faraway place.

Come see what we mean. Visit us at www.simplegoodlife.com. We'll all be there, Mary Ann and Jeannie, Linda, Justen, Ed and Eileen, Rosie, Roland and Scott, Paul and I, and so many more, living a sneak preview of what can be if we choose simplicity within complexity and commit to living in sync with the rhythms that beat in our hearts.

Is it time to turn the pages of your dream? Listen to the beat of your heart and you will know . . .

INDEX